Building an Enterprise-Wide Business Continuity Program

Building an Enterprise-Wide Business Continuity Program

Kelley Okolita, MBCP

CRC Press
Taylor & Francis Group
Boca Raton London New York

CRC Press is an imprint of the
Taylor & Francis Group, an **informa** business

CRC Press
Taylor & Francis Group
6000 Broken Sound Parkway NW, Suite 300
Boca Raton, FL 33487-2742

First issued in paperback 2019

© 2010 by Taylor & Francis Group, LLC
CRC Press is an imprint of Taylor & Francis Group, an Informa business

No claim to original U.S. Government works

ISBN-13: 978-1-4200-8864-9 (hbk)
ISBN-13: 978-0-367-38528-6 (pbk)

**Visit the Taylor & Francis Web site at
http://www.taylorandfrancis.com**

**and the CRC Press Web site at
http://www.crcpress.com**

DEDICATION

This book is dedicated to my husband, Bob—without him, nothing else works; to our children (yours, mine, ours, and extras); and to the people I have worked for, who have given me the opportunity to do what I do best. I thank you because I found something that I love to do and I found a way to get paid to do it, and that is what we all wish for our working lives.

Most of the people I have met in this industry did not set out to be business-continuity or disaster-recovery planners. Most people were given this role, often as only part of their responsibilities, as in "oh, by the way, in your spare time can you do this too?" If they are lucky, the company then ships them off to an industry conference to "learn something about it." Sometimes that helps, and sometimes it just overwhelms them even more.

This book is also for those people.

CONTENTS

CHAPTER 9   Documenting the Plan

CHAPTER 10   Training and Awareness Programs

CHAPTER 11   Testing the Recovery Plan

CHAPTER 12   Coordinating with Public Agencies

xiii

APPENDIX B   Sample Initial-Response Plan for Small Sites

APPENDIX C   Test-Planning Guide and Sample Test Plan for Business-Unit Exercises at an Alternate Site

INTRODUCTION

A business-contingency plan is a set of procedures that defines how a business will continue or recover its operations in the event of an unplanned disruption to normal procedures. The plan needs to include the recovery of the critical technology that supports the business operation as well as the business environment itself.

The objective of this book is to provide the reader with the knowledge and tools to build a program in any enterprise, large or small, public or private. Through each chapter, we will build a step-by-step process for an enterprise-wide business-continuity program. We will also talk about the evolution of the industry and industry regulations that have influenced or in some cases mandated that organizations build programs within their businesses that will ensure their continuation "no matter what."

My intent is to provide the reader with the knowledge and tools necessary to build a successful business-continuity and disaster-recovery program. This book is not just about why we should do this or the theory behind it; it provides actual tactical tools to help you get the job done. Lots of books will tell you what you need to do. This one will, too, but it's also going to tell you how to get it done with examples and tools and stories about the experiences I have had in building programs and actually doing recoveries for real.

As of this writing, I am not a consultant and never have been. I have always been an employee of a company, doing this work through real disasters, small and large. I decided to write this book because of the requests I received at presentations through the years at various industry conferences. For the last nine years or so, I have "taught" a full-day tutorial called "Business Continuity 101: an Introduction for the New Planner" twice a year at the Contingency Planning and Management conference. I have presented topics in this field to a variety of audience—to groups such as the Association of Contingency Planners, Sungard Users Group,

Contingency Planners of Ohio, the American Red Cross, and the New England Disaster Recovery Information Exchange—and to conferences sponsored by Gartner, DRJ, Continuity Insights, IBM Common, Comdisco, and others.

I have presented in the United States, Canada, Singapore, Australia, France, and Germany, and what I have found in all these presentations is that what people appreciate, what they want and need, is not theory on why they should do this or descriptions of what they are supposed to do but real-life practical tools on how to do it. Where to start, how to sell it, and tools to use. Several years ago I did a presentation at a SNUG meeting in New Jersey, and after the presentation a man came up to me and said, "I saw you present here about 10 years ago, and you gave everyone there a sample plan and toolkit to start to build a program. I wanted you to know that really made a difference for me. I was able to take what you gave me and start to build something. Ten years later, what we have all started with what you gave me that day."

That's why I am writing this book.

I tell a joke at the start of all of my presentations. I have no recollection of where or whom I got this joke from, but it goes like this. Everyone knows the Peanuts cartoons by Charles Schultz, featuring Lucy, Charlie Brown, Linus, and other characters. Well, in the joke, Lucy and Charlie Brown are standing on the deck of a cruise ship, and Lucy turns to Charlie Brown and says, "You know, Charlie Brown, some people go through their life with their deck chairs facing forward, looking over the horizon at where they are going, how they will get there, and looking to the future; and others go through their lives with their deck chairs facing backward, looking at where they have been, what they have accomplished, and how they feel about their life and how they have lived it." She turns to Charlie Brown, who is pondering what she said, and says, "So, Charlie Brown, which way is your deck chair facing?" He gets this really perplexed look on his face and says, "I never really figured how to get mine open."

I tell people that the point of the joke is that there is no way that I can give them every answer they ever looked for, but hopefully at the end of the session they will have their deck chairs open. This book cannot possibly answer every question you have ever had about business continuity and disaster recovery either, but I hope at the end you too will have your deck chair open.

1

Where It All Began from Someone Who Was There

Chapter Objectives

- A Brief History, or How This Field Started
- Business Continuity vs. Disaster Recovery
- Job Description of a Business-Continuity Planner

It all started in the data center. Once computers became part of the business landscape, even before the introduction of personal computers, it became clear that we could not return to our manual processes if our computers failed.

My first exposure to this industry was in the mid 1970s when I worked for a well-known and prominent financial-services firm. In the middle of the night, the mainframe computer went down on a catastrophic I/O (input/output) error and no one could figure out why. The data center and all of the applications the business used to run its operations were down for almost 18 hours. Once the crisis was over and the applications were brought back online, the very first thing the organization did was to purchase a second mainframe and put it on the floor right next to the first one. Well, now at least they had *two*. Of course, that would not help if the problem was in the building itself, which this same company would learn a few years later.

One of the business leaders was charged with coming up with a plan for how the company would survive without the data center. After all, the company had been in business since the 1940s, and computer systems were a relatively new introduction. It was thought that we should be able to go back to the way we used to do it—manual spreadsheets, handwritten order forms, and such. How hard could it be?

Time went on, and no plan was published. There is nothing like a good disaster to get people's attention, but as things get back to normal and regular day-to-day issues and concerns regain the spotlight, the intensity of the need to develop a recovery plan tends to fade. When I asked that leader what he came up with as a plan 6 months later, he said,"Well, the first day without the computer, we could process financial transactions manually and just postpone everything else. The second day, we could really only process certain types of financial transactions, and by day three we would really have to close the doors." The real plan was to keep our resumes up to date, because, as a financial-services firm, if we closed the doors until we could bring in a new computer and begin processing again, when the doors opened, most of our customers' business would leave. You cannot take away access to people's money and expect them to continue to do business with you."

The company was growing rapidly and struggling to keep up with all the new business, new technology, and new services it was offering its customers to really think too long about the lack of a plan, so despite the report to management, the organization did not develop a plan for recovery of the data center until three years later, when within a few months the organization faced both a fire in a business area one floor above the data center and a long-term power outage. These disasters occurred before data centers had UPS systems and generators to support power when the utility power fails. Leadership finally took it seriously enough to begin a disaster-recovery program focusing on technology.

The fire occurred first. It was an electrical fire that started in an unoccupied business area in the middle of the night. Because the building had both fire doors and sprinkler systems, the fire was contained to one area on one floor. But it was one floor above the data center. When sprinklers are going off on the floor above the data center, I bet you can guess what was happening *in* the data center. It was raining! Equipment was being covered with tarps, and wet vacuums were being used to try to keep the water from going under the raised floor and impacting the computer equipment in the data center.

The power outage occurred a few months later. At that time, all of the business operations of this company and its one and only data center were located within several blocks of each other in a major eastern city. The electrical wires—which I am convinced were put in by Thomas Edison—finally gave out and caused an underground explosion that threw a manhole cover 30 feet into the air. The power outage caused the entire downtown area to lose power for a full day, and only limited and unstable power was available for almost a week following the explosion.

We were pretty smart. We called Rent-a-Tool®, and within a few hours we had a diesel generator in the alley behind the data center building. It was an old building that actually had windows that opened, so the generator cables were pulled through the windows on the data-center floor and snaked through the hallways into the data center; in about 16 hours we had one CPU, one bank of tape drives, all of the DASDs, and one elevator working.

We set up card tables inside the data center, put up 16 dumb terminals (remember, this is before PCs), and had users come down and do critical data entry so we could run the batch cycles. We learned some really interesting things during this recovery. We learned that it would have been good to have some calculators that did not plug into the wall. We learned that after the emergency lighting goes out, it is *really* dark in the restrooms and the stairwells, and it would be really nice to have more flashlights around. We learned that we were pretty resourceful, but we also learned that despite how resourceful we were, it would be really good to have a plan and to figure out how we could have recovered if we had lost the building, not just the power.

That's when this company got serious about disaster recovery and started a project to build a plan for the data-center environment. It did not think about the business environment yet. That would not happen for a few more years.

DISASTER RECOVERY VS. BUSINESS CONTINUITY: WHAT IS THE DIFFERENCE?

With the introduction of computers to the business world, the business model had changed. The work that people did in general ledgers, in ledger books, or with their hands in a manufacturing environment were now done more consistently, with fewer errors and many times faster, by computers. If those computer systems failed, there were not enough people to do the work, nor did the people in the business still have the skill to do it manually. The disaster-recovery industry was born! Even today, the term "disaster recovery" or "DR" commonly refers to recovery of the technology environment. "Business continuity" tends to refer to the recovery of the business in total, of which the data center is a part.

In the beginning of this industry, the people who ran the data center were the first to build recovery strategies for the technology environment. They knew that the technology was important because every time there was a problem in the data center that caused batch cycles to be late or online systems to not be available, someone, usually lots of someones, complained.

Planning usually started with redundant technology within the data center itself, but for many companies this soon became cost-prohibitive, and they also realized that the additional technology within the data center would only address a hardware failure, not the loss of the building itself. Granted, hardware failures were much more common than a complete loss of a data center, so some redundancy was still prudent, but it did not address the other risk.

This need was met by companies such as IBM, Sungard, and Comdisco, which began to offer contracts to recover your data-center environment. Because these organizations sold the same services to multiple companies, the cost was significantly less than having a second data center and redundant technology funded completely out of your own pocket. It still is.

Just like today, the organization would sign a contract with a vendor to provide technology—in those days, the mainframes and associated peripherals—to recover your business. The organization then worked with the operations teams to develop procedures to IPL the mainframe and with application teams to create disaster-recovery backups of the data needed to recover an application and make sure those backups were sent offsite. Once that was in place, the teams went offsite to the recovery vendor to test the recovery.

In the early days of disaster-recovery testing, we sent teams of operations, network, and applications folks to the alternate-site data center with hundreds of backup tapes and tried to re-build our technology environment from scratch over the course of three or more days of testing. If we got the mainframe up and ran a batch cycle, we consider the test a success.

In the best-case scenario, this recovery strategy for the data center would have it up and running in five to seven days. Yes, it was done in three days in a test, but the test neglected to take into consideration that in a real event, all those tapes we used to restore the systems would have to be packed, shipped, unpacked, and racked in volume-serial order *before* a recovery could even begin. Yet, in the business plan for this financial-services company, it was documented that after three days they would have to suspend operations until we got the data center back online.

In the early days of the disaster-recovery industry, it was common that only the technology people went to the test, and we often neglected to consider that we needed a network from the alternate-site data center to the business sites for the business to be able to use the recovered applications. Application systems will run and online systems will come up as long as all the data the systems needs is available. It does not have to be the right data; it just has to be all the data. The idea that not only should we be able to run a batch cycle but that we should compare the output from the batch-cycle run at the alternate-site data center with the output from the production batch cycle to validate that we recovered the right data did not occur until the program began to mature and the business got involved in the testing. The same held true with the validation of the recovery of the online systems. If the online system came up, the technology people considered the test a success. Until an end user validates that not only did the system come up but that he or she can navigate through all the processes of the application, the recovery is not complete.

In those days, we never thought much about the people. We did not even build a network from the alternate-site data center to where the people who used the applications worked. But when the auditors came in and began asking if we had a disaster-recovery plan and did we test it, we could proudly say "yes."

THE TRANSITION FROM DATA-CENTER-DRIVEN TO BUSINESS-DRIVEN

It took some time, and for many industries it was not until after the events of September 11, 2001, to realize that it really did not matter if we recovered the data center if there were no business people to use it. When technology became a business unto itself, those who ran data centers sometimes forgot that the only reason we have data centers is for the business to run and that, if it were not for the business, the people who make the money, we would not need the data center at all. To them, the technology was the business. Technology is not the business; technology enables the business.

As the technology that runs a business moved out of the glass house (the data center) and onto employees' desktops, the environment continued to become more complex as business partners discovered the power of the technology on their PCs. In the old days, if they wanted a new report, they would ask the applications team to build a new report that showed them what they wanted and the application team would say, "Well, now, that will be 1000 man-hours of programming time at a cost of $10,000 to modify the system to be able to produce a report that showed the data in that way." That was what would happen!

Now, the business could respond with, "Well, I can take the data as a download from the mainframe onto my desktop and then put it in an Excel® spreadsheet or an access database, and then I can look at the data anyway I want. No thanks, systems, I will do it myself." This became so useful as a business tool that companies wanted to share data across business units. They put this access database or Excel spreadsheet onto a networked server so that it can be shared with others.

Networked servers were designed and implemented initially to provide shared printing capabilities so that every PC did not have to have a locally attached printer. That was great, but the business had other ideas on how to utilize this capability, and it just exploded from there. Now the data that runs the business no longer lives in the data center. It is everywhere. The business model changed again.

From a recovery perspective, the data-center folks continued to focus on the applications that ran in the data center, built their recovery strategies, and tested the recovery capabilities for those applications that stayed inside the glass house, ignoring again that the business model had changed just as it had changed when computers were first introduced. Computers did not only live in data centers anymore; technology was in the hands of the user.

Unfortunately, what often happened is that the person who built the access database left the company and, three end users later, all that the business person knows is that he or she clicks on the icon on the desktop. When the database ceases to work, usually because the software on the desktop has been upgraded but no-one updated the database program, the end user calls in a ticket to get it fixed and no-one in the technology group knows what he or she is talking about.

Over time, it began to occur to the technology teams that if they only recovered the infrastructure and applications that ran in the data center, they might be missing something.

I remember exactly when that became abundantly clear in the company I worked for at the time. The business group that was responsible for pricing mutual funds had begun downloading data from the mainframe onto a PC. The data was then loaded into Excel to produce the pricing reports. The data was then uploaded later in the day to the mainframe pricing system. The data-base where all this pricing data lived was stored on a server (really a PC tied to the network) in the business unit. It was actually (I am not kidding here) housed in a coat closet. One weekend, the building management was doing work on the HVAC units so the air conditioning was turned off. Well, as you can imagine, the "server" sitting in the coat closet got overheated and failed. That was OK, though, because the business unit had the data backed up to another "server" right next to it in the same coat closet. The backup failed as well. We missed the papers that Monday. Prices are published in the newspapers, but you have to come up with the prices by the paper deadline or you will not have your prices in the paper. Because this database that the technology group did not even know existed had to be restored before we could price, we missed the deadline.

We needed to recover the whole business, not just the data center. It was time to come back together, and the business-continuity industry began.

The folks in the data center started to ask the business people to participate in deciding what was important to recover and what could wait. The recovery planning was still driven by the data-center operations and application teams but with input from the business partners when they could get their attention. Getting their attention was the hard part. Business people and technology people don't speak the same language. They often don't even call applications by the same name. The business deals in business terms; the technology staff deals in hardware and software.

In companies that have mature business-continuity and disaster-recovery programs, the programs are now driven by the business, not by the technology group. It is the business groups that decide what technology needs to be recovered and when, based on what business operations need to be recovered and when. The ability to "continue the business" is the driving factor, not whether we could restore a mainframe or run a batch cycle.

Business continuity is about recovering the whole business. It involves the data center and the business people working together to define what keeps the business running. If the business does not continue, then no-one has a job. Whatever technology the business uses, whether it is in the data center or on the desktop, if the business needs it to survive, then we need to recover it.

I am often asked to whom a business-continuity-program manager should report and what skills he or she should have. A lot depends on the size of your business and the type of business you are in, but as I have to in most of this book I will generalize.

In a large organization with a mature program, business continuity and disaster recovery should report under enterprise risk management. Enterprise risk management includes BCP and DR as well as information security, physical security, operational risk management, records management, vendor risk management, and often legal, compliance, and internal audit.

In a smaller organization, the role should report to the chief operations officer (COO) or to both the COO and the CTO (chief technology officer).

In my career I have reported to the physical security organization, the audit organization, the technology organization, and the risk organization.

To be successful in the role of business-continuity-program manager, I think that you need a combination of skills and talents. The difference between a skill and a talent is that you can teach a skill—you can teach someone how to configure a server or, more simply, how to type. People can become more or less proficient at a skill, depending on how much they use the skill. You cannot teach a talent. A talent is an innate ability. You could give me voice lessons, and my singing voice I am sure would improve, but no matter what you did or how hard I practiced, I will never sound like Barbara Streisand, and trust me when I tell you that you really do not want to hear me sing.

The talents that I believe make you successful in this job are as follows:

- Communication—generally, finding it easy to put thoughts into words
- Self-assurance—confidence in your ability
- Belief/passion—believing in what you are doing and making others believe too
- Achievement—ability to work hard and deliver results
- Command—executive presence, ability to take charge in an event and make decisions

The skills you need to be successful in this job are as follows:

- Organization—there is lots of data to be organized
- Technical knowhow—ability to understand the technology environment
- Writing—ability to express yourself coherently
- Presentation—join Toastmasters® if you need to
- Financial—basic cost benefit analysis (CBA), return on investment (ROI), budgeting

I have put a job description for a business-continuity-program manager in the appendix for your reference.

2

Selling the Program

Business continuity is a hard program to sell. Management thinks that if you never have a disaster, then all that work was for nothing, and, really, what is the chance that there will be a disaster? No one believes in the "big one." Even after September 11, convincing leadership of the need for a plan is hard. There are so many other competing things to spend time and money on. You need to come in ready for battle. Here are some battle plans for you to use.

In my first full-time job in business continuity, I worked for the executive vice president (EVP). After he hired me, in my first one on one with him, I asked him how serious he was about having a plan. His response was that of course he was serious—after all, he hired me. I replied that that only meant that the auditors said that he had to have a plan; what I was asking was whether he wanted a plan that worked. There is no sense in spending even $1 on a plan unless you build something that actually works.

I told him that I had been there long enough that I could write a plan that looked good for the auditors, and if that was all he really wanted, then I would do it and go on to something else, because it is generally not career-enhancing to do something that leadership does not think is

11

important. The real plan, then, would be to keep our resumes up to date, because if a disaster happened for real, the company would not recover. If he wanted something that actually would work in a real disaster, that was going to take time, resources, and money.

To convince leadership of the need to build a viable business-continuity plan, you need to help people understand the risk they are accepting by not having one and the cost to the corporation if a disaster were to occur. The risks to the corporation are found in three areas: financial (how much money the corporation stands to lose), reputational (how badly the corporation will be perceived by its customers and its shareholders), and regulatory (fines or penalties incurred, lawsuits filed against them). There is also the potential that the leaders of the organization could be held personally liable, financially and even criminally, if it is determined that they did not use due care to adequately protect the corporation and its assets.

FINANCIAL RISKS

Financial risks can be quantified in many cases and are generally used to help determine how much should be spent on the recovery program. You are most likely going to be able to defend spending only the amount of money that is actually at risk from a disastrous event. One of the ways financial risk can be calculated is using the formula $P \times M = C$. This translates to the probability of harm (P)—the chance that a damaging event will occur—times the magnitude of harm (M)—the amount of financial damage that would occur should a disaster happen—equals the cost of prevention (C)—the price of putting in place a countermeasure preventing the disaster's effects.

The amount of money you spend on the program should be in direct relation to the amount of money at risk in a disaster. How much money do you make in a minute? In an hour? In a day? If your systems were unavailable for a week, how much business would you lose vs. business that would simply be deferred to the next week and written then? Your industry, your product, your competitors, your contractual obligations to your customers; these are all factors that should be considered when talking about the need for a plan. In today's world in many industries it is a fact that your competitor is just a click away. If you cannot satisfy the needs of your customers when required, it is not hard for them to find another company that will.

RISK TO THE COMPANY REPUTATION

Reputational risk is harder to quantify, but there are many examples of a negative impact to stock price in the wake of a crisis that is not managed properly. When I teach a class about business continuity and disaster recovery and define what needs to be recovered and when, I use the example of regulatory requirements and customer requirements. Regulatory requirements tell me that I have to do something within a certain period of time, and customer requirements that tell me that if I don't do this, the customer will be dissatisfied and could take their business elsewhere. For example, a mutual-fund company is required by regulation to price its mutual funds every day that the market is open. If the company does not do this, it could be penalized and the fund even be closed. Mutual-fund companies are not, however, required by regulation or law to answer their phones. How long do you think a company would last if it did not answer its phones, particularly if it was widely known that the company experienced some type of disaster?

Rory F. Knight and Deborah J. Pretty recently produced a research report, sponsored by the Sedgwick Group, titled "The Impact of Catastrophes on Shareholder Value." The report examined 15 catastrophes that had happened to publicly quoted companies since 1980, with total financial losses of around $19 billion.

The report found that the share price of a corporation suffering a public disaster falls by around 5 to 8 percent within the first few days after a disaster. Recovery of the share price then depends on how well the recovery is executed. The "winners" regain the confidence of the financial analysts by demonstrating leadership and management ability in rapidly taking control and reestablishing operational capability. The report goes on to state that the share price of a company that manages its recovery well not only recovers the initial loss but may increase within around 100 days by between 10 and 15 percent compared to the pre-disaster share price. The companies whose disasters are not managed well drift at the lower share price, possibly rallying a little around 75 days following the disaster before settling at a price around 15 percent below the pre-disaster share price.

Reputations are at stake. So are jobs. If you lose 40 percent of your business in the wake of a disaster, you no longer need 100 percent of your staff, and often leadership is the first to go. Ask your managers what they think of when you reference the following examples.

In October 1982, when seven people in Chicago were reported dead after taking Extra Strength Tylenol® capsules, it was reported that an unknown suspect had put 65 milligrams of deadly cyanide into the capsules. This amount is 10,000 times more than what is necessary to kill a human. Once the connection was made between the Tylenol capsules and the reported deaths, public announcements were made warning people about the consumption of the product. Johnson & Johnson had a disaster in the making. Tylenol was this company's most profitable product, and now its safety was in question. Not only that, people died!

Johnson & Johnson was faced with the dilemma of the best way to deal with the problem without destroying the reputation of the company and its most profitable product; it needed to respond.

What the company did was remarkable. It put the protection of people first and property second. McNeil Consumer Products, a subsidiary of Johnson & Johnson, conducted an immediate product recall from the entire country, which amounted to about 31 million bottles and a loss of more than $100 million (Lazare, *Chicago Sun-Times*, 2002). Additionally, it halted all advertising for the product.

Although Johnson & Johnson knew it was not responsible for the tampering of the product, it assumed responsibility by ensuring public safety. The reaction cost them money in the short term, but in the long run consumers came back to Tylenol because they trusted Johnson & Johnson's assurances that the product was now safe. In fact, in February 1986, when a woman was reported dead from cyanide poisoning in Tylenol capsules, Johnson & Johnson permanently removed all of the capsules from the market.

What a different story for Exxon®. On March 24, 1989, the Exxon Valdez supertanker went aground, and some 10.8 million gallons of crude oil poured into the pristine waters of Alaska's Prince William Sound. The name of the tanker has since become synonymous with environmental disaster.

Exxon was widely criticized for its slow response to the event. The reputational outcome to Exxon was huge. The company lost market share; the stock value dropped $3 billion; the company slipped from largest to third-largest oil company and became a target of a consumer boycott. After the spill, the owner of the tanker, Exxon Shipping Company, spent $3.4 billion to try to clean up the mess and compensate thousands of commercial fishermen and other Alaska residents hit by the catastrophe. In 1994, a group of 32,677 Alaskans harmed by the oil spill sued Exxon, seeking compensation and additional punishment for the company.

The plaintiffs' lawyers alleged that Exxon managers assigned a relapsed alcoholic, Captain Joseph Hazelwood, to command the supertanker. The jury found that Captain Hazelwood acted recklessly. But the jury found that Exxon acted recklessly, too. Hazelwood was ordered to pay $5,000 in punitive damages, and Exxon was ordered to pay $5 billion. (The verdict was later reduced to $2.5 billion.)

Johnson & Johnson's crisis management was very effective because of its leadership's quick response to the product tampering. Exxon, on the other hand, waited a long time before responding to the oil spill and sending aid to Alaska. For example, it was 10 days after the spill before Exxon ran an advertisement in the newspapers, and two weeks passed before Exxon's chairman, Lawrence G. Rawl, flew to Alaska to view the damage and the cleanup efforts.

Exxon never seemed to take responsibility for what happened. On the other hand, even though it was proven that Johnson & Johnson was not associated with the tampering, it still immediately assumed appropriate responsibility for the wellbeing of its customers. This in turn restored confidence in the consumer about the safety of its product. Exxon completely failed at this task.

Effective business-continuity and disaster-recovery programs can be the difference between a company surviving an event and a company ceasing to exist. A common statistic is that 40 percent of companies that experience a disaster and do not have a plan for recovery go out of business within two years of the event.

REGULATORY RISK

Regulatory risk is clearly defined by the industry the organization is a part of, and we will discuss specifics in a later chapter; however, no matter what industry you are in, what is commonly referred to as the prudent-man law applies: *exercise the same care in managing company affairs as in managing personal affairs.* Since the events of September 11, a huge number of new regulations have been established to require or at least encourage business-continuity and disaster-recovery planning.

HIDDEN BENEFITS OF THE PLANNING PROCESS

At any company, contingency planning is a necessity that has turned out to be beneficial in more ways than ever expected. We all know that contingency planning greatly helps to ensure business viability during and following a disaster. What we have also discovered is that the contingency-planning effort has led to significant improvements in the daily operations of many businesses.

While researching and documenting contingency plans, hundreds of single points of failure (SPOFs) have been found. A SPOF is any single input to a process that, if missing, would cause the process or several processes to be unable to function. Once identified, these SPOFs can often easily be eliminated or at least have their damaging potential reduced. Many companies have also witnessed process improvements as a direct result of their contingency-planning efforts, particularly while exercising business-resumption plans.

There are many more benefits to contingency planning. No other process really makes a business function think about what it does, how it does it, and how to make it better. When managers start thinking about how to operate when they are out of their building, missing half their staff, without connectivity or something equally detrimental—that's when things happen.

WHY NO ONE BELIEVES IN THE "BIG ONE"

If I had built a tabletop exercise scenario where all the airports in the country were closed and every plane was grounded before the events of September 11, 2001, I would have been laughed out of the room. No one would believe that could happen. Even today, I work for a company in a small city that is clearly not viewed by the leadership as a "hotbed" of terrorism. If I tried to use a terrorist attack on the company as a scenario, I would get the same reaction: "That is not going to happen here." You have to find something the leadership can believe in.

The first scenario I used for a drill with my current leadership team was a workplace-violence event. I work for a property and casualty insurance company, and this was six months or so after Katrina. The scenario was a claimant who had evacuated to Texas because of Katrina and was still there. He was still there because we denied his claim on his property in New Orleans because it was caused by the flood. Flood is not a covered event under a homeowner's policy; you have to have flood insurance. He was not happy with us.

After making a number of threatening phone calls to the 800 number for claims, he looked up the address of our office in Dallas on our website and went there with a gun. Our Dallas office is not a claims office, but he did not know that. He then proceeded to kill three people, injure one more, and then turn the gun on himself. He recovered from his wounds, and of course there was a trial. Because of the Katrina link, it became a media issue—the big, bad insurance company against the homeowner

16

who lost everything. Our employees were frightened for their safety; the Dallas office was a crime scene; and so forth.

I made this up, but it was realistic enough for the leadership team for them to believe that it *could* happen and that we needed a plan. This scenario was not the "big one." It was not catastrophic to the firm from the standpoint that we did not lose our data center and our Dallas office is a small regional office, not the home office with 3000 people, but the team believed it could happen and it helped them to understand the need for a plan and the need for them to be a part of it.

Most events are not "big ones," which is why it is hard for people to believe that it could happen to them. They are rare. But little ones happen all the time—events such as small fires, power outages, water leaks, hardware failures, and car accidents. If you use these, people believe they can happen.

I once worked for a company that had 1000 people who worked in an office building that was built on a pier overlooking a harbor. It had huge pane-glass windows looking out on three sides at the harbor. It was directly across the harbor from a major international airport. It was 1/4 mile away from the largest construction project that city had ever seen, which was just about to begin. Tour boats tied up on either side of the building every day and pulled in and out of the pier several times a day. The front bottom half of the building was an exhibition hall large enough that workers constantly pulled 18-wheelers into the loading-dock area with conference exhibits such as boat shows. This particular region was subject to the occasional hurricane. LNG tankers moved in and out of the harbor daily, delivering natural gas to terminal and storage facilities less than four miles away as the crow flies.

It truly was a beautiful place to work, but its location clearly presented risks. Unfortunately for me, the leadership did not buy into any of the above-mentioned risks. The company was too big, and these events rarely happened. What finally sold the team on the need for a plan was that during the build-out of this space to house employees, we pulled additional voice and data network capacity from the downtown area to have redundant network capabilities. That cable was pulled across a bridge that was originally a drawbridge. That's right—the bridge was originally designed as a drawbridge to let boats in and out of the inner harbor area. When the cable was pulled, the city promised it would never open it again. Of all the hazards the team faced, that is the one that finally spurred them to action. They did not believe in the hurricane, the airplane crash, or the construction accident, but they believed that that bridge might get opened on purpose or by accident.

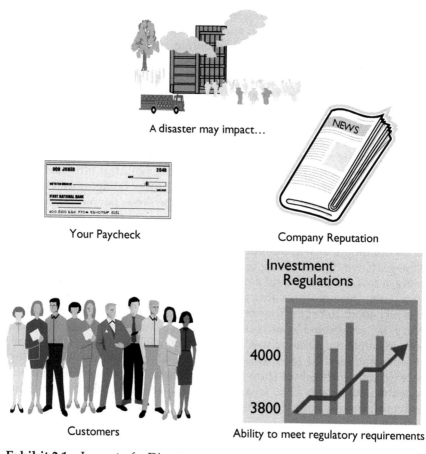

A disaster may impact...

Your Paycheck

Company Reputation

Customers

Ability to meet regulatory requirements

Exhibit 2.1 Impact of a Disaster.

The key to gaining executives' support is to find something they can believe in.

It is also important to approach this as a project directly involving the managers. Management understands project terms like deliverables and resources. It doesn't as clearly understand that you are building a program. Ongoing program requirements will come later. First, we need to get the commitment to get it done. Remember as shown in Exhibit 2.1, a disaster may impact your customers, your company's reputation, the ability to meet legal or regulatory requirements and, more importantly to you, your paycheck.

3

Project Initiation and Management

Let's begin with the first step in building the business-continuity program, project initiation and management. During this phase, we will do the following:

- Obtain senior management support to go forward with the project—without this the project will fail.
- Define a project scope, objectives to be achieved, and the assumptions we will make.
- Estimate the project resources we will need to be successful, both human and financial.
- Define a timeline and major deliverables for the project.

DEFINING THE SCOPE OF THE PLANNING EFFORT

Defining the scope of the planning process is otherwise known as, what is it exactly that you are planning for? It is very simple to get caught up in the "what if" in this business, so it is important to understand the scope of the events you are planning to build a recovery from. The five types of plans every business should consider as part of its program are:

- Loss of site
- Loss of technology
- Information security
- Workforce impairment
- Crisis-management plan

Every business needs to have a plan to address losing a site where you conduct business and losing everything that is co-located with you in your site, including technology. If your business operates in multiple sites, then you need a plan for each of those locations.

Whether you are a small company that conducts all of its business on a laptop or a major corporation with multiple data centers, your technology is an integral part of how you conduct your business, and you need a plan to recover it.

Workforce impairment can result from a pandemic, a labor strike, transportation issues, and the like; your building is fine, your data center is fine, but your workforce is unable or unwilling to come to work.

An information-security event is a breach of confidential information, such as customers' credit-card information being inadvertently released or compromised by hackers or a virus or worm that impacts your technology environment. This event requires a different type of response than a loss of technology due to hardware failure or a facility event that impacts the technology.

A crisis-management plan is a plan for how the business will manage a crisis event. It may often be utilized in one of the other event types but also may be needed when none of those other things have occurred. During the Tylenol tampering, there was no impact to Johnson & Johnson's technology or buildings, but the organization still had a crisis. Crisis management is about leading the firm back to business as usual.

For example, you may need to invoke a crisis-management plan if the president of your company is killed in a plane crash or car accident or has to resign suddenly amid some type of personal scandal. You may need to invoke a crisis-management plan if a product you produce results in injuries or deaths to consumers or if an employee is attacked or killed on your property or during the course of doing business on behalf of your organization in a workplace-violence event. In all of these cases, your building, your technology, and most of the employee population is fine, but the organization still has a crisis.

You need to agree with leadership on the scope of the planning effort, as that will define the project resources you will need, the timeline to complete the project, and the deliverables the leadership team can expect as the project progresses.

I recommend that you focus on the site- and technology-recovery plans first and move to the other plans as your program matures. Much of the work that you will do in support of building those plans will be a foundation for the other plans.

DEFINING A TIMELINE

A general timeline for building a plan where none currently exists within a medium-size company with an experienced planner running the program and a commitment from leadership to support the effort is as follows:

- Emergency-notification list (1 month): To respond to an emergency situation at all, you must first be able to reach the people in your organization who can and will respond.
- Vital records backup and recovery (within the first 6 months): To be able to recover from a disaster situation, you must have access to your vital records at the time of need.
- Business-impact analysis (first 6 months): Identify business functions; the capabilities of each business unit to handle outages; the priority and sequence of functions and applications; and resources required for recovery and interdependencies.
- Strategy development (6 to 9 months): Assess various available strategies, perform cost-benefit analysis, and make recommendation to leadership for approval.
- Alternate site selection (9 to 12 months): Prepare RFPs, perform site surveys, select vendor and/or build-out and equipment of internal site, and negotiate contracts.
- Contingency-plan development (12 months): Consider emergency response and restoring of critical business functions to normal business operations.
- Testing, plan maintenance, and periodic audit (ongoing)

We will go over each of these tasks in detail as the book progresses. The purpose of stating them here is to give you some basic information about what the steps are to help you build a timeline to submit to management as part of your project plan.

COMPANY POLICY OR STANDARD

Organizational leadership must support a corporate policy requiring compliance with the BCP/DRP development program to facilitate assignment of resources from the various areas of the organization that will need to participate. The policy should state the following: "The senior leader of each functional area of the company is responsible for ensuring that a business-continuity plan exists for his or her area of responsibility, for the contents of the plan itself, and for affirming his or her concurrence with the plan annually by signing off on the plan document."

Having this as a policy will allow you to use the policy as an enforcement tool to get resources assigned to the project and to produce reports on the functional areas and their compliance to the standard.

RESOURCE REQUIREMENTS

When we have agreed upon the scope of the planning we will be doing, we can determine the resource requirements we need to accomplish the plan. I promise you that you cannot write this plan yourself. You will need to get at least one person from every functional area of the company to become part of the planning team—and in some cases, more than one person. If you have more than one site, you will need someone from each site to represent each functional area within that site.

Financial resources will also need to be defined for the planning process. Monies may be spent hiring outside consultants to help facilitate the planning in the initial stages or for software tools to assist in data collection and plan development. Travel may need to be budgeted for the lead business-continuity planner to go to each site to work with the planning teams.

A word about the use of consultants, since I am often asked about them. Consultants can be invaluable in helping with information gathering and in performing the business-impact analysis, but I strongly encourage you not to have them write the plan for you. The same holds for the use of software tools. The software tools in this industry are terrific relational databases that can help you keep track of what is in each site and who your planners are, but they will not write the plan for you.

I have always used Microsoft Word® to write my plans. I do not have to train anyone on how to use it. It is readily available no matter where I go. I don't have to have any special software at the alternate site to read or print my plan. I have used planning software for other things but not for the actual plan document.

PLANNING PHASES AND DELIVERABLES

The lead planner should develop a project plan outlining each phase of the planning process, the resource requirements needed, the amount of time each phase will take to complete, and the deliverables to be produced from each phase of the planning process.

When developing a new plan or updating a significantly old plan, the following phases are recommended:

- Planning team and critical staff: You need to identify and build contact lists by site for the planning team's site leadership and critical staff. The theory is that if you can at least get hold of your people, even without a plan you have some hope of recovery. The deliverable from this phase is the emergency notification list (ENL).
- Vital records: Validating that all the records needed to rebuild the business are stored offsite in a secure location that will be accessible following a disaster is essential. This includes backups of your technology as well as paper records. Most companies are pretty good about their traditional vital records, but you must also consider items such as procedure manuals, forms, letterhead—things that are unique to your business and part of how you do your job every day. This continues the theory that if you have your people and now your stuff, you have even more hope of recovery, even if you did not have a plan before the disaster occurred. The deliverable from this phase is a list of your vital records, where they are stored offsite, how to retrieve them, and who is authorized to retrieve them.
- Risk and business-impact analysis: This is where the planning really begins, where you make decisions about which risks you will mitigate against and which processes you will recover and when. The deliverable from this phase of the planning is a list of risks by site and recommendations to be implemented to reduce the impact of the risk. You cannot mitigate against every possible risk because of the cost to do so.
- Strategy development: In this phase you review the different types of strategies for the recovery of business areas and technology based on the recovery time frame you have identified for each, do a cost-benefit analysis on the viable strategies to be selected, and make a proposal to leadership to implement the

selected strategies. The deliverable from this phase is the recommended strategies for recovery.

- Alternate-site selection and implementation: In this phase you select and build out the alternate sites you will use to recover the areas of the business or technology. The deliverable from this phase is a functional alternate site.
- Documenting the plan: This phase is where all the information collected up to this point is combined into a plan document. There should be a plan for each site where the company performs business. The deliverable from this phase is the documented plan for recovery for each site.
- Testing, maintenance, and update: This final phase is where you validate the recovery strategies you have implemented through testing and establish a maintenance schedule for the plan and an update schedule for the plan documentation. The deliverable from this phase is the ongoing results from validating the plan.

The phases as well as other components of the planning process will be discussed in greater detail in later chapters.

4

Your Planning Team and Your Vital Records Program

Chapter Objectives

- Finding Your Planning Team
- Vital Records—What Are They?
- RTO/RPO
- Backup Strategies

Remember my first full-time job doing business continuity within a company when I asked my boss whether he was serious or not about having a plan? He replied that of course he was serious—after all, he hired me. I said that clearly he wanted a plan, but what type of plan did he want? I needed to understand whether he wanted a plan that looked good to the auditors or one that would actually work. I told him that I had worked for the company long enough that he could sit me in a room for three months or so and I could write a plan that looked really good on paper, one that he could show to the auditors and they would smile and agree that we had a plan, and then I would go off and do something else because it really wasn't career-enhancing to do something that management did not consider important. If that was all he wanted, that is what I would do.

You should challenge your leadership's commitment to building a real plan as well. To build something that really works, you need lots of people helping you build and validate the plan. Once the plan is built, you need commitment to maintain the viability of the plan, with lots of people continuing to help you keep the plan up to date and the resources ready to respond.

It is important that you not only get someone assigned but that you get the right someone to participate in building this plan. When I took over as planner in a systems group years ago, the first thing my boss said to me was that the emergency-notification list needed to be updated, and he handed me a copy. I looked at it and laughed. It wasn't an emergency-notification list—it was a who's who of the systems group. If you were important, you were in this book, and it listed everyone by department name. There had to be over 300 names.

I handed it back to him and said that I was going to build something that was actually useful in a disaster, because that list was so big that when an event occurred, by the time I got to everyone on it, the event would either be all over or it would be too late.

To do this, I took a look at what this organization did for a living. The technology group for the company had two primary roles. First, it ran data centers and all that that entails (hardware, software, applications, networks, development, support, operations) and secondly, it was responsible for the voice and data networks in every site we did business in, whether there was a data center there or not.

This particular company had three major data centers. I went to one of them and sat down with people who made that production environment work every day. I asked them who they would need if a disaster happened for real and we lost this data center and had to recover it somewhere else? I made a list of those people and then welcomed them to my team for the data center at that site. I did the same thing for the other two data centers and then also identified who was responsible for the data and voice networks in each of our sites.

You need a team from each site you do business in because generally speaking disasters occur by building, not by business line or by application. Your planning team, whether for business or technology, needs to be the people who would do the recovery if the disaster happened for real. Only the people who do this job every day, day in and day out, understand everything it takes to get it done and how it all fits together.

The people assigned to represent their functional areas will have tasks to complete in support of the project. The initial time the planning team will spend on the project will be spent understanding the business processes within their area and the impact to the firm if those processes are interrupted by an unexpected event. Additional tasks will follow as the planning process continues.

Once you have identified your planning team, you should hold a kick-off meeting with each group to go over the steps you will take to build a plan for the site, the tools you will have for them to use, the timeline for deliverables, and what will be achieved when the project phase is complete.

I try to make it as easy as possible for the planning teams to do what I ask. Try very hard not to be a seagull. When I go to branch-office locations with my current company to work on the recovery plan for their site, I tell them the seagull story: I am coming out here from the home office, and I am going to ask you to do some things for me, but when I come here or when I ask you for something, I am going to have a very specific agenda and, whatever I ask you to do, I will give you all the tools to do it because I am not a seagull. Usually, I get a blank stare or maybe one or two people smile. I then explain that a seagull is someone who flies in from the home office, drops shit, and leaves. Don't be a seagull.

The first task for you and your team is to build an emergency-notification list for the site. I usually have three teams per site, but I may only have one if the site is small. The first team is the executive team. This team consists of the senior leaders who have responsibility for the business conducted in this site. They may or may not be physically located in this site but would need to be involved if there were a significant event impacting the site.

The second team is the emergency management team. These are the senior leaders who are physically located in that site and would generally have decision-making authority over events that occurred in that site, such as whether to close a site due to severe weather.

The third team is the emergency response team. These individuals are usually the planning-team members who would be responsible for executing the recovery from an event if it were required. They work at the direction of the emergency management team.

A sample ENL is shown in Exhibit 4.1.

Emergency Management Team – Home Office

Title	Name	Home phone	Work Phone	Page/Cell phoner
Emergency Mgmt Team Leader	John Smith	508-555-3546	508-855-1234	508-555-3452
Human Resource Team Leader	Mary Flounder	508-555-6765	508-855-2779	508-555-9876

Exhibit 4.1   Sample Emergency Notification List.

VITAL-RECORDS PROGRAM

For both business functions and applications, the company also needs to determine the amount of work in process that can be at risk in an event. The data that is on employee's desks when a fire occurs would be lost forever if that information was not backed up somewhere else. The information stored in file cabinets, incoming mail in the mailroom, and backup tapes that have not yet left the building are all at risk.

The planning team needs to make decisions about all types of data because data is what runs the business. How much data is it acceptable to lose? A minute's worth? An hour's worth? A whole business day? This is commonly referred to as the recovery-point objective or RPO. This is the point in time that the planner will recover to. The vital-records program, backup policies and procedures for electronic and hard-copy data, needs to comply with the RPO established by the business.

DATA STORED IN ELECTRONIC FORM

Backup strategies for data used to restore technology are varied and are driven by the recovery-time and the recovery-point objectives needed to support the business requirements. Some organizations have begun tiering data based on its importance to the business and frequency of use. The more time-sensitive data is replicated offsite either synchronously or asynchronously to ensure its availability and currency. Other data is backed up to tape and sent offsite once or more often a day.

If the data needed to rebuild the technology environment is stored somewhere else besides your alternate site, the time it takes to pack and transport the data must be included in the recovery-time objective. Factors such as how the data is stored, how far away it is, and how it will be delivered to the recovery facility will determine how much the recovery time could be increased. Delivery of offsite data to the recovery facility could delay the recovery by hours or even days. To reduce the recovery time, the data that will be used to recover your systems and applications should be stored at the recovery site whenever possible.

It is vital that the data that is stored offsite include not only the application data but also the application source code, hardware and software images for the servers and end-user desktops, utility software, license keys, etc. Application data alone cannot rebuild an application.

REMOTE REPLICATION/ OFFSITE JOURNALING

Remote replication involves moving data over a network to secondary storage devices in another location. Remote replication is an expensive solution but one that will meet the needs of an application RPO that is immediate or near immediate. Remote replication can be done either synchronously or asynchronously.

In synchronous replication the data is written to the production-environment disk and to the remote disk at the same time. Until both "writes" occur, the next process cannot begin. There are distance limitations on doing synchronous remote replication as well as network bandwidth requirements that can be extremely expensive. Synchronous replication has the potential to impact production but is the best solution when time to recovery and data loss matter. This type of replication is commonly deployed in multiple data-center environments where applications are load-balanced between two or more sites but can be used for other strategies where the currency of the data, not the actual time of the recovery, is key.

Asynchronous replication occurs when the data is written to the production environment and then is queued to write to the backup environment at scheduled intervals, depending on the RPO for the data. This can occur several times a day, several times an hour, or several times a minute, depending again on the need for data currency.

Asynchronous data replication's advantage is that it does not impact production performance, as it occurs offline from the production environment and provides long-distance, remote data replication while still providing disaster-recovery data protection.

Remote replication does not eliminate the need for point-in-time copies of the data. If data in your production environment becomes corrupt, your replicated data will also be corrupt. A point-in-time copy of your data is still required for restoration from this type of event.

BACKUP STRATEGIES

Most companies, no matter what strategy they employ for storing data offsite, start by performing full backups of all their data followed by periodic incremental backups. Incremental backups take copies of only the files that have changed since the last full or incremental backup was taken and then set the archive bit to "0." The other common option is to take a differential backup. A differential backup copies only the files that have had data changes since the last full backup and does not change the archive bit value.

If a company wants the backup and recovery strategy to be as simple as possible, then it should only use full backups. They take more time and hard-drive space to perform, but they are the most efficient in recovery. If that option is not viable, a differential backup can be restored in just two steps. The full backup of the data is restored first, then the differential backup on top of it. Remember, the differential backs up every piece of data in the file that has changed since the last full backup was taken.

An incremental backup takes the most time in restoration because you must lay down the full backup first and then every incremental backup taken since the last full backup. If you take daily incremental backups but only monthly full backups and you are recovering on the 26th day of the month, you will have to perform your full backup restore first, and then 26 incremental backups must be laid on top in the same order that they were taken. You can see how the backup method you use could have a significant impact on your recovery timeline.

The recovery-time objective (RTO) for a business process or for an application determines the recovery strategy for the process or application. The more time that can elapse before the recovery needs to occur, the more recovery options are available. The more time-sensitive an application or function is, the fewer options you will have in selecting a recovery strategy. We will determine the RTO for applications following the business-impact analysis.

HARD-COPY DATA

I remember when I worked for a company in the early 90s and the goal for the business areas was to be "paper-free in '93." Here we are 15 or more years later and paper is far from gone. We certainly have a lot more of our data on image systems and the like, but paper is still with us.

Some common vital records are shown in Exhibit 4.2. When considering vital records to be available to rebuild your business, you need to think not only about the traditional vital records but also the things that are on people's desks that they use every day to do their job that would not be readably available at the alternate site unless they are planned for.

In my first full-time job doing business continuity, when I held my first meeting with my planning team, I told them that I already had an alternate site for them and that it had everything they needed to do their jobs. (I was lying, but I was trying to make a point.) This was in the days before PCs were on everyone's desk, so I told them that I had a room full of dumb terminals. Every desk had a phone, paper, pen, pencils, rulers, paper clips, calculator, calendar, etc., but, I explained, when you got there, you would not have your Rolodex®; could you still do your job? (Rolodexes, for those of you too young to remember, were small paper turnstiles that sat on

---

Business Records

- Databases and contact lists for employees, customers, vendors, partners or others that your business unit deals with regularly or at time of emergency (this includes your ENL)
- Your business unit's contingency plan(s)
- Procedure / application manuals that your employees normally use and procedure manuals for operation in your alternate site if different from above
- Backup files from production servers / applications owned by your business unit that support your critical functions
- Reference documents used by your employees on a regular basis
- Calendar files or printouts – particularly if your business unit schedules appointments with customers
- Source code

Legal Records

- Anything with a signature
- Customer correspondence (statements, letters back an forth, requests, etc)
- Customer conversations (recorded interactions with customer service reps)
- Accounting records
- Justification proposals / documents
- Transcripts / minutes of meetings with legal significance
- Paper with value - stock certificates, bonds, commercial paper, etc.
- Legal documents – letters of incorporation, deeds, etc.

Exhibit 4.2 Common Vital Records.

your desk and had all your contact information. We did not have PDAs, Blackberrys, and cell phones then.

So what is on the desks of your folks? Procedure manuals, forms, letterhead—stuff that they use every day. Make certain that you consider those as part of the vital records to rebuild your business.

5

Risk Evaluation and Control

Chapter Objectives

- Understanding Risk
- Mitigating Strategies

RISK MANAGEMENT 101

As part of the planning process, you will need to perform a risk assessment to determine which threats your organization has and where you should spend mitigating dollars to attempt to reduce their impact.

There are three elements of risk. The first is the threats themselves. A threat is an event or situation that, if it occurred, would prevent the business from operating in its normal manner if at all. Threats are measured in probabilities, such as "may happen once in ten years," and have a duration of time where the impact is felt.

The most common threat that impacts a business' ability to function normally is power. Power outages cause more business interruptions than any other type of event. The second most common type of event is water, either too much (flooding, plumbing leak, broken pipe, leaky roof) or not enough (water-main break). Other common events are severe weather, cable cuts resulting in network outages, fires, labor disputes, transportation mishaps, and, for the data center, hardware failures.

Refer to the threat matrix in Exhibit 5.1. As you go through the list of threats, you will notice that some of them are fairly localized and others,

- Earthquake
- Hurricane
- Tornado
- Volcanic eruption
- Flood
- Power outage
- Falling aircraft
- Transportation mishap
  —Rail
  —Road
  —Boat
- Labor strike
- Workforce illness (Pandemic)
- Scandal
- Severe weather
- Workplace violence
- Fire
- Smoke
- Denial of access from Contamination
- Civil disorder
- Water damage
- Bomb threats
- Sabotage/vandalism
- Mechanical breakdown
- Hardware failure
- Software failure
- Computer virus/worm
- Breach of confidential info
- Sudden loss or death of leadership

Exhibit 5.1   Potential threats.

such as a hurricane, have a regional impact. When there is a regional impact, not only your business but the homes and families of your employees may be at risk.

The second element of risk is assets. If you do not own anything, then you are not concerned about risk because you have little or nothing to lose. The more assets you have that would be impacted by an event, the more you are concerned about how you manage the risk. Assets are comprised of many elements—information assets, financial assets, physical assets, human assets—and when considering the impact of a risk, you must also consider additional costs to recover, fines or penalties you may incur, and lost goodwill or competitive advantage.

The third element of risk is mitigating factors. Mitigating factors are the controls or safeguards you put in place to reduce the impact of a threat. You cannot eliminate a threat. You cannot prevent power outages from occurring. You can, however, mitigate the impact of a power outage on your organization by implementing battery backup UPS (uninterruptible power supply) systems and generators to provide you with power until the utility company returns your street power. You cannot eliminate the criminal element in society, but you can prevent it from working for your company by performing background investigations, and you can make it harder for it to gain access to your building by implementing access-control systems. These are all mitigating factors.

I worked for a company that had 800+ people in a building across the street from the World Trade Towers in New York. We had hardened the facility against all types of risks—power, circuit failure, carrier failure, cooling system failure, etc. Despite all of that, the building itself was still a single point of failure. When the attack occurred on September 11, 2001, our infrastructure actually stayed up for 22 hours, basically until the generator ran out of fuel. However, the building was in the middle of ground zero, and though it was not one of the ones that collapsed, it did suffer significant damage. We did not gain access to the building for the first two weeks. Two weeks following the attacks we were allowed to take a certain number of people with special passes to the building but only to retrieve the contents of our vault and personal things our staff left behind. We had to be escorted by the National Guard throughout the time we were in ground zero. It was significantly longer before we had full access to the building, and the employees were in their alternate sites for *15 months* before moving back to New York.

THE MOST COMMON RISKS AND WAYS TO MITIGATE THEM

The table in Exhibit 5.2 shows the most common risks and the mitigating controls you can implement to control their impact on your company. After all, the purpose of performing the risk analysis is to determine where to spend whatever mitigating dollars have been allocated to the project. It would not be cost-effective to mitigate against every risk, so you must focus on the risks that have the highest potential to occur and would have the highest impact if they did occur.

To do this, you need to determine the risks your particular business is subject to. You need to look at natural-hazard risks based on the location of the business, industry risks based on the type of business your company is in, crime risks based on the location of your business, man-made hazards such as transportation accidents based on proximity to highways, train lines, airports, etc., and proximity risks based on other industries near where you conduct business such as chemical plants or natural-gas storage facilities and recommend mitigating strategies to protect your business where appropriate.

35

Threat	Mitigation
Power Outage ⟶	UPS/Generators
Fire ⟶	Sprinkler systems
Earthquake ⟶	Anchor equipment
Mechanical Breakdown ⟶	Regular maintenance
Flood ⟶	Flood wall
Theft ⟶	Access control
Lightening ⟶	Lightening Rod/Grounding

Exhibit 5.2   Some Potential Threats/Mitigations.

Natural-Hazard Risks

You can check with the United States Geological Service for a natural-hazards map of your area. Some common natural hazards include:

- Earthquake
- Tornado
- Flood
- Hurricane
- Ice storm
- Blizzard
- Tsunami

Let's talk about some natural-hazard risks and how to mitigate against them. You cannot prevent an earthquake, and earthquakes are fairly common events. Every day on average there are two earthquakes somewhere in the world that are of a magnitude of 2.0 or greater on the Richter scale. The most earthquakes occur in the Pacific Rim, but they can occur anywhere in the world. In the US only Florida, eastern Texas, and the Midwest seem to be immune to earthquakes. We always think of California when we think of earthquakes in the US, but New England, where I live, has had two earthquakes in the last 200 years with a magnitude of 6.0 or greater.

So what can a business do to mitigate against an earthquake?

- Make sure your office is located in a building that was built to withstand earthquakes to reduce the risk of structural failure.
- Heavy or breakable equipment should be positioned as near to ground level as possible.

- Secure equipment to the building structure—for example secure an equipment rack or a bookcase to the wall with anchors. High racks should be secured together on top and to the floor on the bottom. Secure PCs to the desktop, and secure cabinet doors with positive latches.
- Store hazardous materials correctly and educate all your employees about them. Secure freestanding, movable partitions. A good rule of thumb is to secure anything above desktop level.
- Check for diagonal bracing wires suspended in ceilings. Ensure proper restraint of "stem" light fixtures and fluorescent light panels. Securely attach decorative ceiling panels, spotlights, speakers, air-conditioning units, etc. Check above suspended ceilings for poorly attached ducts, cables, etc.
- Secure any electrically powered equipment. Shock hazards exist if unsecured electrical equipment breaks its connection or exposes energized lines. Unsecured equipment may short out the power in your office building.
- Have a backup power generator for emergency lighting and to protect computers against data loss. Ensure that generators, fuel tanks, battery packs, and fuel lines are all properly secured.
- Seismic anchoring of floors helps to prevent them from collapse.
- Secure water heaters, furnaces, boilers, fans, pumps, and heating, ventilating, and air-conditioning equipment and the ducting or pipes that go with them. Large, heavy equipment like HVAC or generators should be secured to the actual fabric of the building. Loss of plant equipment may prevent you from continuing your business after a quake.
- Secure large containers of production chemicals or cleaning supplies. Ensure that all toxic items are in the correct containers and properly labeled. Unsecured or improperly stored hazardous chemicals may force your business out of an otherwise undamaged building.

Not in an earthquake zone? How about something nearly all of us have experienced at some time in our life—severe weather? Severe weather occurs at times nearly everywhere. Lightning strikes can occur in almost all regions. They can cause severe disruption to a facility unless power-surge protection and grounding are deployed. Power outages and fires can be caused by lightening strikes as well as damage to cables and wiring.

In my home in Massachusetts, I had an underground electric dog fence that was attached to the device that caused the small electric charge into the dog's collar when he crossed over the wires buried a few inches deep around the perimeter of the yard. The device that controlled the fence was mounted on a wall in the basement. During a thunderstorm, lightening struck somewhere near the house, and the electrical charge was picked up by the wire fence and carried into my house. The device was blown off the wall in my basement, and every piece of electronic equipment in the house had to be replaced because of the power surge. Luckily there was no fire, but the explosion left a large color pattern on the wall that showed us how lucky we were.

Some protections against lightning and the impact of severe storms in your facility include:

- Install lightning rods and appropriate grounding systems.
- Ensure that all buried and overhead entries into your building are bonded to a grounded system.
- Use surge protectors on all sensitive electronic equipment.
- Use UPS systems to filter the power coming into your sensitive electronic equipment.
- Consider weather-monitoring equipment and proactively move to generator power until the storm threat is over.

Heavy snowfall can cause a roof that is not reinforced to collapse. When the snow melts, it can cause water leaks into a building, ice dams on the roof, or flooding in the street.

If you are in an area where floods can occur (check your USGS flood zones), either due to the frequency of storms capable of heavy rainfall such as hurricanes, because your office is located in proximity to *any* body of water, or you are close to the coast and subject to storm surge, you need to protect your business from the impact of flooding.

My house is located on a small river in western Massachusetts. The river is behind the house, and on the right side of the house is what the town calls a seasonal stream. We have only lived here for about four years, but we have already been awed by the power and the changing face of the water we live on. The height of the river varies, as one may expect, by the season, but the stream varies based on the weather *today*. The stream is sometimes barely noticeable and at other times a raging torrent of water. We have seen the stream height rise by more than five feet in an hour.

But water problems are not only caused by floods. They can be caused by roof leaks, plumbing leaks, sewer failures, and water-main breaks. Simple condensation from an air-conditioning unit can cause water damage if the water pools or drips in the wrong place.

Recently, in a building my company leased, the roof was being repaired. The contractors left for the weekend, and there was an exceptionally heavy rainstorm. They had not sealed the roof properly against this type of storm, and of course my office space, being on the top floor, got soaked.

My home office had a small electrical fire on the second floor. It occurred on the weekend, so very few people were in the space, which was a good thing. The sprinklers went off above the workstation where the fire occurred, so that workstation and the six closest to it had significant water damage—particularly after the fire department came in with their hoses and dumped more water on them. There was soot on every single surface in the space. Every ceiling tile on the second floor had to be replaced over the weekend. Every single surface had to be dusted. Take a look at your desk and imagine a fine layer of soot on every surface. Pictures, books, keyboards, monitors, printers, papers. The soot damage was terrible, but the water was worse!

Water goes wherever it wants. It was contained on the second floor to the area of the fire, but on the floors below the water travelled everywhere. It went into an electrical closet and damaged one phase of a three-phase transformer on the first floor, then traveled into the UPS room and caused at least some water damage to nearly a quarter of the workstations on the first floor.

A plumbing leak in the clinic one floor above the data center that went unnoticed caused damage to the tape silo in the data center before it was stopped. An air-conditioning-unit condensation drip pan overflowed, leaked onto an electrical panel, and short-circuited the power to an entire floor. I could not make this up!

Some mitigating tips for water threats include water sensors under raised floors in the data center to set off an alarm when the first drop of water hits the floor (instead of waiting until it actually impacts a piece of equipment before it is discovered), water pumps, watertight doors, and flood walls around a facility, all of which can prevent flood waters from entering into your building.

When problems do happen, it is so much easier to recover if you can catch them when they are still small instead of waiting until they cause something to fail. I had an office in Tulsa, Oklahoma. It was a small branch office with a limited budget; when the air-conditioning unit broke in the server room, the regional vice president decided that he did not want to pay to have it fixed. Instead he cut a hole in the server-room door and put a fan up against it. In Oklahoma. In the summer. Well, like most building-management companies, this one turned the air conditioning virtually off over the weekend when no one was in the space. The server room stayed cool enough during the work week and over the cooler evenings, but come that first weekend, the room heated up, and the sever went down on thermals and had to be replaced.

If we had been monitoring the temperature in the room, we would have known when the temperature started to rise and we could have remotely shut down the server to protect it until someone could get to the office and address the issue. Instead, the server had to be replaced, and that little office was out of business until we could rebuild a server from the backups and bring it back online.

Industry Risks

Some risks are associated with the business you are in. Convenience stores have a greater threat of robbery than manufacturing plants. Banks may face robbery but also need to be concerned about money laundering. Department stores are frequent victims of shoplifting and also need to worry about identity theft. Insurance companies sometimes face threats of workplace violence from claimants who are dissatisfied with the handling of a claim. Some common industry risks include:

- Robbery/theft
- Workplace violence
- Money laundering
- Identity theft
- Theft of trade secrets
- Fraud
- Loan defaults
- Market risk
- Credit risk
- Labor disputes

As we go through these risks, you should begin to become aware that business continuity touches all sorts of other areas within the company. Remember, it is much easier to prevent a disaster than to recover from one, so you will want to work closely with other risk-management areas in the company to influence better risk-management practices across the organization.

Don't Forget the Neighbors!

Some neighbors you may want to check out:

- Nuclear-power plants
- FBI/CIA
- Oil-storage facilities
- Hazardous-waste producers
- Chemical factories
- Biomedical research labs

If they are already your neighbors, there is not much you can do unless you are ready to move someplace else, but clearly if you are selecting a location for your business operations, who is nearby should be one of the factors you consider when selecting a site.

Your local fire chief and your town hall may be able to provide you with information about companies that pose hazards to the community at large, but even if you are not located near enough to one of these to be concerned, other factors such as proximity to highways, waterways, railways, and airports also present risks you will want to be aware of.

I have had two events in my career where a transportation mishap has caused a cloud of toxic gas to head in the direction of one of my facilities. It was only a change in wind direction that kept us from having to evacuate all the staff to safety.

RISK-MANAGEMENT PRACTICES

As shown in Exhibit 5.1, there is significant interrelationship between business continuity and other risk-management areas such as information security, physical security, records management, vendor management, internal audit, financial risk management, operational risk management, and regulatory compliance (legal/regulatory risk), as they are all part of the context of the overall risk-management framework.

There is a great deal to be gained by partnering with these other areas during this phase of planning your business-continuity and disaster-recovery program. How well and in what way other areas manage the risk within their space will influence the business-continuity program. You will also share common concerns in the management of specific risks that, jointly presented, may influence management decisions.

It does not matter how strong the firewall is or how good the password enforcement is if the physical security practices are so poor that unauthorized individuals can easily gain access to the company space. It does not matter if the company has an alternate site if the records-management practices are so poor that the data needed to recover the business is not available offsite.

All of these efforts are enterprise-wide in scope; they intersect one another at various points, and the extent to which we do one well and another poorly can impact all the other areas. Each of these areas needs to work collaboratively to effectively manage risk. Our risk-management effectiveness is only as good as our weakest link. We can have the best information-security practices in the world, but if people put their passwords on Post-It® notes under their keyboards or our physical security allow unrestricted access to our space, it may not matter.

Physical Security

We will talk more about implementing physical security in Chapter 16. Floor wardens, evacuation drills, and workplace violence all fall under the physical-security domain. Physical security is more than just guards and gates. Protecting our people and our workspaces is an important job and one that influences many other areas of risk management.

Physical security is also about access control. Wearing badges physically on your body at all times when in the workspace means that employees can be identified. If you make a visitor wear a badge but employees don't have to wear badges, then, unless every employee knows every other employee by sight, all I have to do to be an employee is take off my visitor badge and I look just like an employee. Even employees should only have access to the spaces where they belong, not everywhere in the building.

Physical security is also about key management. I remember getting a facility tour from a building engineer who kept opening all these doors with a key. So I asked him, "Is that a master key?" Yes, it was. So I asked, "How many people have this key?" Roughly 30. " Wow," I said, " how many times have you had to replace all these locks because someone either lost the key or left the company without returning it?" Blank stare. "Um, never." That's a problem.

Master keys are a bad idea unless they are strickly controlled, and even then they are still not a great idea. It is better to secure critical access through card readers at minimum. Biometrics are even better. Card readers allow you to track who has accessed what space when and to quickly and easily disable access to people who have left the company, even if they did not return their badges when they left. You don't have to replace the lock; just disable the badge.

Physical security is also about background investigations on anyone who has unrestricted access to the workspace. Not just employees but contractors, vendors, cleaning staff—anyone who gets to walk around the space without an escort.

Physical security is also about visitor procedures. I tell a story to highlight the importance of strictly enforcing visitor procedures. In one of the smaller offices of my company, one that is small enough that everyone knows everybody else's husbands, wives, kids, grandkids, etc., one employee's husband came into the office one day with a single red rose in a vase. He told the person who came to the door that he only wished to leave the rose on his wife's desk as a surprise gift and sneak away quietly. Of course, the person who answered the door recognized him and thought, "Aw, how sweet!" So she let him go unescorted to his wife's desk. He did leave the rose but also took her car keys, her credit and bank cards, her checkbook, and her cell phone. It seems they were having marital difficulties, and she did not inform the entire office. No unescorted visitors to the space—*none*.

Physical security is also about cameras and lighting, escort services, landscaping, facility siting, security patrols, alarm monitoring and more.

Information Security

Information security is the risk-management area that is responsible for the security and protection of the information assets of the company. Information security is about policies and practices involving strong passwords, firewalls, intrusion detection, virus protection and response, cyber investigation, standard logical access definitions, login ID management, internet policy, usage monitoring, and other items related to the protection of electronic data. It is also about access to physical records, proprietary waste disposal, clean desk policies, and confidential information management. Information security has a policy arm, a process arm, and an enforcement arm.

The policy area is where policies regarding the protection of information assets are established. For example, an organization should have a policy on passwords: how long the password needs to be, how frequently it needs to be changed, what the password must consist of (numbers, letters, capitals, symbols), how frequently passwords can be reused, etc.

In the process area in this example, there would need to be a process defined for establishing passwords when a new login is created and how an individual can change a password when it expires. There would also need to be a process for how forgotten passwords can be reset, who can reset them, and how an individual identity would be validated before a password was reset.

The enforcement arm in this example would mean having a process that forced a password to expire after a defined period of time and requiring the user of the login ID to change the password when it expired before gaining access to systems. The process would enforce the policies about the new password: that it not be one that had been used before and that it be of sufficient length and contain the appropriate type of characters before it could be changed. Password-management systems make the enforcement of those types of policies automatic and company-wide.

Firewalls are appliances that act as policy-enforcement agents for information access from outside the internal corporate network. Intrusion detection is a software tool that monitors attempts to get through the corporate firewall so that any attempted or successful breach can be addressed. Anyone who accesses the internet regularly knows what virus protection is. Without it computer viruses or worms can impact the corporation's ability to use its computer systems.

You need at least a basic understanding of the policies and technology that supports your information-security environment because you are going to need to implement at least some components of it in your disaster-recovery plan for your technology.

The protection of paper records and electronic media is the responsibility of the information-security organization, working very closely with the next risk-management area, records management.

Records Management

Records management is about which records you need to keep and for how long and which you do not need to keep and how they should be destroyed. It is about how records are stored, where they are stored, how long they should be stored, how to retrieve them, how to return them to storage, and how to protect them from modification or unlawful destruction.

Every piece of information that is used to run your business needs to be defined as to its level of confidentiality, its retention schedule, the media it is to be stored on, and the process for reproducing the record as needed and for destroying the record once the time of retention has passed. It is not just about what you should keep and for how long but also about what you should *not* keep. You have to establish a retention schedule for every type of record that is based on the legal and/or business requirements that govern that type of record. Then you have to enforce it.

If you have business records that go back 40 years and you are in a lawsuit of some type that makes those records discoverable, then you have to produce those records even if 40 years ago they were all on paper and could be in one of 2000 boxes in offsite storage. Even if you have to pay someone to go through each and every one of those boxes until the record is found. If you have it, you have to produce it. If you do not legally need to keep it anymore, don't. The same is true of electronic media.

Information security and records management have a close alignment with the next risk-management area on our list, privacy.

Privacy

Privacy laws have been implemented in the last decade to protect consumers from the propagation of information about them that is not publicly available. Companies that conduct business in the United States and increasingly in other countries as well must comply with the privacy laws of that jurisdiction. They include who you can share private information with and under what circumstances, how it is to be shared, and what you must do if private information is inadvertently shared or stolen. Every company needs to establish a privacy policy, share it with its customers, and have processes in place through its records-management and/or information-security practices to protect information that is not publicly available from unauthorized or inadvertent disclosure. Certain types of records such as Social Security numbers, credit-card numbers, bank-account information, and health records are especially subject to privacy regulations under various laws and regulations.

Vendor Management

Vendor management is an area of risk management that is also a concern of the business-continuity planner. One of the things we discovered during the September 11 recovery was that some of our vendors were in trouble too, and not all of them had adequate business-continuity and disaster-recovery plans that put them back in operation as quickly as we needed them to be.

As part of your vendor-management process, it is important that critical vendors be identified and that their risk-management practices, including their business-continuity program, be reviewed before contracts are signed. It is a necessary part of your due-diligence process for vendor selection. A lack of a plan or an insufficient or untested plan should be a warning signal to the vendor-management process as much as a poor credit rating or poor financial position. If a vendor's programs are insufficient, a response must be in place so that either another vendor is selected for the business, a backup vendor is identified and contracted with, or remedial plans for the program be agreed to contractually and audited for compliance.

You can have the best plan in the world, but if a critical vendor cannot supply a critical service or part at time of need, it could all be for naught.

Operational Risk Management

Almost every single fraud investigation I have ever been a part of or heard about has been about managers not paying attention. Operations-risk controls only work if they are understood and enforced by the management team. If a manager signs off on an expense report without reviewing it against corporate policy, then the manager opens the door to an employee submitting fraudulent expense reports. Operational risk is about understanding the types of risk your operation is subject to and implementing proper controls to mitigate that risk. For example, an employee should not have the ability to both change the registration on an account and process a withdrawal from the account. Most employees are honest, but allowing that type of access could allow an employee to change the name and address on an account and process a withdrawal. There would be a record of the transaction, but it could take months or even longer to identify the fraud, particularly on the account of an individual who is recently deceased or for whom you do not have a correct address.

Managing operational risk is one of the ways we prevent a disaster instead of having to recover from one.

Internal/External Audit

Saying you are from the audit department is sometimes interpreted with the same dread as saying, "I am from the IRS; I am here to help." I have found that auditors can often be very helpful in promoting better risk-management practices and in supporting your business-continuity and disaster-recovery program. Auditors generally have standards or industry best practices, and identifying a gap in an audit report can go a long way to convince management of the need to close that gap. Remember, there is no point in spending a single dollar on your program if you are not building something that actually works. If you have a fatal flaw, put it on the table and get the audit department to support addressing the gap.

MANAGING THE RISK

When you identify a risk, you need to make choices about how to respond to that risk.

You can accept it. If the risk of occurrence is so small, the impact so minimal, or the cost to mitigate it so substantial, you can simply choose to accept the risk.

You can transfer it. This is where insurance comes into play. If a risk is too costly to mitigate against but too big to just accept, you can choose to transfer the risk by purchasing an insurance policy. Similar to car insurance, business-interruption insurance is often used to transfer the risk of an event that cannot be mitigated either because of cost or some other factor.

You can mitigate against the risk. It is much easier to prevent a disaster than to recover from one. If you can put controls in place to prevent the most likely of risks from having an impact on your ability to do business, you will have fewer actual events to recover from. Risks are from natural hazards such as hurricanes, earthquakes and tornados; from man-made hazards such as human error, sabotage, arson, and workplace violence; and from technology hazards such as hardware, mechanical, and software failures. The ones you mitigate against are the ones most likely to occur. You would probably not choose to anchor equipment to a desktop or wall to mitigate against an earthquake if you are not in a region where earthquakes are a common threat.

A business-continuity plan is one type of mitigation. In fact, a business-continuity plan is what we implement when all other mitigating factors fail.

The table in Exhibit 5.3 shows an example of a risk matrix. A risk matrix is used to present to leadership the identified risks, the probability of those risks occurring, and the recommended mitigation to be implemented to control them.

Location	Risk/Probability	Recommended Control
Home Office – Boston, MA	Hurricane/Low	Business Continuity Plan
Home Office – Boston, MA	Power outage/High	Backup generator UPS on critical systems
Field Office – Kansas City, KS	Tornado/Med	Tornado shelter on site Tornado drills Property insurance Weather radios
Field Office – San Francisco, CA	Earthquake/High	Anchor equipment to walls/desktops Secure hazardous items
Field Office – Miami, Fl	Hurricane/High	Backup generator Business Continuity Plan

Exhibit 5.3   Risk Matrix.

6

Business Impact Analysis

Chapter Objectives
- What is a Business Impact Analysis?
- How to Perform a BIA
- Why It Is so Important to Get It Right

WHAT IS A BIA?

The next step in the planning process is to perform a business impact analysis (BIA). The BIA becomes the foundation of the plan you will build for your recovery. This is the process that will determine what needs to be recovered and how quickly. It is one of the most difficult tasks to perform and one of the most critical to get right. The more time you have to bring a business function back in service following a disaster, the more your recovery options increase. The BIA is invaluable for identifying what is at stake following a disaster and for justifying spending on protection and recovery capability. Nobody but you will mind your own business.

Why It Is About Time Sensitivity, Not Criticality

I dislike the use of the terms "critical" or "essential" in defining the processes or people involved in this phase of the planning. I prefer to use the term "time-sensitive." Generally speaking, organizations do not hire staff to perform non-essential tasks. Every function has a purpose, but some are more time-sensitive than others when there is limited time or resources available to perform them. A bank that has suffered a building fire could easily stop its marketing campaign but would not be able to stop processing deposits and checks written by their customers. The bank's marketing campaign is essential to its growth in the long term, but in the middle of a disaster it will take a backseat, not because it is not critical but because it is not time-sensitive.

The organization needs to look at every function in this same light. How long can the company not perform this function without causing significant financial losses, significant customer unhappiness, or significant penalties or fines from regulators or from lawsuits?

How To Do This and Get It Right

It is all about impact. It is all about what keeps the business running and what can wait till later. When I was doing mid-range and client-server DR for a company, I had to speak to the business unit that managed the general ledger for the company. The general ledger is concerned with accounts payable and receivable. It is just like your checkbook. It is where a business keeps track of the monies coming in for payment of goods or services and those going out to pay for expenses such as payroll. In this company, the general ledger ran on an AS400, and my job was to figure out how long I had before I needed to bring back the system. When I met with the business unit, the first response was that it had to be back by day one after a disaster.

My response was that I was willing to build whatever recovery strategy the business needed and was willing to pay for, but before I priced this strategy, I wanted the team to think about something. This is a financial-services firm. If we did not run the general-ledger system for 30 days, it would be ugly. There is no question that we would have to cut manual checks to keep critical services going and have to maintain a manual general ledger until the system was brought back. I would not want to be the accountant who had to reconcile all the manual-ledger entries into the application once it was restored, but the firm would survive as a business if it did not run the general ledger for a month. How long do you think we would survive as a business if we did not answer our phones? Price our mutual funds? Process our customers' transactions?

It is not about being important. When business is normal, the general ledger is very important. It is about what keeps us in business. It is about surviving. Disasters are not about business as usual. Management metric reporting is very important when business is normal. My CEO expects his management reports on his desk at 7:00 a.m. every business day. But if the home office burnt to the ground, I know he would be willing to forgo seeing them for a few days!

All business functions and the technology that supports them need to be classified based on their recovery priority. Recovery time frames for business operations are driven by the consequences of not performing the functions. The consequences may be the result of business lost during the down period: contractual commitments not met and resulting in fines or lawsuits, lost goodwill with customers, etc. Impacts generally fall into one or more of these categories: financial, regulatory, or customer retention. Remember, these were the same categories we talked about in Chapter 2.

What steps can you give your planning team to conduct a business impact analysis? It starts with simply identifying the processes or functions performed in their area. Working with the management team, list everything that is done by that group. Once the business processes are understood, each one must be analyzed against three areas: financial risk of not performing that function, regulatory risk of not performing that function, and customer or reputational risk of not performing that function.

Financial risks may include loss of revenue, loss of interest on bank balances, the cost of borrowing to meet cash flow, loss of revenue from sales, interest value on deferred billings, penalties from not meeting contractual commitments or service levels, opportunity lost during the downtime, and losses from processing transactions at market risk as of the date received.

Regulatory risk may include penalties for not filing financial reports or tax returns on time, fines or penalties for noncompliance with regulatory requirements in place for your business, or the need to pull products off shelves because of lost product-testing information.

Customer or reputational risk includes loss of customer confidence and market share, liability claims, customer dissatisfaction with service, media coverage of customer complaints, loss of goodwill, and loss of competitive advantage.

It is all about impact. What happens to the company if we do not do this?

Once your planning team has a list of functions and what happens if they are not performed, the next question to be answered is, how soon do we start to see the impact? Is it as soon as we stop doing something? A customer call center that has been evacuated due to a fire stops performing its function immediately. Unless there is another call center someplace else that is fully equipped and staffed to take calls, the impact to your customers is immediate. How significant this impact is depends entirely on your business—how many calls you get and what the calls are about.

Let's say your call center receives an average of 1200 calls per hour and on average, 72 percent of those calls result in a sale with an average value of $57. Do the math: $1200 \times 0.72 \times \$57 = \$49,248$, the potential loss per hour that the call center is not operational.

If your customers or potential customers find your product or service and place their orders on your website and it goes down, you have an immediate impact. Again, how significant the impact is depends on your business—how many orders you take, how much each order is for, and whether the customers will wait and order from you later or take their business elsewhere.

After your planning team has a list of functions, an idea of what happens when they stop, and how quickly you start to see the impact, the next question to be answered is, how much impact? You can use quantitative measures such as actual dollars per minute, hour, or day of downtime or qualitative measures, which predict certain outcomes based on the knowledge or experience of the individual.

Once all that information is pulled together, you have a view of everything the company does, what impact it would have if the function could not be performed, how quickly that impact would be felt, and how significant the impact will be. This information is the start of what we need to develop the appropriate recovery strategies for each site we do business in.

A SIMPLE BIA FORM

Exhibit 6.1 shows a simple BIA form for classifying functions and determining their time-sensitivity code, which is shown in Exhibit 6.2. To use this form, the planner will need to adjust the factors to reflect the business being evaluated. The factors that may need to be adjusted are "time before impact," what would be considered high, medium, or low in the "customer impact" and "regulatory impact" columns, and the dollar values in the "financial impact" column.

Have each of your planning-team members complete the form for his or her functional areas and return it to you. You will then need to add it up by site to understand the functions in each site that you will be planning for and the recovery time frame associated with that function.

A common question I am asked during this phase of the planning is, what if this particular function is only time-sensitive at specific times of the month or year, like month-end or year-end? My response is that you

Functional Area	Functional Name	Mail-zone	Risk Code F=Financial C=Customer R=Regulatory	Time Before Impact 0=week 2 or more 1=week 1 5=up to three days 10=day 1 20=4 hours 40=immediate	Customer Impact 0=none 1=Low 3=Med 5=High	Regulatory Impact 0=none 1=Low 3=Med 5=High	Financial Impact 0=none 1=0 to 10K 2=>10K but <100K 3=>100K but <500K 4=>500K but <1 Mil 5=>1 Mil	Rating Total Sum of 1 thru 4	Recovery Time Sensitivity Code	Alt. Site
Customer service	Call center	Z 45	C & F	40	5	1	3	49	AAA	Surviving sites then Smith Road
Customer service	Customer account maint.	Z 37	C	1	3	0	0	4	D	Work from home
Customer service	Customer monetrary	Z 38	C & F & R	10	3	3	4	20	A	Smith Road

Exhibit 6.1   BIA Form.

Rating total of 45 or more =
  AAA Immediate Recovery
       Must be performed in at least two geographically dispersed locations
       that are fully equipped and staffed.

Rating total of 25 to 44 =
  AA Up to 4 hours to recover
       Must have a viable alternate site that can be staffed and functioning
       within the four hour timeframe required.

Rating total of 15 to 24 =
  A   Same Day Recovery
       Must be operational the same business day and must therefore have
       a viable alternate site that can be staffed and functioning within the
       same business day.

Rating total of 10 to 14 =
  B   Up to 3 days
       Can be suspended for up to 3 business days, but must have a viable
       alternate site that can be staffed and functioning by the fourth busi-
       ness day.

Rating total of 7 to 10 =
  C   Week 1
       Can be suspended for up to a week, but must have a viable alternate
       site that can be staffed and functioning the second week following an
       interruption.

Rating total of 0 to 6 =
  D   Week 2 or greater downtime allowable
       Can be suspended for greater than one week.
       A maximum number of days should be identified for this function.

Exhibit 6.2 Business Function Recovery Time Sensitivity Codes.

should rate that function at its highest level. If you have a disaster and it is
not the time when the process needs to be resumed quickly, those resources can be used for other things, but it is better to plan for the worst-case
scenario for each function because disasters are very good at occurring
at the worst possible time. Ask Murphy. In fact, like many others, I think
Murphy was an optimist.

7

Resource Requirements

Chapter Objectives

- Defining Requirements for Recovery
- Technology Reviews
- Interdependencies

HOW MANY, WHAT TYPE, AND WHERE

Once all the business functions have been identified and a recovery time frame determined, the planning team then needs to identify all the resources necessary to perform each of those functions. Resources include applications systems, minimum staff requirements, phone requirements, desktop requirements, internal and external interdependencies, vital records, printers, fax machines, copy machines, unique equipment, etc.—everything that business function needs to perform its job.

Technology Review: Business People and Technology People Speak Different Languages

The recovery priority for application systems is also identified during this process. It is the business that decides which application systems need to come back and when, based on the recovery priority of the business functions those applications support.

This technology-review process is sometimes difficult for the business to perform. The average desktop user knows that he or she clicks on an icon and an application system launches. Most workers have little comprehension of where the application resides (mainframe, midrange, server, desktop), where the data resides (central storage, network server, the desktop), or where the executable resides.

These are important considerations in building a recovery plan. If the application is co-located with the business, then the recovery for that application must be part of the recovery plan for that site. If the technology for that application is not co-located in that site with the business operation, then when planning for the recovery from loss of that business site the planner needs only to provide network access to where the application resides, not recovery of the application itself.

When I began working with the business partners in New York about five years before the events of September 11, 2001, to do the technology review, it took us almost six months to get it done. Business people and technology people call applications by different names. Business people inherit icons from former employees and have no idea what the application behind the icon is. When asked for a list of applications that they use to run the business, we would often see descriptions such as "Joe's spreadsheet" or "monthly management report." We then needed to sit with the end user and figure out exactly what the applications were.

Here are some of the considerations in identifying recovery priorities for applications:

- Application name
- Business functions that use that application
- Hardware platform the application runs on
- Physical location of the hardware
- Alternative applications or manual processes available
- Location of application data
- Location of application executable

All applications, like all business functions, need to be classified as to their time sensitivity for recovery even if they do not support business functions that are time-sensitive. For applications, this is commonly referred to as "recovery-time objective (RTO)" or "maximum tolerable downtime (MTD)." This is the amount of time the company can function without that application before significant business impact occurs.

To collect the data on application recovery times, have your planning team identify on the BIA the applications used by each business function and whether alternate systems or manual processes could be used in place of them for a period of time in a disaster. Remind them that this is not about service levels when everything is normal; this is about recovery times in a disaster. The remaining information about the application will be completed by your technology team.

Once the company has determined the time frame for recovery of the different business operations and identified the applications that are essential to perform those functions, you can establish the RTO for each of the applications to be recovered by the technology plan. The RTO will define for the technology-recovery team how much time can elapse between the time the disaster occurs and the time the application is recovered and available to the business.

Resources for recovery go beyond applications. They also include PCs, telephones, printers, fax machines, photocopiers, answering machines, scanners, postage meters, mail carts, and many other things. You can purchase paper, pens, and pencils at a time of disaster because they are readily available, but many other supplies that are needed to run our business are not available in large quantities quickly without preplanning.

Desktop Image

Unless you are depending strictly on a central server (thin client) for all your applications, most desktop images are hardware-dependent, meaning that you need to build an image on the hardware that you will recover; otherwise your desktop image may not work. The hardware in your production environment may be obsolete at the time of disaster at not available for purchase.

Though many business units have unique desktop images that include the applications used by that operation, I strongly recommend that you create one desktop image with all possible applications rather than trying to maintain multiple images. Generally individuals cannot access applications unless they have both physical and logical access to it, so having the application appear on the desktop is not a security risk.

Routing Calls

Call routing must be considered for recovery, particularly if you are recovering a call-center environment. Building the ability to reroute your inbound toll-free traffic to your alternate site before a disaster occurs saves time and prevents customer dissatisfaction. If you are not in your building, phone calls are not being answered or are being held in a queue indefinitely if your phone switch is still working. If your phone switch is not working, customers are getting either dead air, no answer, or a message such as,"The number is not in service at this time."

If you are routing calls to an alternate site that is not your own, such as a site with a contracted vendor, you need to rebuild all of your phone groups at the alternate site. You will be routing the 800 number to a phone number on the phone system in the alternate site. The phone system in the alternate site must then be configured to deal with the call once it gets there.

For each number you route to the alternate site, you have to design what happens to that call. For example, let's say that the call comes into the phone switch and first goes to an auto-attendant. The customer hears, "Thank you for calling ABC Company; your call is important to us. If you wish to speak to someone in sales, press 1; if you need to speak to a customer-service representative, press 2...." Once the customer presses 1, he or she is forwarded to a sales agent. But if all agents are busy, what do callers hear? Does the delay message repeat? Do you have music while on hold? Do you give them an option to leave a voicemail message? Are your phone calls recorded? How many agents are in each group? If the unanswered queues for a particular group get too large, do you want to send the calls to an overflow group? I encourage you to keep the routing during a recovery as simple as possible. If you end up in your alternate site for longer than a few days, you can always add the complexity of additional prompts and skill sets to the plan. The most important thing initially is that the call gets to you at all.

It is expensive to reroute DID (direct-in dial) lines, but you can do it. DID lines are like the phone number at your house. They are directly dialed without having to enter an extension. It is possible to reroute the DID number that sits on your desk to your home or cell phone at a time of disaster, but it will take awhile to do this if you have not built a plan with your carrier before the disaster happens.

Printing, Faxing, and Copying

How much printing is done by each group, and what type of printer does it need? There are generally three types of printing that occur in a business:

- Print mail—invoices, checks, bills, customer statements, etc., that are printed, stuffed in an envelope, and mailed
- Batch-cycle printing—reports that go to multiple end users
- LAN printing—files sent from the desktop to a printer in the work area

Each of your planning-team members needs to define the type and volume of printing that will need to be recovered.

In addition, fax machines are an integral part of many business operations. It is important that your planning team identify the type of faxing and volume of inbound and outbound faxes needed to be available in the alternate site.

Photocopy machines are also part of the business landscape. How many do you need and what types of features are important? A desktop copy machine will copy one page at a time in black and white and make 20 copies at once. That won't be a good model if you need to make 20 copies of a 25-page color presentation for a customer.

Unique Equipment

Your planning team will need to identify any unique equipment it uses as part of business operations. Scanners, time-stamp machines, postage meters, mail carts, insertion machines—just to name a few specialized equipment types that, if forgotten, can slow a business-operations recovery.

Interdependencies: Who Else Needs to Know/Who Else Needs to Help

Interdependencies, both internal and external, need to be understood and documented. Interdependencies include all the inputs to a function or application and where they come from and all the outputs to a function or application and where they go. They include external dependencies such as the post office and your key vendors and internal dependencies such as other business units. When I moved 850 people from New York City to New Jersey after 9/11, for example, it was important to let the post office know where they went. To assist the planners in collecting this information, I use an alternate-site development kit which appears in Appendix E. Ask the following questions of each business function:

1. How many seats will you require in the alternate site?
2. What applications and proprietary software (software from other vendors) do you need to perform your functions?
3. How many phones will you require at the alternate site?
4. Do your phones need international dialing capabilities?
5. Do your require any of your phones to have call recording? If so, how many?

6. Do you have phone numbers that will need to reroute to the alternate site? If so, please provide appropriate details.
7. Do you require any modems?
8. Is outbound dialing only on any modems acceptable?
9. Do you need to establish automated-call-distribution (ACD) groups? If so, please provide information.
10. Please identify any other specific requirements you may have. Consider such things as scanners, time-stamp machines, postage meters, mail carts, printing calculators, etc. Do not include items such as paper, pens, pencils, staplers, and other general office supplies.

THE BUSINESS-FUNCTION INDEX

At the end this process, you should now have in your possession a list of every business function, its recovery time frame, and its resource requirements, including all types of technology and interdependencies. You are now ready to look at recovery strategies.

8

Recovery Strategies

SELECTING A RECOVERY STRATEGY FOR BUSINESS OPERATIONS

Recovery strategies are driven by the recovery time frame required by the function or application to be recovered. Some strategies the planner may consider for business operations are as follows:

- A surviving-site strategy is implemented so that, while service levels may drop, a function never ceases to be performed because it operates in at least two geographically dispersed buildings that are fully equipped and staffed. This strategy is commonly employed for call centers and trading floors where downtime is unacceptable.
- In a self-service strategy a business transfers work to another of its own locations that has available facilities and/or staff to manage the time-sensitive workload until the interruption is over.
- In an internal arrangement, training rooms, cafeterias, conference rooms, etc., may be equipped to support business functions

while staff from the impacted site travels to the temporary site and resumes business. When I worked for the financial-services firm in New York, our alternate-site strategy was a combination of contracted vendor sites and internal sites. Having a bunch of seats sitting there waiting for the big one is not a plan that management could get behind easily. Most of the internal sites designated as alternate sites were dual-usage spaces. Of the 520 internal seats we had in one facility, 160 were in training rooms that were already equipped to support call-center training, and 280 were in the cafeteria. The equipment to populate the cafeteria was stored onsite and 1/4 of the cafeteria was built out four times a year for testing. On September 11, 2001, all 280 seats in the cafeteria were built out in four hours.

- In reciprocal/mutual-aid agreements, other similar businesses may be able to accommodate those affected. For example, one law firm may be able to provide office space to another in the event of an outage. This could involve the temporary suspension of non-time-sensitive functions at the business operations not affected by the outage.
- Dedicated alternate sites are built by the company to accommodate business function or technology recovery.
- Today, many companies have the capability to have employees work from locations that are remote from a physical office environment, such as a satellite office or home. Just remember that during a natural disaster where employees homes are impacted as well, this strategy may not work.
- A number of external suppliers offer facilities covering a wide range of business-recovery needs from full data centers with a variety of platforms to mobile units that can be transported to the company site and temporary staff to provide services when the employees cannot.
- For low-priority business functions or applications it may not be cost-justified to plan at a detailed level. The minimum requirement would be to record a description of the functions, the maximum allowable lapse time for recovery, and a list of the resources required.

If you are going to use any type of reciprocal or mutual-aid agreement, make sure you get your commitments in writing and that they are reviewed annually to be certain the option is still viable for both parties—

life happens, things change. If the agreement includes the need to displace staff, make certain you have the logistics worked out before the event. Consider things such as, whose voice mail is that? Are you bringing your own PCs or are you planning to use theirs? How will you schedule conference-room time? Should you bring your own coffee? I know it sounds silly, but if you do not do this type of planning, what will most likely happen in a real event is that you have a crisis in one site and you will create a crisis in the other.

If you are planning to move large numbers of people significant distances from their homes to support recovery, make certain that you do your logistics planning *before* the disaster. I had a business operation with two almost identical locations, the same number of staff doing the same job in each site. The initial recovery strategy was to have the surviving site carry the load, but if the event was going to continue beyond a few days, the company was going to fly 125 people from the impacted site to the surviving site. (This, of course, would not have worked on September 11.)

Most of the people would be phone representatives. How many phone representatives do you think they gave corporate credit cards to? If your guess was zero, you would be right. So the first logistic element in this plan was to figure out how they were going to pay for 125 airline tickets, not to mention hotels, rental cars, food, and out-of-pocket expenses. Most phone representatives are young people in their first real job after college. If you think most of these people have enough personal credit to fund a last-minute airline ticket, you are mistaken. Many young people are borrowing from their MasterCard® to pay their Visa®. College loans, credit cards, setting up new apartments, and low incomes make that a reality for many.

Then, of course, there is the question of who can get away from home? Among your workforce, you have single parents, people caring for aging parents, people afraid to fly. One thing that came out very clearly during the recoveries from 9/11 and Katrina was that people did not want to travel away from their families. After 9/11, certain groups in New York were supposed to recover in an internal facility in New Hampshire. They knew that before the disaster. They tested there four times a year, but when managers starting talking to employees on 9/12 about going to New Hampshire for recovery, the vast majority of them said, "Fire me if you want, but I am *not* leaving my family." If you need 125 people to go, you should have a group of 200 who say in advance that they will go. Life happens, things change – "I know I said I would go, but … now I am pregnant" or "I am getting married next weekend" or "I am a single parent" or "My house is flooded and my family is at risk; I am not going."

Then there is the issue of travel/accident insurance. Most carriers have a limitation on the amount of benefit they will pay as a result of a single disastrous event. For that reason, there was a company policy that dictated that no more than seven people from the company could travel on the same flight. Well, how long do you think it will take to get 125 people on different flights from different airports, and who are you going to send first, the managers or the reps?

Once the 125 people get off the plane and into the facility, where are they going to sit? Neither facility had 125 seats just waiting there, so the move required displacing people or moving them to other shifts to accommodate those coming in. Having an understanding up front with the groups to be displaced is very important. Again, logistics are very, very important. If you do not do them up front before the disaster occurs, you will have a disaster in one site and you will create a disaster in the recovery site.

SELECTING A RECOVERY STRATEGY FOR TECHNOLOGY

Depending on how much downtime you have before the technology recovery must be complete, recovery strategies selected for the technology environment could be one of the following:

- A dual-data-center strategy is employed for applications that cannot accept any downtime without impacting business. The applications are split between two geographically dispersed data centers and either load-balanced or hot-swapped between to the two centers. The surviving data center must have enough head room to carry the full production load in either case.
- An internal hot site is standby-ready with all necessary technology and equipment to run the applications recovered there. The planner should be able to effectively restart an application in a hot-site recovery without having to perform any bare metal recovery of servers. If this is an internal solution, the business will often run non-time-sensitive processes there such as development or test environments, which will be pushed aside for recovery of production when needed. When employing this strategy, it is important that the two environments be kept as close to identical as possible to prevent problems with O/S levels, hardware differences, capacity differences, etc., from halting or delaying recovery.
- In an external-hot-site strategy equipment on the floor is available but the environment must be rebuilt for the recovery. These ser-

vices are contracted through a recovery-service provider. Again, it is important that the two environments be kept as close to identical as possible to avoid problems with O/S levels, hardware differences, capacity differences, etc. Hot-site vendors tend to have the most commonly used hardware and software products to attract the largest number of customers. Unique equipment or software would generally need to be provided by the organization either at the time of disaster or stored there in advance.

- A warm site is a leased or rented facility that is usually partially configured with some equipment but not the computers. It will generally have all the cooling, cabling, and networks in place to accommodate the recovery, but the actual servers, mainframe, and other equipment are delivered to the site at time of disaster.
- A cold site is a shell or empty data-center space with no technology on the floor. All technology must be purchased or acquired at the time of disaster.

There are advantages and disadvantages for each of these recovery strategies. The advantages of a dual data center:

- Little or no downtime
- Ease of maintenance
- No recovery required

The disadvantages of a dual data center:

- Most expensive option
- Requires redundant hardware, networks, staffing
- Distance limitations

The advantages of an internal or external hot site:

- Allows recovery to be tested
- Highly available
- Site can be operational within hours

The disadvantages of an internal or external hot site:

- Expensive—internal solution more expensive than external
- Hardware and software compatibility issues in external sites

The advantages of warm and cold sites:

- Less expensive
- Available for longer recoveries

The disadvantages of warm and cold site:

- Not immediately available
- Not testable

COST-BENEFIT ANALYSIS

Each of these strategies can be considered for both business and technology recovery. The ones that are recommended need to have a cost-benefit analysis (CBA) performed to determine if the costs of the strategy fits within the amount of risk or business loss the business is trying to avoid. The company would not spend $1,000,000 a year on a recovery strategy to protect $100,000 of profit. Every business does not need a dual-data-center recovery strategy. The strategy selected must fit the business need. I recently analyzed a dual-data-center project for the company I work for to see what it would cost to provide the same level of recovery as the company currently has in place with a vendor internally. As much as the company would like to internalize the recovery, our profits don't justify the expense.

The cost of implementing the recovery strategy recommended needs to include the initial costs associated with building out the strategy as well as ongoing costs to maintain the recovery solution and, where applicable, the cost of periodic testing of the solution to ensure that it remains viable.

IMPLEMENTING RECOVERY STRATEGIES

Once the strategy has been agreed to and funded, the planner must then implement it. This may involve negotiating with vendors to provide recovery services for business or technology, doing site surveys of existing sites to determine excess capacity, wiring conferences rooms or cafeterias to support business functions, buying recovery technology, installing remote replication software, installing networks for voice and data recovery, assigning alternate site seats to the various business areas, and the like.

The implementation phase is a project unto itself—perhaps multiple projects, depending on the complexity of your environment and the recovery strategies selected. It is strongly recommended that, as you implement each component of your recovery strategy, you test that piece to make certain that it works as designed. Ultimately, you will need to test all the pieces together, but we will talk about final testing later.

9

Documenting the Plan

Once recovery strategies have been developed and implemented for each area, the next step is to document the plan itself. The plan includes activation procedures, the recovery strategies to be used, how recovery efforts will be managed, how human-resource issues will be handled, how recovery costs will be documented and paid for, how recovery communications to internal and external stakeholders will be handled, and detailed action plans for each team and each team member. The plan then needs to be distributed to everyone who has a role.

The documentation for recovery of the technology environment needs to be detailed enough that a person with a similar skill set, having never executed the procedures before, could use them to perform the recovery. Documentation tends to be the task that no one really likes to do; however, there is no guarantee that the people who perform this function in the production environment or the person who restored the infrastructure and application at the last test is going to be available at the time of disaster. In addition, disasters tend to be chaotic times when many demands are being made at once. Without the proper documentation, a practiced recovery strategy can fall apart and add to the chaos. Restoring an application can be challenging; restoring an entire data center just destroyed by a tornado can be overwhelming if not impossible without good documentation.

The documentation needs to be stored at the recovery facility, and every time the recovery is tested, the documentation should be used by the recovery participants and updated as needed. Once the level of confidence about the documentation is high, have someone who has never performed the procedure attempt it with the expert looking over his or her shoulder. It may slightly delay the recovery time of that particular test but, once complete, confidence in the documentation will be strong.

WHAT ARE THE COMPONENTS OF THE PLAN?

The components of the business-continuity plan are as follows:

1. Purpose, objectives, and assumptions: This section defines the purpose of the plan document, the objectives to be accomplished, and the assumptions made.
2. Recovery strategies: This section describes the strategies the company has developed to respond to an emergency situation.
3. Recovery management: This section describes the organizational structure of the recovery teams and the roles of the management members.
4. Human-resources management: This section describes how the company will manage the various human-resource issues that may arise during the recovery effort; providing for temporary or contracted help, financial assistance to employees, and help in dealing with family issues.
5. Logistic and administrative support: This section describes how administrative functions such as food, travel, and lodging for recovery staff will be managed.
6. Finance issues: This section identifies how finance issues will be handled during the recovery, including procedures for ordering of equipment or supplies, expense reports, identification of the cost center for recovery expenses, etc.
7. Recovery communications: This section identifies how communications will be handled during the recovery process. This includes communication to other employees and business units, communication about the status of the recovery, problem management, and external communications.

8. Plan activation: This section begins by describing the normal process by which an emergency situation is communicated, how the damage assessment is performed, and how a decision to activate the plan is made and by whom. Once the plan is activated, it describes the establishment of the command centers and the emergency-notification process to the recovery teams.
9. Site recovery: This section details the recovery process and the actions that will be executed by the recovery teams as a result of losing the physical site where business is performed. This section includes a checklist for each recovery-team member during the recovery effort.
10. Business-application recovery: This section details the recovery process and the actions that will be executed by the recovery teams as the result of losing the business applications required by the business. This section includes a checklist for each recovery-team member during the recovery effort.
11. Appendices: These sections provide additional information and procedures referred to in the main document.
12. Recovery procedures: This section provides detailed recovery procedures.

Quick Reference Guide

Since very few people will actually read the entire plan, it is important that you include either with the plan or as a separate document a quick reference guide with basic information that will be needed quickly. When an emergency happens, everyone needs to know what to do next. Very few events that occur are smoke and rubble events where it is really clear because of the burning crater that was your building that you have a disaster on your hands. Most events start small or the initial impact is unclear, and an assessment must occur before a decision is made to declare an emergency. The process in any event is for team members to *gather, assess, decide, mobilize, communicate,* and *recover.*

1. Gather employees and tell them exactly where they are supposed to go. You need to tell them where they should go if you can still occupy the building and where to meet outside the building if you have to be evacuated. If they have been evacuated and it is clear they are not going to get back into the building anytime soon, release the general staff and head to the gathering place. I usually

select hotels in the area because they are always open, they usually have a room you can rent, they usually have internet access, and they have phones and food service available.

2. Assess the situation. Should staff be sent home? What part of the business has been impacted? Do we need to go to our gathering location? How long will we be unable to operate normally if at all? Who owns the problem? Who else needs to know? Who else needs to help?

3. Decide what to do. If it is just your company, wait to declare an emergency as long as necessary; if other companies are impacted, declare first and apologize later. Once you move a data center, it is a *long* process to come back, but you generally can start at least preparing to recover at the alternate site while still trying to recover the primary site. Business operations are comparatively easy and less expensive to move if you have local alternate sites. If your business operations cannot or should not wait while you finish assessing the situation, send people to the alternate site to work immediately.

4. Mobilize. Once you have decided on the initial response, you need to mobilize the appropriate responding teams and put contingency plans in action. Business teams in each business unit in the impacted site should have at least one planner who has built a response plan for the business operations. Once activated, planners will begin to assemble their teams to execute the business recovery based on their plans. Technical teams need to execute their plans based on the site impacted, the type of event, and the technology impacted. This could include rerouting phones, activating voicemail recovery, retrieving data from offsite storage for recovery of technology, building desktops in the alternate site, rerouting networks, traveling to the alternate site to execute data-center recovery, and activating email recovery. The logistics team needs to provide logistical support for recovery teams, such as travel arrangements, rental cars, and hotel rooms. GPS devices, alternate-site supplies, laptops, printers, cell phones, etc., as requested by the responding teams, may also be needed.

5. Communicate. We need to communicate to our employees, our vendors, our customers, and possibly the media about this event and how we are managing. Employees need to know what to do, where to go, what has happened, and do they still have a job?, Will they get paid? Is everyone else okay? What about benefits? Customers need

to know what services will be unavailable and for how long and how they can reach the company if they need something. Vendors need to know how to find the company and what we may need from them to support the recovery. The media needs a story; if we are going to give them one, let's make it a positive one. One spokesperson, one message, and talking points to all who might be asked to comment.

6. Recover. Provide information on the location of your alternate sites, how to activate them, travel direction to get there, and what is being recovered in each site as well as phone numbers for reaching staff.

Initial Response Plans

If there are multiple locations for your business, there needs to be an initial response plan for each site where the organization conducts business. That plan will document in just a few pages the following:

- What business and/or technology operates at that site
- The recovery strategy in place for the business or technology
- Who the decision makers are
- Where everyone should go if they cannot get back into the building
- The process for declaring a disaster at that site
- The location of the alternate site
- Travel directions to get to the alternate site
- Seat assignments at the alternate site
- Hotels, transportation services, and caterers near the alternate site

A sample initial response plan appears in the Appendix B and can be downloaded as a Word document from: www.kelleyokolita.com.

Communications

Communications are key to a successful recovery. If you find a way to communicate to every one of the stakeholders in a timely manner about what they care about and what they need to do, you will recover. If you do not communicate effectively, your recovery will not be as successful. Because communications are so critical to the recovery, it is discussed in greater detail in Chapter 14.

Detailed Execution Procedures

For each recovery strategy, detailed execution procedures need to be documented on how to execute the strategy at the time of disaster. Again, these procedures need to be written in such a way that someone with a similar skill set or background, having never tested them before, would be able to pick up the procedures and execute them.

What I tell my planning-team members is that if we do the business impact analysis correctly and they complete their alternate-site developments kits correctly, then I can provide them with an alternate site that will have all the resources they need to do their job. What I cannot do is to tell them how to run their business with 25 people instead of 100 people. They need to write that plan. Only the people who have intimate knowledge of the business processes can write that portion of the plan.

If I move a phone representative from a seat in building A to a seat in building B and everything else is the same—same applications, same phone systems, same calls coming in—then I do not need a detailed plan for that. I just need to detail the logistics of getting that person from building A to building B—how he or she will know to go there, how to get there, when to get there, where exactly he or she will be sitting. But if I am going to change how or what is done, then that needs to be in a plan. For example, due to resource constraints in an emergency, we make a decision that we will only process transactions that have a financial impact of some kind, not maintenance transactions. We then need to document in the plan a process for sorting incoming work to make certain that only financial transactions are given to staff to execute and that all other transactions are sorted by type and date received, to be addressed later in the recovery.

When documenting the plan, don't forget some of the simple things that we take for granted when business is normal. Some of the lessons I learned during the recovery from the events of 9/11 were details such as planning for delivery of office supplies to the alternate site, setting up a package-delivery account for the alternate site, having a postage meter for the alternate site, and knowing where the post office is located.

If the company uses some type of mail zone for internal delivery between sites, make sure the plan sets one up for the alternate site as well. Be prepared to have a "switchboard operator" at the alternate site until the company can publish a new phone directory for the employees working from the alternate site. This operator would manage a central phone number that can be published quickly to the appropriate stakeholders until the new phone numbers for individuals can be published.

The Human Factor

One common factor left out of many plans is human-resource issues. Disasters are human events, and it is important that the plan document the responsibility of the firm to the employees participating in the recovery. Companies need to recognize the hardships placed on the families of their response teams. To be able to give their best to the company at the time when it is needed most, employees need to have a level of comfort that their family members are safe and the employee's absence during the recovery effort will not place undue hardship on them.

If you are reading this book, then I assume that you too are a human, and so I have made this section about you. I want to talk to you about what it is like to be in a disaster, and I want you to pretend that it is just another normal day at the office. You are sitting in a meeting with a dozen of your work associates talking about whatever it is you talk about at meetings. (Sometimes it seems we spend an awful lot of time talking in meetings about what we should be doing but can't do because we are in all these meetings, but I digress.) Suddenly, without warning, your world is rocked. Literally rocked.

The building sways and your coffee dances and then falls off the conference table. Others in the room try to stand up and are knocked to the ground. Anything not firmly anchored falls from everywhere—from the walls, from the tables, from bookcases and filing cabinets. The shaking seems to stop briefly; you get up, and you notice that the man next to you has hit his head on the table as he fell and is bleeding. You reach out to help and it starts again, only this time the shaking is worse. Bookcases fall over, furniture slides across the room, you hear creaking and cracking sounds as the building sways. You hear glass breaking and people yelling to get out of the building. After what seems an eternity, the shaking stops and somehow all of you manage to make you way out of the building.

Are you there? Okay, so now you are standing outside your building with your coworkers, some injured, some screaming, some in shock, everyone dazed. The sirens start to be heard from the distance. What's your first reaction? "Gee, let's go get that data center up and running, folks!"

Not likely.

Like many others who have faced a natural disaster, your first thoughts are most likely going to be about you coworkers and your family. Are they okay? Did everyone make it out? You need the plan to address the need for taking care of the people in your organization. If their families and homes are at risk, they are not going to be available for your business. But

73

even if the event did not impact their family or home directly, any tragic or catastrophic event is going to take its toll on people.

It was nine weeks after the events of September 11, 2001, before every employee had a place to go back to work. The employees who came to work shortly after the tragedy in some ways were better off than the people who stayed home. People need their work families too, and the sense of normalcy that comes from getting up and going to work every day. The people who were at work had an opportunity to tell stories of a shared experience. The people who were at home talked to their families, but the family members were not there when it happened. They did not see what they saw, hear what they heard. They did not feel the same fear.

We addressed some of that by having company meetings with all employees working at the site, as well as ice-cream socials, group counseling sessions, rotating shifts, and reaching out to employees at home. It is important that people be able to talk about and share their stories. Even those who sat in silence and could not yet speak of what happened and what they saw still benefited from hearing the stories and feelings of others who shared the same experience.

We had mental-health counselors for the employees in the alternate site from day two on. The first two weeks there was a lot of "rah, rah, go team, they cannot take us down," but after weeks of going to wakes and funerals for relatives and friends, commuting to new locations, no personal space in the working environment, etc., we started having a lot of medical situations (panic attacks, heart palpitations) and more human-resource issues than we normally saw. Conflicts and stresses between employees, sick days, crying, emotional breakdowns. Disasters are human events. Don't forget to take care of the humans.

The level of support provided to the recovery-team members will clearly be defined by the nature of the disaster itself. In the case of a natural disaster where the employee's family may be at risk, the company may provide for temporary relocation of family members or allow the family to accompany the employee to the recovery site. Support may range from facilitating dependent-care services, company-paid travel for employees to return home for a visit or for family members to travel to recovery locations, or cash advances to provide for family needs. This section of the plan also needs to document how the company will handle the injury or death of an employee during an event.

Administrative Support

Don't forget to include administrative support as part of the recovery team. Planners do not often think of administrative-support staff as being "time-sensitive," but they are welcome additions in a recovery. They do things no one else has the time to do, such as answering phones, sending communications to recovery staff, making travel arrangements for recovery staff, ordering food at recovery locations, keeping minutes of the status meetings, making copies, arranging courier service, keeping track of the locations of employees, and the like.

Logistics

The logistics team is comprised of members from different groups throughout the firm. The team is responsible for logistical support for any event where staff will be deployed to respond and recover. Their section of the plan documents how they are prepared to support the procurement and deployment of office space, supplies, rental cars, airline tickets, hotel rooms, equipment, cash, and credit as needed for the recovery efforts. The logistics team consists of the following groups:

- Real estate—responsible for providing additional office space to responding teams
- Finance—responsible for cash and credit availability
- Travel—responsible for providing lodging, rental cars, flights, and other travel-related services
- Desktop—responsible for providing hardware and software to responding teams
- Network—responsible for providing network connectivity to responding teams
- Mail room—responsible for redirecting mail from the impacted site to the alternate site(s)
- Procurement—responsible for obtaining supplies needed by responding teams
- Information security—responsible for providing access to responding teams

Finance Issues

For insurance purposes, it is important that costs associated with the recovery effort be tracked and payment for purchases of needed supplies and replacement equipment be expedited. Procedures for handling finance issues must also be included in the plan.

My recommendation has always been that a separate cost center for both expenses and capital be established to be utilized only in a contingency event. All purchases and expenses would be charged to that cost center, utilizing whatever existing expense-management system you have in place. In this manner, you are certain that all expenditures are tracked and categorized appropriately.

Transition Back to Normal Operations

The final parts of the documented plan are about restoration of the primary environment and transition back to normal operations. While other parts of the organization are focusing on resumption of business in the alternate site, part of the staff needs to focus on what needs to be done to restore the production environment of the primary facility.

Ownership of this process is dependent on what was impacted by the event, but in most cases it will be a coordinated effort among the facilities staff to restore the building to its original state or acquire and build out new space, the technology staff to repair or replace technology hardware, software, or network components, and records management to recover lost or damaged records.

The organization's legal staff and insurance agent will play a role in the restoration and recovery from the event. No recovery efforts should begin until both have been contacted, but the area of impact should be secured from further loss and where possible pictures taken of the damage before anything is removed, repaired, or replaced.

The transition back to normal operations is easier than the recovery for the simple reason that it is a planned event. The plan can be to return all at once or to move operations back over time to control issues that may arise from the transition and prevent yet another event. General transition plans should document the process to move back, but detailed plans will need to be written to respond to the specific issues of the transition that results from the type of event that the organization is recovering from. Moving a business operation back to its primary space is challenging but is usually easier than moving a data center. If your data center was impacted by this event, then you need to manage the transition project as a data-center move.

My organization was located in alternate sites for 15 months following the events of September 11 and for two months following Hurricane Katrina. After 9 weeks in the September 11 alternate site, an interim transition plan was executed where employees were distributed between two interim sites while the primary site was repaired and built out. The interim sites used spare equipment and furniture from storage and other sites to populate the space. Once those moves were completed, the "contingency" event was over. After 10 weeks, even though we were not back in the site were we used to doing business, the sites we were in were no longer alternate sites. They were our sites and would be for 15 months before we went back to the original site.

When it was time to repopulate the data center, asset swaps were used rather than moving the technology that was in the alternate sites. In assets swaps you negotiate with the vendor to provide the equipment to populate the new or restored data center. By doing this you allow for the ability to burn in and test the new equipment and the building infrastructure before the actual move instead of having to disconnect and reconnect over a move weekend. After the move back is completed, the equipment in the alternate site was given back to the appropriate vendor, moved back to storage, or sold.

DISTRIBUTION OF THE PLAN

The plan document needs to be distributed to everyone who has a role within the plan. When I distribute a plan document, I usually include a wallet hard card with key phone numbers and information and a one-page sheet at the front of the plan that tells everyone where their role is documented in the plan. Remember, the sample plan includes a checklist for every team and every team member. The checklist is written by the planning-team member and by pointing the person to those pages that refer to his or her role, it ensures two things: the employee can find it at the time of disaster easily, and he or she may actually read it before a disaster. Most people are unlikely to read the entire plan, but if you point out the section that belongs to them, they may read that.

PLAN-MAINTENANCE STRATEGIES

As with any documentation, version control is important, particularly with detailed technical procedures. The use of version-control numbers on the plan helps to make sure that everyone is using the current version of the plan documentation. The plan needs to be distributed to everyone who has a role and also needs to be stored in a secure offsite location that not only survives the disaster but is accessible immediately following it.

It is important that the plan be kept up to date as the business and technology environments of your company continue to change and adapt. Tying plan updates to your change-management process is critical to keeping pace with significant changes in technology. The business plan must be reviewed and updated at least annually, more often if significant business changes occur. Plan updates also frequently occur following tests of the plan, where issues or action items from the test require plan-documentation changes.

USING THE SAMPLE PLAN

The sample business-resumption plan is intended as a guide for business contingency planners to the type of information you would expect to find in a working plan. The sample plan has been produced as one document with a comprehensiv e table of contents; however, depending on the complexity of your plan, it may be too elaborate for your needs. The plan may be adjusted by adding or deleting sections as needed to match your recovery requirements.

The plan is organized in sections. Each section includes the type of information that may appear if this were an actual plan. For example, in the purpose, objectives and assumptions section—instead of stating that this is where you should document the purpose of the plan, the objectives to be achieved, and the assumptions made during the planning process—it uses actual words that might appear in a real plan. It states, "The purpose of this plan is to define the recovery process developed to recover this company's critical business functions. The plan components will detail procedures for responding to an emergency situation that affects the company's ability to provide services to the customers of the company or its ability to meet legal or regulatory requirements."

In my experience, if you give people a place to start and ask them to edit the content, you have much more hope of getting something back than if you ask them to write something from scratch.

For the purpose of the sample plan, a *site outage* assumes that the entire building and all of its contents are unavailable and you must perform the functions at another location. An *application outage* assumes that the facility you are in is intact but you do not have access to the applications required to perform the function. For example, if the data center were to experience an outage, you must plan for how you will manage the business operations without those applications for as long as it takes for the systems to be restored. When the applications become available, they will be current only to the latest backup taken before the disaster occurred. You must plan how you will perform your critical business functions without the applications and how you will "catch up" once the applications have been made available to you.

This is not intended to be a fill-in-the-blank plan. It is a sample from which you can duplicate or borrow as much as is appropriate for your business. Business-recovery planning is a process, not a product. As long as the business continues, technology changes and business functions change, and the plan you develop will need to be continually modified and repeatedly tested.

The sample plan makes the assumption that the business being recovered is a large organization. If your company is small, you may delete teams or team members to more accurately reflect your organization. The detailed recovery procedures included in this document are intended to provide a format for detailing the actual steps to recover a function, whether it is a business function, a server recovery, or a system application recovery. You may include these elements as part of the plan or keep them as separate documents that are referred to in the plan. These are the step-by-step procedures that need to be developed for each critical function performed by your business.

The sample plan appears in Appendix A and can be downloaded as a Word document from the following site: www.kelleyokolita.com.

10

Training and Awareness Programs

It does not matter how good the plan is if no one knows what is in it. It is important that every single person in the firm knows what to do in an emergency. To enable this knowledge, business continuity needs to be embedded into the culture of the organization. To accomplish that, the planner must introduce training and awareness programs that involve all the stakeholders. Stakeholders include everyone from your executive leadership team and your full employee population to your customers, regulators, and vendors.

THE QUESTION

I am often asked by members of my planning team to make a presentation at a staff meeting on the overall program or conduct a learn-at-lunch session for the general employee population of their groups. Sometimes they regret it, because I usually start out saying something like this: "Okay, we are going to pretend that the fire alarms are going off and that everyone has followed the floor warden out of the building. It is really clear as you are all standing outside that you are *not* getting back into this building today. *Does everyone in this room know what to do next?*"

Every single employee needs to know the answer to that question. Even if what they are supposed to do next is to go home until we call them.

DIFFERENT TRAINING FOR DIFFERENT PEOPLE

The type of training needed is different for different populations of the organization. The leadership team needs crisis-management training. Their role in a recovery is not to execute the recovery but to lead the organization back to business as usual. The technical teams need to know not just the procedures for executing the recovery but also the logistics of where they are going and how they will get there.

Training is about people. Having the best plan in the world will not help if no one knows that it exists or what his or her role is. I have a sign outside my office door that says, "If you are reading your plan for the first time and you are in the middle of a disaster ... *you are in trouble.*" I am not a specialist in adult learning, but I have learned over the years what people remember and what they don't.

I can tell everyone that it is really important that they lock their workstation before they leave their desk in order to protect confidential information and unauthorized access. They hear me and forget it 10 minutes later. But if I find someone's desktop unsecured, sit down at the desk, and send an email saying something like, "I was just at your desk and thought about sending an email to your boss and telling him he is a jerk and he smells bad from your email account just like I sent this one to you from you," they remember that. Even if I just tell them (jokingly, of course) that I will do that if I find their desk unlocked, they remember.

I can tell people that they have to lock their laptop into their docking station whenever it is in the docking station. It needs to be a habit—put it in the docking station and lock it. Compliance will be scattered with just a policy statement. But if I find your laptop locked and leave you a free meal coupon, you'll remember that. If I find your laptop unlocked and I remove it, leaving a note saying "missing something?" you will remember that.

Technology is easy. It is black or white, on or off, it works or it doesn't. People are not easy. People are not the same. People respond to different messages in different ways. You need to find ways to stay in front of them, to make it easy to remember what they need to do in an emergency. Your biggest asset is your employees. Without them you cannot recover. With them you can do anything. You need to reach them in various ways and continually reinforce the messages that you need them to understand.

The planner will need to design awareness programs for different audiences. Various vehicles for the delivery of training and awareness programs can be utilized depending on the audience that needs to hear the message.

The intranet portion of the corporate website is one good vehicle for communicating the plan to the general employee population. General information such as life-safety procedures, assembly areas, contingency information phone number, alternate site location, and travel directions should be available to the general employee population on the corporate intranet.

Learn-at-lunch programs, online training self-study courses, new-hire orientation, and awareness campaigns tied to specific seasons such as tornado safety, flu shots, hurricanes, and even evacuation drills can be opportunities to introduce employees to the business-continuity and disaster-recovery plans.

The customers of an organization may want to know that the company has a plan and will be there for them no matter what. They should be aware of the planned course of action in the event of a disaster, alternate contact numbers, and any changes in operational procedures they should expect. The corporate website available to the public may be a good means of communicating information to the customers of an organization. Potential clients may request a copy of your plans or request that you provide statements regarding your recovery plans as part of a request-for-proposal (RFP) process.

Regulators may require attestations from your organization on your programs for both your technology and your business operations. Depending on your industry, you may have to submit information to the regulators or allow regulators to audit your program.

Conducting exercises is also a form of training for those who have a direct role in the recovery. Whether the exercise is a tabletop exercise, an actual exercise at the alternate site, or just a call-notification exercise, the team will practice its role. The more the plan is exercised, the more confident the recovery team will be if or when a disaster happens for real.

Putting a section on the business-continuity-planning program in a new-employee orientation session is a great vehicle for introducing the program when an employee starts with the organization. The information provided can explain the overall scope of the plan, what to expect if a disaster were to happen, and where to get additional information on the program.

The employees need to know basic information about the plan and their role in it. This includes assembly areas following evacuation, leadership-team members, how they will be communicated with after an event, alternate site location including directions, and when they should report to the alternate site.

My current firm has an annual business-continuity day in each site. We hand out stickers for the back of employee badges with the contingency information number as well as directions to the alternate site. We give out raffle tickets for prizes if employees have the sticker on their badge and if they can name their floor warden.

When we do evacuation drills in smaller sites, I try to attend and make a one-minute speech while everyone is outside the building in the assembly area. Usually I say, "Thanks for participating; we want to make certain that everyone knows how to evacuate the space safely and where to assemble outside to get information on what to do next." Then I ask how many people have their wallets with them? Purses? Car keys? I remind them that in a real event, they may not be able to get back in the building for weeks if at all. Then I ask if anyone knows what to do next if he or she were not going to be allowed back in the building.

My leadership team at each site, even the home office where the operating-committee members are located, have had at least one evacuation drill where they were not allowed to go back in the building after the all-clear but had to go to their assembly location for a brief meeting and then to their alternate site.

This is what I have learned about what works and what doesn't. What works:

- Reinforcing/recognizing good habits/behavior
- Recognizing and calling attention to behavior that you want to discourage
- Providing examples that people can relate to
- Repeating messages through orientation, exercises, and workplace training
- Making it easy to find information when it's needed
- Leading by example

What does not work:

- Doomsday scenarios
- Providing examples that people don't relate to
- Policy statements with no reinforcement
- 500-page documents
- Long emails

11

Testing the Recovery Plan

Chapter Objectives

- Explain the Different Types of Tests
- Planning the Test
- Reporting Test Results

Once the plan has been completed and the recovery strategies fully implemented, it is important to test all parts of the plan to validate that it would work in a real event. It is often wise to stop using the word "test" for this and began to use the word "exercise." The reason for this is that when the word "test" is used, people think "pass or fail" as if they were in school. In fact, there is no way to fail a contingency test. You see, if we knew that it all worked, we wouldn't bother to test it to begin with. The reason to test is to find out what doesn't work so it can be fixed before it happens for real. No test is a failure as long as it provides opportunities to better the recovery process so that if it happened for real, you are more likely to recover.

You need to continue to repeat this rationale to leadership over and over again. I have been with my current organization for four years and have built the program from the ground up. When I joined the company, it had no business-continuity plan beyond severe weather events and its data-center recovery contract would not have recovered the company's data center.

In one of my more recent data-center exercises, nearly half the applications did not recover. We tried something new in the test, something that was very important to try. Every test we had conducted since we implemented remote replication a year and a half ago assumed a recovery point of 5:00 a.m. Saturday morning, a very convenient time for a disaster, since all the systems were inactive. We had proven repeatedly that we could recover at that point in time. Unfortunately, disasters are not usually that accommodating, waiting to occur at the best possible time for your business. For this test, we decided to pick a time out of hat and try to recover—and it failed miserably for some of the platforms.

When I reported to the leadership team, I stressed what a good test this was because we learned so much. As a result of this "failure" we learned that we had to make changes to be able to recover for any point in time, which we then proved in a subsequent test.

FIRST RULE OF TESTING YOUR PLAN

My first rule for conducting tests of your recovery plans is that you are not allowed to create a disaster by testing for one. No matter what type of test you are conducting, it is important to protect the production environment and make sure all participants recognize that this is a test, not a real event. In my early days of testing, we conducted a test that included a simulated fire. When the test participant called security to report the fire, she neglected to mention that this was part of a test, and the security staff contacted the fire department. Fire departments do not find this amusing.

TYPES OF TESTING

There are many different types of exercises that the planner can conduct. Some will take minutes, others hours or days. The amount of exercise planning needed is entirely dependent on the type, length, and scope of the exercise. The most common types of exercises are call exercises, walk-through exercises, simulated or actual exercises, and compact exercises.

In a call exercise (see Exhibit 11.1) the planner attempts to call everyone on the emergency-notification list to see how long it takes to reach them and if they are prepared to respond.

Call exercises can be conducted by using a method in which one person calls five people, who in turn call five people, and so forth, or the organization can use some type of automated system for making calls. If the planner has an automated system, it is important to periodically use the "manual" way to reach out to people just in case the automated system is not working at the time of a real event.

What to do:

- Call everyone on your Emergency Notification List and validate their phone numbers are accurate and that your team is prepared to respond.
- How to do it:
    Call their cell phone
    Call them at home
- Page them. If they do not respond within a certain timeframe, try again or try reaching the backup—require a response
- Page them and have them call into a conference bridge

Why to do it:

- Validate the phone numbers are accurate
- Find out how long it takes to reach everyone
- Determine what percentage of people are unavailable
- Exercise call notification procedures

Exhibit 11.1   Call Notification Exercise.

When conducting call exercises, it is common to have the participants reached call into a conference bridge to acknowledge receipt of the communication so that the team can communicate with one another as they would if this event was real. It is an opportunity to have people talk to each other and validate the team's readiness to respond.

I once had a person call me the day after conducting a call test. He told me that he only reached 58 percent of his staff in the two hours of the test and wanted to know if that was enough. My response was, "I don't know. How many people do you need?

The purpose of the call test is to find out if you can reach the people you need to support the recovery of the business. You not only need the right number of people but the right people with the right skill set to respond. For key roles, it is important to have multiple people who can play the role in a recovery. You never know who will not be available at a time of disaster. Your key network person could be on a cruise ship in the Caribbean when the disaster strikes.

The next type of exercise is a tabletop or walkthrough exercise (Exhibit 11.2). When the organization has a new plan, the best type of tabletop

---

What to do:

- Walkthrough all or a portion or your recovery procedures with your teams

How to do it:

- Set up meeting date and time
- Contact Team Members and invite them
- Walkthrough the plan with the team members
- Take notes of comments, action items

Why to do it:

- Use as Training and Awareness for Team Members
- Identify plan weaknesses or deficiencies
- Improve recovery capabilities

Exhibit 11.2   Walkthrough Exercise.

exercise is a walkthrough of the actual plan document with everyone who has a role in the plan. Even the planning team is unlikely to read the entire document, and walking through the plan helps to ensure that everyone knows the whole story and everyone's role. Walking through the plan with the team will help identify gaps in the plan so that they can be addressed.

Once the planner has conducted a walkthrough, he or she can begin scenario-based tabletop exercises. In these exercises the planner will gather the team in a meeting and pretend that something has happened; the team members are supposed to respond as if it were a real event. The planner could pretend that there is a power outage; based on what is backed up by alternate power sources such as UPS and generators and what is not, the team would discuss how the technology or business would be impacted and how they would exercise the portions of the plan to address that scenario.

Tabletop exercises are used to validate the plan within an actual scenario without having to actually execute the recovery procedures. The planner will "talk through" what the team would do; the team will not actually do it. These types of exercises are especially helpful in working through the decision processes that the leadership team will confront when faced with an event and in providing an opportunity for other teams to talk through recovery options based on the scenario being presented in the exercise.

After working with the planning team to build the overall crisis-management plan for my current firm, we conducted a walkthrough of the plan document with all the primary and alternate members of the team. They provided us with some fine-tuning for the plan document and made sure that everyone understood the different roles within the plan and how they fit together. We then scheduled a walkthrough exercise using a scenario.

No one knew what the scenario would be, but they all expected some type of network failure, power outage, or fire simulation. Instead, I hit them with a workplace-violence event. This event allowed all members of the planning team to exercise their portion of the plan. The leadership team, the HR staff, the corporate-communications staff, facilities, technology, finance, legal—everyone had a role to play in this scenario.

The next type of exercise is a simulated or actual exercise (Exhibit 11.3). The only difference between a simulated and an actual exercise is compliance to the first rule of recovery testing, never create a disaster by testing

---

What to do:

- Simulate execution or actually execute recovery procedures at the alternate site

How to do it:

- Create test scenario
- Obtain Management approval
- Team members respond to scenario by executing recovery procedures
- Take notes of comments, action items

Why to do it:

- Use as Training and Awareness for Team Members
- Identify plan weaknesses or deficiencies
- Improve recovery capabilities
- Validate alternate site readiness

Exhibit 11.3   Simulated/Actual Exercise.

for one. The planner must make every effort to ascertain that what is being tested will not impact the production environment, whether business or technical. For example, the first time we test the routing of call-center calls from a primary site to an alternate site, we don't take live calls. We wait until the call center is closed, or we set up a dummy 800 number to test the routing, messaging, queues, and overflows at the alternate site. In that way we limit the possibility of a live customer call coming into the alternate site or, worse yet, not going anywhere but getting lost in the cloud during a test.

The purpose of this type of exercise is to validate alternate-site readiness, whether this is the alternate site for technology recovery, for business operations, or both. The planner should run this exercise as closely as possible to the way it would happen if it was a real event. Because exercises are planned events, the planner will have an opportunity to reduce the actual timeline by prestaging certain aspects that could not be done if this were an unplanned event—things such as pulling backup tapes or hard-copy information from offsite storage and having it delivered to the alternate site, ready for use on the day of the exercise. What the planner should not do as part of the planning is to plan for success. Remember, the reason we test is to find out what does not work so we can fix it before it happens for real.

A manager once said to me that he checked with his peers in other companies, and no one else tested as much as we did. Did we really need so many tests? My response was to say that as soon we stopped having issues in every test, we would cut back on testing.

Test as often as you reasonably can. One of the major lessons learned in the September 11 recovery was that testing was the key to the success of our recovery. When it happened for real, everybody knew their role and executed it. Backup personnel performed their roles well for those who were too traumatized by the event to come to the recovery facility. Everything worked. Did we still have issues? Of course, but over little things we had not thought of, not the big things that make the difference between being able to recover and being out of business.

An actual exercise should be considered successful if the required resources, equipment, and connectivity of voice and data are recovered to the satisfaction of the business unit at the designated alternate site within the time frame required. An actual exercise should also be considered successful if the above *didn't* happen, because the planner can fix it before a real incident. There truly is no way to fail a contingency-plan exercise. The only time the planner will fail is if it happens for real and the business does not recover.

The final exercise is a compact exercise. Here, the planner will begin with a call exercise and continue through an actual exercise. It is sometimes done as a surprise exercise where very few people know in advance when it is going to happen. I once conducted a compact exercise that began with an unannounced evacuation of over 4000 employees from three buildings on the same campus. The general-employee population was allowed to go back into the building, but the business-continuity and disaster-recovery teams were not allowed back into the space. They had to gather their leadership teams, get them to make a "decision" to go to the alternate site, assemble their full teams, go to the alternate site, and "execute" their recovery.

The local police, fire, and EMT participated in the exercise with us. We had some folks pretending to be injured. We even had one person walking around with a movie camera, pretending to be the media. We learned a lot from that exercise, and not everything went the way we expected. It is amazing how different a conference call can be when you are standing outside with 2000 other employees and sirens blaring in the background. How important it suddenly became that all the leadership assemble in the same spot outside. What people will say to a video camera. How not having your wallet and car keys becomes a problem very quickly. How a fire truck blocking the exit out of the parking area could impact the plan.

After every exercise the planner conducts, the results need to be published and action items generated to address the issues that were uncovered by the exercise. Action items should be tracked until they have been resolved, and where appropriate the plan should be updated. It is very unfortunate when the same issue recurs in subsequent tests simply because someone did not update the plan.

PLANNING THE EXERCISE: EXERCISE CHECKLIST

You can and should plan for your testing. Just don't plan for success. You want to conduct exercises that provide an opportunity to validate that the plan or portions of the plan work. Or don't work, as the case may be. When implementing a new strategy, I often planned testing around each piece of the strategy first before trying to test the whole. That gave us an opportunity to focus on just that piece with a limited number of people and to address any issue with it before going forward.

Below is a checklist to use as a guide in your exercise planning. Not every question will apply to every exercise you conduct.

Tasks required for every exercise:

1. Define type and scope of exercise
2. Define exercise objectives
3. Review business functions or technology to be tested
4. Obtain management support to conduct the exercise

Logistics Tasks

Logistics tasks include:

1. Define exercise scenario—use your risk analysis or check out the exercise ideas in the Appendix D
2. Develop the sequence of events that will occur as the scenario unfolds
3. Develop messages, mini-scenarios, data to be used
4. Coordinate efforts of internal and external response organizations if needed
5. Secure logistics support (people, facilities, food, paperwork)
6. Develop mockups, props, diagrams
7. Complete exercise manual/plan
8. Identify exercise participants, controllers, and evaluators

Participants are the people who are testing the recovery. Controllers are people who are going to help you manage the flow of the exercise; evaluators are going to watch the exercise unfold and take lots of notes about what they see and hear.

A sample test plan is included in the Appendix C and can be downloaded from this site: www.kelleyokolita.com.

Getting Ready to Test

Here is the procedure to follow:

1. Conduct a technical walkthrough of the exercise with the controllers and evaluators
2. Distribute pretest information to the participants
3. Validate logistics one more time

The technical walkthrough, if needed, is where you and the people who are going to support the test walk through the execution plan, make sure everyone knows their roles, the scenario, and the timing of each action, and answers any final questions people may have.

The pretest information sent to participants includes a thank-you for participating as well as a statement as to why it is so important that they participate in the exercise, such as: "Thank you for your participation in the exercise today. Our company is committed to creating and maintaining a business-contingency plan in the event of any disaster—small or large. In order for the plan to be successful, it is imperative that we conduct these exercises to learn how to streamline the process to make it as easy as possible for you to conduct business in our alternate-site facility in the event of a business interruption. While everyone is very busy in his or her day-to-day activities, it is vital that we 'do our homework now' so that in the event of an emergency the plan will come together with precision."

The package will also include the following:

- A list of goals and requirements for this exercise
- A contact list of the support staff and person(s) in charge
- A timeline that will guide participants through the events of the day
- A listing of the business functions to be addressed by this exercise
- A listing of the applications to be recovered
- An issues log to document any problems with the desktop or the exercise in general
- A questionnaire to fill out to enable you to make improvements in the process

One last time: validate that the alternate site is expecting you, that the caterer will arrive with the right amount of food, and that the support teams are ready.

Exercise Begins

As the exercise begins, complete the following steps:

1. Activate alternate-site environments as required
2. Complete technical build-out of environment to support test—network connections, desktop hardware, desktop image, reroute phones, printers, fax machines, copiers, etc.
3. Welcome exercise participants and provide them with evaluation forms

4. Conduct the test
5. Conduct a quick debriefing with participants while the exercise is still fresh and collect evaluation forms

Post-exercise Tasks

Once the test is over, your post-exercise tasks may include:

1. Conducting a full debriefing with participants and support team
2. Generating an exercise report
3. Revising the plan and training based on lessons learned
4. Publishing a thank-you letter to participants and attaching the issues list from the exercise
5. Assigning the action list from the exercise

Recovery-Team Review

Upon returning to your production site, your recovery team should be brought together for an in-depth review to assure that any problem areas or potential improvements identified are documented or resolved prior to your next test.

The following questions can serve as an agenda for this discussion and may be modified to suit the specific needs of your organization. Be sure to update your business contingency plan based upon the results of this review:

- What were the objectives, scope, and approach for the test?
- Were the objectives/scope, and approach documented?
- Did all participants understand them?
- Were test objectives met?
- What problems were encountered?
- Were problems documented?
- How will the plan be revised based upon problems encountered?
- Was a detailed test plan prepared?
- Were task assignments made?
- Were task assignments completed?
- Was the test plan followed?
- Were documented procedures followed during the course of the test?

- Were these procedures adequate?
- How could they be improved?
- Were expected results identified?
- Were they clearly understood?
- Was a detailed walkthrough conducted prior to the test?
- Were problems uncovered during the walkthrough?
- Did all test participants attend the walkthrough?
- Were all required vital records available at the offsite storage location?
- How were they delivered to the alternate site?
- Were there any problems retrieving data from offsite storage?
- In what way was the participation of alternate-site personnel required?
- Was their performance satisfactory?
- Overall, how would you rate this testing experience?
- What might you do differently for the next test?
- Are there any recommendations for the next test?

PUBLISHING THE RESULTS

Once the exercise is complete and all post-test reviews have been conducted, a post-exercise report should be published and distributed to everyone who participated in the test and to the leadership of the organization. A sample post-exercise report is included in Exhibit 11.4

Data-Center Exercise Reporting

Reporting the results of the technology-recovery exercise is different than that for a business-recovery exercise. In a business-recovery exercise, the question to be answered is whether the company is able to do business in the alternate site. A data-center exercise has different questions. A sample data-center exercise report in included in Exhibit 11.5. Note that the report contains the following information on each platform and application recovered:

- The name of the technology or application restored
- The recovery-time objective (RTO) for the application
- The date last tested
- Whether the application was recovered in the RTO committed to the business

95

Sample Exercise Results

Business Recovery Exercise Results, Exercise Date 7/17/08

On 7/17/08 a recovery exercise was executed by this company's recovery teams with the support and cooperation of the technology group. An outage was simulated at our primary site, a disaster was declared, teams were contacted and assembled at the alternate site and our recovery plans for the critical functions at the primary site were executed. The primary objectives and results of this exercise were as follows:

- Validate that recovery procedures exists for all critical functions at this site COMPLETE
- Validate the current recovery procedures will be available at the alternate site at the time of need COMPLETE
- Validate that the facilities at the alternate site are sufficient and properly equipped to allow for recovery of the critical functions within the timeframe required PARTIAL
- Validate the desktop connectivity at the alternate site is complete to support the critical functions PARTIAL
- Validate the recovery procedures are complete and accurately reflect the steps required to execute recovery of the critical functions COMPLETE

A complete list of actions items is included for your reference.

Sample Exercise Action Items

Action Item	Responsible	Estimated Complete	Issues or comments
1. Update ENL with corrected phone numbers	BCP	7/20/08	4% of staff unreachable due to inaccurate phone numbers
2. Update recovery procedures to reflect changes identified	Business Function Team	8/15/08	
3. Include missing data in offsite storage	Off site storage Team	7/25/08	Missing manual to be included
4. Provide connections to SASVTAM for 3 desktops identified	Tech Team	8/3/08	
5. Install 2 additional phone lines and larger white board in the Command Center	BCP	8/15/08	

Exhibit 11.4   Sample Post-Exercise Report.

June 2008 Disaster Recovery Exercise Report

Application/Platform	RTO	Last Tested	Documented Plan Offsite	Recovery met RTO	Recovered Successfully	End User Validation	Batch 1 Successful	Batch 2 Successful	Support Team
APPLICATIONS									
Call Center Application	24 hours	Jun-08	NO	NO	NO	NO	NA	NA	Joe Smith
Corp. Fin. - ABC	72 hours	Jun-08	YES	NO	YES	YES	NA	NA	Dave Brown
Corp.Fin - Peoplesoft GL	72 hours	Jun-08	YES	NO	NO	NO	NA	NA	Linda Jones
Corp.Fin. - Peoplesoft AP	72 hours	Jun-08	YES	NO	NO	NO	NA	NA	Mark Sawin
Corp.Fin. - Treasury Ops	72 hours	Jun-08	YES	YES	YES	YES	NA	NA	Scott Gray
Account Applications	24 hours	Jun-08	YES	YES	YES	YES	YES	YES	Mike Beta
Corp.Serv. - Employee Database	72 hours	Jun-08	YES	YES	YES	YES	NA	NA	Michael Green
INFRASTRUCTURE									
AS400	24 hours	Nov-07	YES	YES	YES	NA	NA	NA	Joe Myer
CAT Switch	12 hours	Nov-07	YES	YES	YES	NA	NA	NA	Bob Gerawn
CICS	12 hours	Nov-07	YES	YES	YES	NA	NA	NA	Chris Alpha
Cisco Routers	12 hours	Nov-07	YES	YES	YES	NA	NA	NA	John Crank
Cleartrust	24 hours	Nov-07	NO	NO	NO	NA	NA	NA	Tom Skye
DB2	12 hours	Nov-07	YES	YES	YES	NA	NA	NA	Lucy James
DNS/DHCP Gateway	12 hours	Nov-07	YES	YES	YES	NA	NA	NA	Ned Young
DS3	12 hours	Nov-07	YES	YES	YES	NA	NA	NA	Dave Anderson
LAN	12 hours	Nov-07	YES	NO	NO	NA	NA	NA	Sam Okra
LINUX	24 hours	Nov-07	YES	YES	YES	NA	NA	NA	Frank Perry
Mainframe IPL	12 hours	Nov-07	YES	YES	YES	NA	NA	NA	Mike Knight
RS6000	24 hours	Nov-07	NO	NO	YES	NA	NA	NA	Jim Dyer
SUN	24 hours	Nov-07	YES	YES	NO	NA	NA	NA	Liz Harris
Alt Site Network	2 hours	Nov-07	YES	YES	YES	NA	NA	NA	Mike O'Toole
Windows	24 hours	Nov-07	YES	NO	NO	NA	NA	NA	Lucas Kerry

Exhibit 11.5 Sample Data Center Status Report.

- Whether the application recovered at all, even if it did not meet the RTO
- Whether current documented repeatable processes for recovery execution are stored offsite
- If the application had a batch cycle, was it run and was it successful?
- Application owner
- Did the end user validate the application recovered?

CHANGE CONTROL

All team members have an obligation to participate in the change-control process. The plan document and all related procedures will need to be updated after each exercise and after each material change to the production technology or business environment. The procedures should be reviewed every three months, and a formal audit of the procedures should be conducted annually. The exercise reports produced following each exercise should be provided to the internal-audit department, which should include review of the plan documentation and test results as part of the regular audit cycle.

TEST SCHEDULES

As part of the ongoing program to maintain the viability of the recovery plans you have built, you need to establish regular test schedules. As stated before, I recommend that you test as often as you can, but at minimum your organization should test your plan according to the following schedule:

- Call exercise—twice per year
- Walkthrough exercise—once per year
- Alternate-site test—twice per year
- Compact exercise—once per year
- Data-center exercise—at least twice per year

12

Coordinating with Public Agencies

Chapter Objectives

- Defining the External Agencies that May Assist in Recovery
- Establishing Relationships Before an Event

WHAT YOU CAN EXPECT FROM PUBLIC AGENCIES

There are numerous public agencies that can provide support to you during the planning effort or following a disaster. You should proactively reach out to those authorities before something happens so that you understand what you can expect from them. In an event that only impacts your building, the support and attention you receive from the responding authorities may be different then they would be in an event that has regional impact, such as a hurricane.

WHOM YOU SHOULD HAVE RELATIONSHIPS WITH BEFORE THERE IS A CRISIS

You should build relationships in your community with the local police, fire, and EMT services, as well as local government authorities such as the building inspector and the Department of Public Health. If they know you and your company, you are much more likely to get the services you need and not the ones that you do not want.

I will use a story to help explain the benefits of establishing these relationships. We had an electrical contractor on a ladder with his head inside the false ceiling in one of our buildings after hours. He lost consciousness and fell from the ladder. Some other contractors nearby called 911, and the responding authorities came into the building. While they were preparing to transport the contractor to the hospital, they smelled a suspicious odor, decided that the building had an air-quality issue, and closed the building until the Board of Health could send an air-quality expert to investigate the odor and determine if it was safe to be in the building, a process that could take up to three days.

Here we were; we had no problem with the building or the technology, and yet our employees were not going to be allowed in the space to work the following business day. We had a relationship with the local fire chief and we called him—in the evening, at home. Because he knew us and knew how we managed our facilities, he intervened on our behalf and got the local authorities to agree that we could bring in our own air-quality expert to certify that the building was safe for occupancy. We were open for the start of business the next day. (The odor was actually caused by the glue from new carpeting that was being laid down and was not a health hazard or the cause of the contractor's fall.)

HOW TO ENGAGE THEM IN YOUR PROGRAM

Invite the fire department for a tour of your building. Share the building's fire-evacuation plan. Show the firefighters where all the fire-suppression equipment and the maintenance records are in your building. Show them the location of the emergency power off (EPO) button and identify any power equipment that would not be turned off by the EPO, such as generators or UPS systems. Fire departments do not like to send their firefighters into a building with water on the floor from sprinklers and electrical power still running. Invite them to attend one of your floor-warden training classes and to participate in your evacuation drills. Introduce your liaison, the person who would be responsible for coordinating between responding authorities and your business in a disaster.

Ask the local police department to do a facility assessment of your physical security and safety. Ask the Board of Health how you can support their pandemic-planning efforts. Support the Red Cross by having an employee blood drive. Donate to community causes such as building playgrounds. Ask your local mayor or council member how your business can support the community. Be a good neighbor.

Here is a helpful list of local agencies, services, and entities that can be called upon to provide response and support in an emergency:

External Agency	What It Does	How to Establish Relationship
Fire department	Responds to fires; available to assist in site pre- and post-incident evaluations	Have physical-security staff or business-continuity planner reach out for evacuation drills, floor warden training
Local building department/building inspector	Provides occupancy permits—if you have an event that significantly impacts your facility, once your repairs are complete, occupancy permits will be required	Have facilities staff or business-continuity planner reach out during planning process—these people should also be able to tell you about your neighbors and any risks they may present
Police	Respond to emergencies, assist with evacuations and crowd control	Have physical-security staff, legal staff, and/or business-continuity planner reach out as you are building your crisis-management plan, ask them to participate in your drills
Local hospitals	Provide medical care and triage; can assist with medical emergency-response planning	Have physical-security staff and/or business-continuity planner reach out as part of crisis planning
Local EMT	Can assist with medical emergency-response planning	Have physical-security staff and/or business-continuity planner reach out as part of crisis planning
Local emergency-management services	Will take control of response to major incidents	Have business-continuity planner reach out to identify liaison for incident management, ask to participate in any local drills and ask them to participate in yours

(continued on next page)

External Agency	What It Does	How to Establish Relationship
CDC/WHO	Provide information on medical emergencies (e.g., pandemics)	Website has great information on planning for medical emergencies and pandemics
FEMA	Provides housing, food, security in regional disasters	Contact local administrator; web-site—lots of information available on preparedness
Military	Provides security in regional disasters and civil disturbances	Contact, identify a liaison to work with them
Red Cross	Provides food and shelter in widespread emergencies	Contact local chapter. Offer to do a blood drive in your company
SEC	Will give waiver from reporting requirements (10-K, 10-Q, annual reports) in emergencies	If in the securities industry, legal or compliance staff should have contact information
Municipal government	Will give incentives to protect jobs following a disaster	Get to know your local councilman and mayor if possible, support community activities and volunteering
OSHA	Will provide safety inspections	Human Resources should get to know the local OSHA administrator

13

Crisis Management/ Event Management

EVENT MANAGEMENT

In addition to the actual recovery procedures, the planner also needs to document the process that will be used to manage the recovery from any type of event. Event management is about communication and response, and because those two elements are needed even when the problem is not at disaster level, they can and should become part of the fabric of an organization. The goals of an event-management program are shown in Exhibit 13.1

In my experience, most organizations are quite good at responding to an event, particularly in the data center. For example, if an application becomes unavailable due to some type of hardware failure, the application and infrastructure teams responsible are quickly paged to repair or replace the hardware and bring the application back online very quickly. What most organizations are not good at is talking to one another.

- Single Source of Information
- Triage
- Rapid Escalation
- Consistent Problem Management
- Rumor Control
- Make sure everyone who needs to know does
- Allow the problem solvers room to solve
- Playbook which documents key roles and responsibilities

Exhibit 13.1   Goals of Event Management.

I can remember sitting in a facility of the company I worked for at a time when a momentary power outage occurred. The lights went off and then quickly back on. Since I was sitting in the area where the facilities people worked, everyone in the area got up and went to validate that the building was fine and that everything came back up cleanly. They spent maybe 15 minutes on the event itself. We spent two hours responding to the rumors about what happened.

There was a rumor that the entire trading floor went down. Actually, *one* trading desk did go down, but only because it had not been properly attached to the UPS system. There was a rumor that the power failure occurred because the electric company was doing some work during the daytime when they should not have been working. That was completely untrue.

It occurred to me then that though we had handled the actual event very well, we had not done a good job of communicating what had happened to the people directly impacted by the event. Because we had not handled that aspect well, people made up their own versions of what had happened. In response to this event, we developed an event-management process to make certain that not only did we respond well when something happened but that we also communicated well.

We took a look at the types of events that commonly occurred and realized that, other than small events impacting individual applications, most of our events happened in a facility—a power issue, a network issue, an evacuation of a building, for example. So we decided to build our initial strategy around each building we did business in.

We implemented a pilot program by building, did a proof of concept for a month, and then had some follow-up conference calls with all the parties involved to discuss what they thought of the process. During that call, we had a long discussion with the real-estate team as to whether or not a momentary power outage was an event. An event had been defined as anything that either already had caused or had the potential to cause a business impact.

By this definition from the perspective of the Real Estate group, if everything that was attached to the UPS stayed up (critical infrastructure) and the power was not out long enough for the generator to kick in, then the building behaved exactly the way it was supposed to and therefore there was not an event.

I explained that the business had made a conscious choice not to connect the call-center desktops to the UPS. The call centers operated in six different regional sites and were designed so that one could go offline without any impact to call-center service levels. When there is a momentary power failure, all the desktops fail at once and, because there are hundreds of them, it takes a long time for them to reboot, log in, and be available again. The real-estate people said, "But the calls did not drop; the phone switch is attached to the UPS system." True statement; however, since the desktop is not available, we cannot service the customer.

An event does not necessarily mean that someone has done something wrong. In the above case, everything worked exactly the way it was designed to work, but it still was an event because there was a business impact.

In the early days of the event-management process, we would get a closure communication such as, "226 Main Street building evacuated 350 employees for 20 minutes due to a false fire alarm – no business impact." I would think to myself, what do those 350 employees do that they can be out of the building for 20 minutes and *not* cause a business impact? It took a while for everyone to understand what the event-management process was, what an event was, and what the term "business impact" meant.

We adopted this process to manage any type of event, big or small. Because we used it for everything, we used it every day and it became part of the way we did business. Because it was used all the time, everyone understood how it worked, what their role was, and how they would be communicated to. We used it to manage communications about events as small as minor plumbing leaks to major catastrophes such as September 11, 2001, and everything in between.

The program was built building by building initially. Every building we did business in had three teams—an assessment team, a first-escalation team, and a general-response team. Whenever an event occurred, a communication would be sent to the assessment team for that building to evaluate the event and determine what if any additional communication needed to occur. The reason the assessment team is needed is that it is a not a good idea to wake up 30 people at 3:00 in the morning and tell them that the UPS went into alarm but nothing happened, so they can all go back to sleep now. People only want to hear about it if it impacts them, and if you call them unnecessarily, they will stop listening and responding.

The job of the assessment team is not to fix the problem. That is already happening through the normal problem-management responders. The assessment team's job is to figure out if the event has caused or could cause a business impact. If it determines that an impact has occurred or may occur, a communication is sent to the first-escalation team. A conference bridge is used to manage the communication. The general-response team would be communicated with after the first conference call to report on the status of the event.

Any event-management process has to have a trigger, something that causes the process to begin. The trigger is an event. An event is defined as "anything that happens that either already has or has the potential to cause a significant business interruption." Occurrences such as a hardware failure, a power outage, a network failure, or a building evacuation are examples of events.

Once an event is identified, it must be reported to a central communications group, which will then be responsible for initiating the communications to those who must respond to the event and those who are impacted by the event. The group that gets this initial report from the problem finder needs to operate seven days a week, 24 hours a day because problems happen 24/7. Everyone in the organization should have this central number available to report problems. Commonly, these communications would go to an organizations help desk, technology operations center, physical-security staff, or whomever in the organization is responsible for alarm monitoring.

In support of this communication, emergency-notification lists are built by event type, because different events have different event owners. A facility event such as a power failure, a water leak, or a fire would be owned by the facility staff, whereas a network outage would be owned by the network-communication staff. In addition, each event would impact different business-people depending on their physical location or the technology they used.

Any event that occurs would first be reported to an assessment team. The assessment team's sole purpose is to determine if the problem that has been reported requires further escalation and, if so, who else needs to know about it and who else needs to help fix the problem.

If it is determined that the event requires further escalation and communication, the first-escalation team for that event type would be contacted. The first-escalation team consists of the event owner, the event responders, and anyone else who has determined that when this type of disruption occurs, it directly and immediately impacts their ability to execute the business done in that space.

If you make it the responsibility of the individuals in the organization to sign up for communications on the events that they care about, you will never again hear, "Why didn't you tell me?" In my programs, we build teams by location and event type. Each location has the three teams mentioned previously—an assessment team, a first-escalation team and a general-response team. Only the event owner and the business-continuity-program manager are allowed on the assessment team, but anyone can sign up to be part of the first-escalation team.

It is difficult these days to be able to understand, document, and keep current all the interdependencies that exist among the technologies in different buildings, much less the business operations. By allowing individuals to sign up for communications about the aspects they care about, you make certain that everyone who needs to know about an event that is occurring does know.

As you can imagine, if you have 25 people who have signed up for communications about an event impacting a certain facility, the challenge is to communicate with all of them quickly. You may need hours or even days to respond to and fix a problem, but those impacted by the event want to know as quickly as possible what is going on and how long it is going to last. The use of some type of notification software that can contact a large number of people quickly facilitates this type of communication. I have recently seen this type of software used by school systems to contact parents when there is a snow day. There are a number of vendors who provide this type of software.

In the early stages of any event, there is often little to say to those impacted, because we have not had time to diagnose the problem. Very few events are smoke and rubble events, where it is really clear from the moment the event occurs that we have a major problem. Most events start small and are quickly fixed or escalate over time into larger problems. I would recommend that the initial communication to the first escalation team be just a communication that confirms that you know about the problem, are assessing it, and will have a an update as soon as there is something to say. The next communication should be no later than half an hour after the event occurs, even if you still don't know anything yet. If you wait too long, people will think you forgot about them and start calling you for an update.

One of the major reasons for establishing an event-management process is to keep the people responsible for fixing the problem from being constantly interrupted for updates. Updates should occur at planned intervals, and the event owner, not the responders, should provide them to the rest of the team.

The first communication to the first-escalation team may look something like this:"To the first-escalation team from business continuity—a power outage has occurred in the 100 Main Street building. Assessment in process, updates to follow."

The second communication may look something like this: "To the first-escalation team from business continuity—conference bridge to discuss power outage at 100 Main Street building will occur at 3:45 EST. Conference bridge 1-800-888-1234, pass code 123456."

In programs I have built, we manage this communication through the use of a conference call. The conference call acts as a virtual command center to manage the communications and response to the event. One conference bridge can be set up for managing the responders, the people responsible for fixing the problem, and another conference bridge can be held so the event owner can communicate to those impacted by the event. The owner should communicate what the problem is, the current status of the problem, how long it should be before it is resolved, what is impacted, and, if necessary, when the next update will be provided and how.

The best part about using a conference bridge for event communications is that everyone hears the same story at once. People come to trust the conference bridge as the single source of accurate communication regarding the event. Some words of caution about conference bridges, however: Someone, and I do mean *one* someone, needs to facilitate the call. You need to remind people of conference-call etiquette. One person talks at a time; mute your phone if you are not speaking; no guessing, facts only. People giving updates have to be trained not to state what they think may have happened on a call, because as soon as you say it, it becomes a fact. Just state the facts. If you do not know yet, don't guess; say that you do not know but as soon as you do, you will let them know.

The conference bridge should go something like this: The facilitator will take attendance to make certain that everyone who needs to be there is there and then will introduce the event owner for an update. Once the update is provided, the facilitator will open the floor for questions and document any outstanding questions that could not be answered on the call. If the issue is still outstanding and further communications will need to occur, the facilitator will get agreement from the attendees and the event owner on the timing of the next status update. If there is a change of status before the next scheduled call, additional communications can be sent to the team to bring them back to the call sooner.

My experience has been that what matters most in any type of event and in how the event is perceived after the fact is almost entirely dependent on how well communications are managed during the course of the event. If people know what is going on and know what to expect, they can manage the impacts and responses to those impacts effectively within their own space. When a system is down or a building is without power, the people who work in that building or who use that application need to know how to deal with the business impacts resulting from the problem. If they know that the system will not be back for at least two hours, they won't tell the customer to call back in 10 minutes. If the leadership team knows that the building will be without power for the rest of the day because there has been an electrical problem in the building, they will release their staff while it is still light enough to walk down the stairs.

The third team identified consists of people who do not need to be part of the initial response to a problem, nor are they directly impacted by the event, but they need to know that something happened. We call this the general team. Team members need to get involved only if the problem escalates, but otherwise they simply need to be informed that a problem has occurred, who was impacted by it, how long it lasted, and what the root cause was. A communication to them would look something like this: "To the general team from business continuity—500 people in the 100 Main Street building were evacuated at 10:18 a.m. for 15 minutes due to a false fire alarm caused by construction crew. No further updates."

Unless from the very start of an event we are clear that we have a major issue, the leadership team generally does not need to be a part of the initial response to an issue, but it often needs or wants to be made aware that the issue exists and that if the problem persists or has a significant impact, that it may be called in to make decisions on how to manage the business impacts caused by the event and to coordinate the larger-scale response.

Every event that the firm is confronted with can and should be managed through this process, from a small event like a plumbing leak that has impacted workstations on the floor below to large events like September 11 and Katrina. If the planner will commit to that, then it is not something that is used only in a disaster but becomes part of the fabric of the business. Everyone understands how they will be communicated to and where to go to get the right information or help that they need when a disaster occurs. Event management takes practice, and a disaster is a really, really big event.

WHEN AN EVENT BECOMES A CRISIS

The event-management plan is part of the business-continuity/disaster-recovery plan. Making a decision to execute the BC or DR plan is one possible response to an event. The event-management plan needs to identify who is authorized to declare a disaster, how a declaration is made, when the decision to "declare" is made, and how it will be communicated to the teams that need to respond.

Leadership in Crisis

The executive emergency-management team is a team that consists of the senior executives within the company who have an overall responsibility for the recovery of the business and services to others. As needed during the emergency, these individuals will participate in the command centers, virtual or physical, established for the recovery efforts and in the execution of the plan. The crisis-management-plan documents cover both a formal integrated response process for management and onsite coverage/support in emergency situations.

The executive team does not directly manage the day-to-day operations of the organization under normal circumstances and is not expected to have day-to-day responsibilities in managing the recovery efforts from the emergency situation. However, the team will respond to and assist in the resolution of issues that need their direction. It will provide the spokesperson for the organization to the media and make decisions on how the organization will manage the business impacts of the event.

The executives of most organizations are concerned with strategic issues, not with tactical delivery. While the next team, the emergency-management team, needs to be held accountable for the tactical response to the event, the executive team needs to focus on the strategic response. It is the executive team that will lead the organization through the crisis; it will not manage the crisis itself. Exhibit 13.2 shows the difference between crisis management and crisis leadership.

Crisis leadership is not taught in an MBA program, yet a crisis can threaten the viability of the organization. We somehow think that our leaders are just born with traits that are needed to lead an organization during times of crisis. But the fact is that a true crisis event is so rare that most senior leaders have never seen one in their tenure as leaders. A crisis has the potential to dismantle an organization, and, since it generally falls under close media scrutiny, it can be a turning point in an organization as well as a defining moment, negatively or positively, for the leaders of that organization.

In a true crisis it is helpful if at least one of your senior leaders has already been through a crisis, but since that is often not the case, it is important that the senior leaders of the organization participate in walkthrough exercises that train them in the role of crisis leadership. The exercises do not prepare the leaders for everything, because a simulation does not inflict the physiological effects of stress, nor does it coincide with external factors that can occur, such as their houses being destroyed, their cars being underwater, their personal finances being impacted, and their every action being scrutinized by the media.

After building the crisis-management plan for my current organization, we did a series of walkthrough exercises with the executive team to enhance their preparedness to respond to a real crisis. The organization had gone through some difficult times and had hired a turnaround leader about four years before. He had done what he was hired to do, and the organization was moving forward with momentum.

For the first crisis-management exercise, I used a scenario in which the CEO and the COO were visiting clients and got into a car accident.

Crisis Management	versus	Crisis Leadership
React		Anticipate
Short-term		Long-term
Process		Principles
Narrow		Wide focus
Tactical		Strategic

Exhibit 13.2 Crisis Management versus Crisis Leadership.

The CEO was killed and the COO was in intensive care, a true crisis of leadership. There was no building burning or system down, but the organization faced a crisis. Our organization's recent success was built around a charismatic leader, and now he was gone. How do we convince the stakeholders that our company will go on and will continue its success without him?

The next scenario was an employee sabotage that caused a facility fire and the deaths of three employees. The employee was charged with arson and manslaughter, but the firm was under media fire because the employee said that he did it for all his fellow employees whose jobs had been outsourced to other countries, while the executives raked in millions of dollars in salary and stock options.

It is important for the leaders to be able to understand the context of an event and how it will be perceived by stakeholders. Some context implications include whether the event is a man-made or natural disaster (9/11 vs. Katrina), whether people have been killed or injured or whether it just involves money (Tylenol poisonings vs. Enron), whether it is only their company under scrutiny or whether other companies have the same issue (Goodyear Tire vs. current credit-market issues impacting banks), and whether the company is somehow at fault for the issue or it too is a victim of the event (Arthur Anderson vs. Cantor Fitzgerald).

The executive team needs to manage the crisis impacts to the firm from a strategic perspective, addressing the needs of all the stakeholders through timely communications that are grounded in a vision that is ethically based, unselfish, honest, and transparent.

The next team, the emergency-management team, is comprised of individuals who would report directly to the command center and have responsibility to oversee the recovery and restoration process being executed by the emergency-response teams. This team is responsible for communicating the recovery status to the executive management team and making the necessary management decisions to support the recovery efforts. The emergency-management team leader has overall responsibility for the recovery team and communications with the executive management team on the status of the recovery and the impacts to the business operations. The objectives and the functions of this team are:

- Make a preliminary assessment of the damage.
- Notify senior management on the current status, impact to business, and plan of action.
- Declare a disaster if necessary.

- Initiate the plan during the emergency situation.
- Organize and control the command centers as a central point of control of the recovery efforts.
- Organize and provide administrative support to the recovery effort.
- Administer and direct the problem-management function.

The final teams, the emergency-response teams, are comprised of individuals who are responsible for executing the recovery processes necessary for the continuity or recovery of time-sensitive business operations impacted by the event. These individuals report to the alternate sites for their critical functions to execute the recovery process. They report to the emergency-management team through emergency-response-team leaders who have overall responsibility for the response teams' efforts in those locations. The response teams may be broken into subteams, each with its own leader, to facilitate the recovery effort.

The primary responsibilities of the members of these teams are as follows:

- Retrieve offsite site records and recovery information from offsite storage.
- Report to the alternate site identified in the procedures.
- Execute the business-recovery procedures for their area of responsibilities in the order of priority identified.
- Communicate the status of the recovery to the command centers as needed.
- Identify issues or problems to be escalated to the management team for resolution.
- Establish shifts for recovery-team members to support the recovery effort 24/7.
- Establish liaison with alternate-site personnel if needed.
- Support efforts to return to normal operations.
- Reestablish support operations affected by the disaster
- Identify replacement equipment/software needed for the recovery effort and return to normal operations.

Command centers are set up at a central location for communications and decision making during an emergency situation. Command centers are set up in response to the disaster and are equipped with a copy of the plan document and other resources that may be needed in a disaster.

PROBLEM MANAGEMENT

The planner will need to document a process for reporting and managing problems that will occur during the recovery. Even if the plan was tested yesterday and everything worked perfectly, unexpected problems may occur. There needs to be a process in the plan to document them, triage them, escalate them, fix them, and report on them. If the company already has a formal problem-management/change-management process, use it. If not, invent one to use in a recovery and test the process when you test the recovery.

If your process for managing problems day to day is to report the problem to a central group, open a ticket, and assign it to a responder, use that process in the recovery. Even during alternate-site tests when business users validate alternate-site readiness or during data-center recovery exercises, make people call in a ticket before a problem is addressed.

14

Crisis Communications

- Understanding the Importance of Communications During Recovery
- Different Communications to Different Stakeholders

RECOVERY COMMUNICATIONS

If I have stressed any point during this book, it is that communications are key to your recovery. If you learn how and when to talk to one another and all the other stakeholders of an event, then your recovery will most likely be successful no matter what struggles you face. There are many types of communications that need to occur during an event. In the event-management section of this book, we talked about how to establish a method of communications around an event that impacts business that becomes part of the fabric of the organization. When an event becomes a crisis or a disaster, other communications are needed to address the concerns of other stakeholders who do not get involved in the minor day-to-day interruptions. The focus of this chapter is on managing recovery communications.

Communications surrounding the event itself and the recovery from the event need to be coordinated through the corporate communications staff, working with the crisis leadership team and, where appropriate, human resources. Remember, disasters are human events, and we need to manage the communications to the various stakeholders to make certain that everyone is hearing the same story and that they are hearing the part of the story that concerns them and what they care about.

EMPLOYEE NOTIFICATION

Employees who are members of an event-management team or an emergency-notification list will be contacted directly in the event of an emergency situation by the responsible management-team member. The planner will need to document the process of how the organization will communicate with the remaining employees about the event and the recovery efforts.

A common method of doing this is to establish a contingency information line for the general employee population to get information about what happened and the progress of the recovery. To keep this number handy, I have put it on a sticker on the back of employee badges and also on a magnet the employees are supposed to take home and put on their refrigerators. To make sure this number is familiar to employees, this same number can be used by the company to communicate office closures or early release or late start notifications in the event of severe weather.

In the event of a natural disaster or some type of event in which an employee's safety may be at risk, this same line can be used as an "I'm OK" line. During the recent hurricanes that have impacted offices where my company does business, we used the same contingency information line not just to reach out to employees but to have the employees reach out to us to let us know where they had evacuated, if they were safe, how to get in contact with them, and whether they needed anything from us.

The line is updated throughout the event to notify employees of the status of the recovery effort, where and when to report to work, and any other communication we want to share with them. During 9/11 and Katrina, we used it to let employees know when there would be "town meetings," ice-cream socials, or other activities that we wanted the employees who were not able to come to work yet to be involved in.

In addition to these tools for managing communications, there are a number of externally hosted software tools that can be contracted for to maintain contact information for employees or others that you may need to reach out to. As I mentioned before, those of you with children in public schools may have been called by one of these notification systems to let you know of school snow days. These same tools can be used by business to reach out during an event to keep people up to date. Most of these tools allow you to build dynamic teams based on particular criteria (such as location) and predefined teams of specific people (such as network teams).

The advantage of these tools is that they can rapidly communicate with large groups of people over various types of devices—pager, home phone, cell phone, work email, home email, SMS—virtually any device that can receive either a voice or text message. The other advantage is that everyone not only gets the information very quickly but they get the same information. Information that is relayed between several intermediaries can sometimes get lost in translation. Many of these tools also have the ability to require a response from the receiving individual to specific questions like "Are you okay?", "Did you understand this message?", or "Can you report to the alternate site tomorrow?"

As noted in the chapter on crisis management, in the early stages of any event, there is often little to say to those impacted, because we have not had time to figure out what is going on and how we need to respond. Whether the event you are dealing with is a smoke-and-rubble event where it is clear from the moment the event occurs that we have a major problem or an event that starts small and escalates over time into a larger problem, I would recommend that the initial communication to everyone be just a confirmation that we know about the problem, we are assessing it, and that we will have an update when we have more information. Again, don't wait too long—people will think you forgot about them and start calling you for an update.

COMMUNICATIONS AMONG AND
TO YOUR RECOVERY TEAMS

In the crisis-management/event-management chapter we talked about how and when we make the management of events part of the fabric of the company and use it all the time. When an event becomes a crisis, we use the same process, only the number and level of people involved escalate. It is really just an issue of scaling the event so that you have clearly defined, based on the event level, who else needs to know and who else needs to help.

I use a color scale—green, yellow, orange, and red—similar to the Homeland Security scaling of threat levels.

A green event is a part of the normal fabric of the business day. Individual PCs fail, printers break, single applications have problems, servers go down, or plumbing leaks, and people respond to fix, repair, or replace whatever is broken and the day goes on.

In a yellow event whatever broke is having an impact on business, particularly an outward-facing impact. The website goes down, power goes out at a building and employees cannot work, a virus impacts our email system, we are subject to a denial-of-service attack, employees get evacuated, the roof leaks on an office area and causes water damage to equipment and files. These events are larger in scale, impact the ability of more employees to be productive, or are visible to customers and require a more coordinated response and recovery plan.

A orange event occurs when whatever broke is having a significant impact on our employees' ability to conduct business in a normal manner if at all, we may require an alternate-site activation, and/or our customers have been impacted by this event for a period of time that is no longer acceptable. For my current company, that threshold is two hours. If our website has been down for two hours or more, the event goes from yellow to orange.

A red event occurs when whatever broke is having a significant impact on our employees' ability to conduct business in a normal manner if at all, we will require an alternate-site activation, and/or our customers have been impacted by this event, those impacts are expected to last for more than a day, and/or we have employees at risk.

Who is in charge of the event and to whom the event gets communicated are dependent on the type of event and the event level.

Green events are managed through the normal course of business. If a sink is plugged up in a bathroom or a single server is down, they are fixed. A yellow event has an event owner who is responsible for assembling and managing the team to fix the problem and manage the communications to the impacted parties until the problem is resolved.

An orange event introduces another team to the management of the problem. While the event owner remains the same in terms of the resolution of the problem, the decisions about how the company will respond to the business impacts caused by the problem are moved to a leadership team comprised of legal, human resources, finance, risk management, corporate communications, and the COO. This group will be the decision makers on the need for the alternate site, whether and when we will communicate to the media, what communications need to be made to the employees, and what communications will be made to the customers of the organization.

When an event is a red event or becomes a red event, the problem owner stays the same, but the leadership team expands to include the company president and at times the board of directors.

USING CONFERENCE BRIDGES

During the course of the recovery efforts it may be helpful to establish conference bridges to communicate recovery issues and to coordinate communications among the different recovery locations. Multiple conference bridges can be used for different parts of the recovery. I find that it is best to keep the discussions between the technical groups and the business partners separate, because they simply do not speak the same language.

When it is not possible to have all employees seated at an alternate site, conference bridges can be used for virtual town meetings for management to communicate to all the employees what is going on and to provide an opportunity for employees to ask questions. Bridges can be used for managing staff recovering at different locations and as virtual command centers.

There are a number of conference-bridge services available from a variety of vendors. If you do not use a vendor for this as part of normal business, identifying one before a disaster and working with the vendor to meet your needs would be better than trying to secure the service at time of disaster, especially a regional disaster when many organizations are seeking service.

COMMUNICATIONS TO CUSTOMER, CLIENTS, AND VENDORS

Customers or clients of the firm want to know whether what is going on is going to impact them in some way. Media statements will be one form of communication, but employees who talk with customers and/or clients as a part of their normal business day should be provided with a statement or script regarding the recovery effort. This is often referred to as talking points, usually a series of common questions that a customer may have and the company response. It is important that *everyone* tell the same story. Any customer not satisfied with the response provided should be referred to management or the corporate-communications staff.

If you work for a service provider and have a call center, it is possible for someone from the media to call into the call center to try to get information from one of your representatives. I tell a story when I am speaking at conferences about this subject. I tell them that I am certain that there are representatives from the media who are legitimate customers of my company and they could call, authenticate themselves as a customer, ask a trivial question about their account, and then say, "I heard you have some type of problem going on there. What's *really* going on?" I then explain that our customer-services representatives are trained to satisfy our customers, and if we don't give them a story to tell, then they will make one up based on the information they have. Give them the right information.

Another vehicle for communication is the company's website. A statement about the problem and common questions and answers can be posted on the website for customers. It is important that the communication be framed within the context of the crisis, as discussed in the crisis-management chapter. The communications should take into consideration the following:

1. The firm should demonstrate that it cares about the wellbeing of anyone impacted by the event.
2. The information provided should be open, honest, and transparent.
3. The firm should assume appropriate responsibility for the crisis.
4. All decisions and actions the firm makes should be based on ethical guidelines.

As the recovery progresses, the company will need to provide recovery-status updates to all the stakeholders. It is important that the statements be honest and concise. It is also important to consider each stakeholder's various needs and concerns. Employees may be worried about their jobs, whereas stockholders may be more worried about the impact to the company stock and customers just want to know that their product or service will be there when they need it.

HANDLING THE MEDIA

If you have a crisis that is being played out in the media in a negative way or one that could be played in a negative way, I strongly encourage you to hire outside help in handling the media if you can afford to do so. Specialists have much more experience in handling a media event then anyone on your staff could have simply because that is all they do every day. They have contacts, speak the same language, know best how to counteract negative attention, know when to talk, and more importantly know when to be quiet. If your firm either cannot or will not do that, then you need to make a plan for addressing the media.

First, you need to get several people in the firm media-trained. In large publicly traded firms, it is common that the senior leaders have at least some type of media training. In smaller firms, you should select one or more people from the senior staff who will be trained to act as spokespeople in a crisis. During the actual crisis, only *one* person *ever* speaks to the press; everyone else is taught to refer all questions to that person when confronted by the media. Consistency is very important. It is even risky to give other employees talking points or an approved statement to be made when confronted by the media, since reporters are trained to pick up on that and push to ask further questions, prompting people to improvise an answer.

Everyone needs to understand that there is no such thing as off-the-record with the media. An inadvertent comment made by staff or even the appearance of a leader smiling and laughing in the background during a media event may provoke the opinion that the leaders are insensitive to the crisis.

When a crisis occurs, the leadership team needs to meet and gather the facts of the event as known. They need to look at the crisis, discuss how the situation could escalate, assess the impact on assets, and consider what actions they may take and what the intended or unintended consequences of those actions may be. Discuss each potential stakeholder shown in Exhibit 14.1 and ask what a good resolution of the crisis would look like if they were in their shoes and whether that is possible.

- Employees
- Families of your employees
- Contractors
- External business partners
- Line managers
- Senior leadership
- Board of directors
- Institutional investors/ Shareholders of the company
- Insurance representatives
- Vendors
- Distributors
- Customers
- Government regulators/ politicians
- Competitors
- Media representatives
- Unions
- Local communities
- Internet (users/bloggers)
- Industry activist groups

Exhibit 14.1 Potential Stakeholders In a Crisis.

Remember that you are not required to speak to the press. In the first moments or hours of an event, it may be in your best interest to let others speak. Let the fire chief answer questions about the fire. Let the police chief answer questions about possible injuries. This will give you and your leadership team time to understand the situation better and to formulate a media plan.

Some tips on dealing with the media:

- If the media is at the scene, establish a media briefing center and contain the media to that area to prevent them wandering and talking to random people.
- Deal with the emergency head on—don't hide out.
- Face the media quickly and openly; don't speculate; deal only with the facts that are known—if you don't know yet, say you don't know.
- *Never* report on injuries or fatalities until you are certain that family members have been notified.
- *Never lie*—not even a little white lie.
- *Never go off the record,* especially in an emergency.
- *Never volunteer negative information.*
- Return calls to the radio first, then TV, then the newspapers—this is based on the speed with which the information is released.
- Don't use business acronyms; keep you verbiage simple.

The media is looking for a story that is going to be interesting to its readers. Human-interest stories from the event are especially vulnerable. One bad story published by the media can result in an avalanche of negative media for the firm, resulting in loss of customer and investor confidence. On the other side of the coin, an event that is handled well can instill confidence in the company.

Be prepared, be very prepared.

WORK YOU CAN DO BEFORE AN EVENT

You should at minimum have a framework for crafting messages and communications to be used in an event. The framework can be simply asking questions about the nature of the event at hand to make certain the communication considers all the facets of an event. You can consider crafting messages that can be preapproved for use during an event, with the specifics of the event are updated into the prepared document prior to disseminating. This will speed the process of developing communications following an event when people are more likely stressed and not necessarily thinking as clearly.

Just like every other process, your media team needs to be tested. As you perform walkthrough drills with you crisis leadership team, drill the media piece as well.

15

Pandemic Planning

Chapter Objectives

- Understanding the Flu
- The Current Threat
- Why This Plan is Different

AN INFLUENZA TUTORIAL

"We're due. It is not a matter of if but *when* this will happen. I am far more afraid of a flu pandemic than I am of SARS."—Albert Osterhaus *The Wall Street Journal*, May 29, 2003

Pandemics have occurred throughout recorded history. On a scale of a human lifetime, pandemic influenza is a rarity, but no one seriously doubts that there will be another one. The last influenza pandemic that occurred was in 1968, the Hong Kong flu. Influenza virus has survived throughout history by continuing to adapt through mutations. We have an influenza virus every year, which kills an average of 36,000 Americans, usually the very young, the very old, and the very sick. I strongly encourage everyone to get a flu shot every year. You cannot get the flu from a flu shot. There is no live virus in the vaccine. While the flu shot is unlikely to provide immunity to a pandemic influenza, it will most likely provide immunity to the seasonal varieties. Pandemic Influenza is different from seasonal influenza. The definitions of seasonal flu, bird flu, and pandemic flu are noted below for your reference:

- Seasonal (or common) flu is a highly contagious respiratory illness that can be transmitted from person to person. Most people have some immunity, and a vaccine is available.
- Avian (or bird) flu is caused by influenza viruses that occur naturally among wild birds. The H5N1 variant is deadly to domestic fowl and can be transmitted from birds to humans. There is no human immunity and no vaccine is available.
- Pandemic flu is virulent human flu that causes a global outbreak, or pandemic, of serious illness. Because there is little natural immunity, the disease can spread easily from person to person. Currently, there is no pandemic flu.

Influenza is a respiratory illness caused by a flu virus. The flu has two subtypes, determined by proteins on the outer surface of the virus: hemagglutinin (H), which helps the virus attach to respiratory cells, and neuraminidase (N), which helps the virus penetrate the cells once it is attached. Once the virus penetrates the cells, it begins to replicate and infect other cells. There are 144 different possible H and N combinations. For example, the 1968 Hong Kong flu was an H3N2 virus.

Influenza has thrived over the millennia by adhering to one simple principle, adapt or die. This is why it is possible to get a flu shot and still get the flu. The virus can mutate after the production of the flu vaccine so that the vaccine does not provide immunity anymore.

New influenza viruses occur through antigenic drift or shift. Drift is a subtle mutation within the same subtype (sometimes associated with pandemics), and shift is an entirely new subtype of virus that emerges through either recombination of human and animal antigens (often swine or avian) or a direct leap to humans (more often associated with pandemics).

The general course of influenza in adults is as follows:

- Day 0—become infected
- Day 1–4—disease incubation (average of two days)
- Day 1–6—contagious (one day before to five days after)
- Day 2–9—symptomatic (usually two to five days)
- Day 4 to ?—decreased energy (one week of more)

Influenza is spread through close personal contact. Close personal contact is considered to be three to six feet away. When you breathe, talk, cough, or sneeze, tiny particulates containing droplet nuclei are expelled into the air. These droplet nuclei are 1.5 microns in size and can remain suspended in the air for several hours, depending on the environment.

Sneezing can spread tens of thousands of droplet nuclei up to ten feet away. Look around you right now and see who you are sharing your droplet nuclei with.

When you breathe in that droplet nuclei or touch a surface it is on and then touch your nose, mouth, or eyes, the infection can enter your system. That is why one of the best defenses against getting the flu or any other infectious illness is hand washing. Frequent hand washing reduces the spread of infection at home and in the workforce.

Influenza is a very contagious disease of the respiratory (breathing) system. For most people, the flu makes them feel very sick, but they generally get better in about a week. However, young children, people older than 65 years of age, pregnant women, and people with chronic medical conditions can have serious complications from the flu. These complications can include pneumonia, dehydration, and worsening of medical conditions such as heart disease, diabetes, or asthma.

The following tips can help protect you and your loved ones during the regular flu season, as well as from the threat of bird flu and any cough-related illness:

- Get a flu shot every year—the flu vaccine you get every year does not protect you against bird flu, but it is the best way to protect yourself. Getting the flu shot also means you will not pass the flu to others.
- Ask your healthcare provider if you should get the pneumococcal vaccine—you need this vaccine if you are over 65 years of age or if you have a medical condition such as diabetes, asthma, or heart disease.
- Wash your hands often with soap and water or use an alcohol-based hand sanitizer.
- Cover your mouth when you cough or sneeze—use a tissue or the inside of your elbow, then throw the tissue away and wash your hands.
- Avoid touching your eyes, nose, or mouth—this decreases the chance that you will get the flu virus or other germs into your body or that you will pass the flu on to others.
- Clean things that are touched often—at home, work, or school, clean things like doorknobs, elevator buttons, refrigerator doors, computer keyboards/mouse, phones, and water faucets.
- Avoid close contact with those who are sick. Avoid any unnecessary holding, hugging, kissing of anyone who has a cold or the

127

flu. People with young children, immune problems, or a chronic illness should avoid large crowds unless necessary.
- Stay at home when you are sick. If you have flu symptoms, stay home from work or school and avoid public places for at least five days, seven days for children, so that you do not pass the flu to other people.
- When visiting other countries where bird flu is present, use caution—avoid bird markets, bird farms, and close contact with birds.

PANDEMICS IN THE LAST CENTURY

There have been three notable outbreaks of pandemic flu in the last century:

- 1918 Spanish flu
- 1957 Asian flu
- 1968 Hong Kong flu

The Asian flu was first identified in May 1957 as an H2N2 subtype that originated in Singapore. The new flu virus was reported by the World Health Organization (WHO). Infection rates varied from 20 percent in developed countries with good infection-control practices to 70 percent in third-world countries. The U.S. death toll from the 1957 pandemic was 70,000 in excess mortality. That statistic means that 70,000 more U.S. citizens died of the flu than in a normal year.

In mid-July 1968, a new influenza subtype emerged in Hong Kong. The H3N2 virus was dubbed the Hong Kong flu. Worldwide, the mortality rates were similar in magnitude to those caused by Asian influenza. Age-specific mortality was highest for those over the age of 65, and the U.S. death toll was 31,000 in excess mortality.

The 1918 pandemic was much deadlier that the Asian flu or the Hong Kong flu. The "Spanish" flu first manifested on March 10 at Camp Riley, Kansas. The first wave of the flu pandemic was mild by comparison only to the second and third wave that followed it. The second wave hit in August with a deadly difference. In most flu viruses, the mortality rate is generally highest among those who are very young, very old, or very sick. The Spanish influenza acted differently. Rather than attacking those with weak immune systems, it tended to target the young and healthy members of society. Most victims of the flu were between 21 and 29. Being young and healthy seemed to work against them. It is now believed that the immune systems of the young and healthy put up such a huge defense against the virus that they basically drowned in their own fluids. Individuals could wake up healthy in the morning and be dead by nightfall.

This pandemic occurred during the First World War. Soldiers from the U.S. carried the virus on ships across the ocean and spread the infection throughout the world. Very few places on the globe were untouched by this pandemic. The 1918 virus acted much differently from "ordinary" human flu viruses. Scientists now believe the 1918 strain was probably *entirely* a bird-flu virus that adapted to function in humans.

In the U.S., communities that quickly responded to the virus by closing schools and limiting large gatherings of people suffered much lower infection rates than communities that did not do that or did it too late. The Liberty Loan parade in Philadelphia was held on September 28, 1918 despite the growing pandemic threat. Thousands of people were in attendance, cheering the parade. Within days, the city was struck with a wave of influenza cases.

U.S. communities experienced city-wide quarantines, severe nursing shortages, shortage of caskets, mass burials, school and business closures, panic, and widespread fear. October 1918 turned out to be the deadliest month in our nation's history: 195,000 Americans died of influenza in that one month; 851 New Yorkers died of influenza in a single day. In Philadelphia, the city's death rate for one single week was 700 times higher than normal.

The third wave occurred in February to April 1919 and was again milder but only by comparison to the second wave of the virus. When it was finally over, the worldwide death tolls were staggering. Entire Inuit villages in Alaska were completely wiped out; 20 percent of the population of Western Samoa (7,500) died; 1 out of every 20 citizens of Ghana died over a 60-day period from September 1 to November 1. There were an estimated 50 million deaths worldwide, 17 million in India alone, and 550,000 deaths in the U.S.

Why were there fewer deaths in 1957 and 1968 than in 1918:

- The 1957 and 1968 viruses were less virulent viruses caused by recombination—a human virus that acquired two or three genes from bird-flu-virus strains rather than a direct leap from birds to humans, as is suspected in 1918 pandemic.
- Antibiotic treatment for secondary infections was available—there was no penicillin in 1918.
- Improved supportive care.
- Improved infection control.

SO WHAT IS BIRD FLU AND WHY ARE WE WORRIED?

Health experts have been monitoring an extremely severe influenza virus—the H5N1 strain—for almost 11 years. The H5N1 strain first infected humans in Hong Kong in 1997, causing 18 cases, including six deaths. Since mid-2003, this virus has caused the largest and most severe outbreaks in poultry on record. Beginning in December 2003, infections in people exposed to sick birds were identified. The H5N1 virus has raised concerns about a potential human pandemic because:

- It is especially virulent.
- It is being spread by migratory birds.
- It can be transmitted from birds to mammals and in some limited circumstances to humans.
- Like other influenza viruses, it continues to evolve.

Since 2003, a growing number of human H5N1 cases have been reported.

There has been no sustained human-to-human transmission of the disease, but the concern is that H5N1 will evolve into a virus capable of human-to-human transmission.

This virus is especially virulent. In confirmed cases to date, the virus has been 60 to 70 percent fatal—60 to 70 percent of people who get this virus die. The mortality rate in the 1918 pandemic, by comparison, was 4 percent. Similar to the 1918 pandemic, this virus is attacking the young and healthy—90 percent of the confirmed cases of H5N1 where age was reported have been in individuals under 39 years of age, 75 percent were 29 years of age or younger, and 50 percent were under the age of 16.

On October 21, 2007, an outbreak of the highly lethal H5N1 virus was confirmed at a poultry farm in North-West Frontier Province, Pakistan. To respond to the threat, a group of workers was immediately called to cull all the chickens on the farm to prevent the virus from spreading. Unfortunately, one of the workers handled the chickens without using any personal protective equipment; he developed fever and other symptoms about a week later. Instead of resting at home, he traveled to his family home in another district, where he passed the virus to his brother, who in turn infected two other brothers. A fourth brother was also infected but did not show any symptoms. The culler and two of his brothers eventually recovered, but the other two brothers died a month later. Among the people who attended the funerals was another brother, who was from New York. Upon his return to the United States, he was tested by health authorities, who were worried that he could have brought the virus into the country. Fortunately, he tested negative.

This episode of a limited outbreak of human to-human transmission of H5N1 shows how compact our world has become and how quickly and widely an infectious disease could spread. Influenza is much more contagious than SARS, and yet SARS crossed the globe in a little more than a week. The Spanish flu was spread by soldiers fighting in WWI, but in those days, the spread was slowed by the mode of travel available. With today's world of air travel, the spread of infectious diseases has emerged as a significant challenge. When a pandemic occurs, depending on its virility, millions of people could fall ill or die. The fallout could ripple across the world over a prolonged period of time.

Another lesson learned from the outbreak in Pakistan was that it took time for the public to learn about the cases. Although the infections and subsequent deaths took place between October and November 2007, the first media reports surfaced only in early December 2007. Information was sketchy and sometimes conflicting. It was only in mid-December that the world had a clearer picture of what was happening in Pakistan. We can expect the same uncertainty during the initial stage of a pandemic.

The CDC has estimated the number of people in the U.S. who would be ill, seek outpatient care, need hospitalization, need mechanical ventilation, and die from a mild pandemic similar to 1968 and a severe pandemic similar to 1918.

In a 1968-like pandemic with a 30 percent infection rate, 90 million people would get sick. Of those 45 million would seek outpatient, perhaps more with the introduction of antivirals; 864,000 people would need to be hospitalized, 128,750 of those in ICU, with 64,815 people needing mechanical ventilation. A 1968-like pandemic would produce 209,000 deaths, or an excess mortality of 173,000 people.

A 1918-like pandemic with the same 30 percent infection rate would result in 9.9 million people needing hospitalization due to complications of the flu; of those 1,485,000 would need ICU care and 745,500 would need mechanical ventilation; this flu would result in 1,903,000 deaths in the U.S. alone, or an excess mortality of 1,867,000 people. There are not 745,500 mechanical ventilators in the U.S. today, and many of those that do exist are in use. A pandemic of 1918 proportions in today's world will create some difficult ethical issues for the healthcare community. If you have an 85-year-old woman on a ventilator and a 16-year-old comes into the same facility needing a ventilator and there are no more to be found, what do you do?

The healthcare industry needs to think about these issues before the next pandemic, and though everyone hopes never to be faced with such a choice, having guidelines for extreme situations that were prepared when the world was *not* in crisis will be helpful.

H1N1 FLU

Between the time I completed writing this book and its publication, the world was confronted with the first influenza pandemic of the new century. The World Health Organization moved to pandemic level 6, its highest level, on June 12, 2009 as a result of a novel influenza virus first detected in Mexico in April that has as of that date spread to more than 70 countries. The virus is an Influenza A virus that contains genetic pieces from four different virus sources: a North American swine-influenza virus, a North American avian-influenza virus, a human-influenza virus, and a swine-influenza virus found in Asia and Europe.

From the first news reports in April to the time of the first press briefing by the U.S.Centers for Disease Control (CDC) on April 23, the virus had quickly spread to the United States, carried mostly by people returning from a school-vacation week spent in Mexico.

The two most important pieces of information that we did not know at that point were:

1. How many people were going to get sick from this new virus? Our planning assumption was that 30 percent of the population would get sick in a community outbreak lasting six to eight weeks.
2. How lethal this virus was going to be? Our fears were that it could be a virus as lethal as the 1918 pandemic, which had a worldwide mortality rate between 2.5 and 4 percent (depending on the source), or worse yet, the H5N1 bird flu, which remains 60 to 70 percent fatal.

Whenever an infectious-disease event begins, we will not know the answers to these questions. Therefore the initial response my organization put into action was aggressive. Our primary goal was to keep the infection out of our workspace for as long as possible, so we implemented plans for eliminating any visitors without a business need, screening at the entrances to all our facilities, and implementing mandatory stay-at-home policies for anyone who had recently been to Mexico, had any flulike symptoms, or had been exposed to anyone with flulike symptoms.

The first reports out of Mexico were frightening, but as the virus spread in the U.S., the news was better. As of this writing, currently the attack rates are fairly consistent with what we see with seasonal flu. In a typical influenza season, about 7 to 10 percent of the people in a community may become infected with an influenza virus. And about 20 percent of people in households where infected people reside contract influenza. Though there were some deaths in the U.S., the fatality rate was very low—similar to a mild seasonal flu. Right now we are seeing a mortality rate of 0.15 or 0.2 percent.

The H1N1 flu continues to spread around the world but remains mild. The virus actually met the criteria for level 6, but WHO was hesitant to raise to that level because the severity of the illness is less than what was anticipated. The pandemic levels were designed for a more serious flu virus that was more transmissible and more deadly than this one has proven to be so far. WHO is evaluating the pandemic scale and making adjustments not only to reflect how widespread a virus is but also the severity of the illness. This one could be labled "widespread, but not that bad."

As of this writing, roughly two-thirds of the confirmed cases are in the U.S., though because of the mild illness it presents in most people, the CDC is treating cases in a similar fashion to the seasonal flu. Some facts as of this writing:

- Average age of infection is 16 years.
- Almost two-thirds (62 percent) are 5 to 24 years old. The infection rate for people over 65 is 1 percent.
- *Most* hospitalizations and deaths have occurred in individuals with underlying health issues.
- The CDC is no longer testing every case of flu but presenting information similar to the seasonal flu updates.

There is some speculation that people born before 1957 may have some immunity to this novel flu virus because of exposure to a similar virus circulating at that time. During the seasonal influenza, which occurs every year, attack rates and complications from seasonal flu are more common in those over 65. Similar to most pandemic influenzas, young people are more susceptible to this virus than the older population.

The outbreak appears to have peaked in the Northern Hemisphere and is beginning to slow in most regions of the United States but not everywhere. The reason for this is because the flu season in the Northern Hemisphere is at an end, schools and colleges are closing for the summer, and people are outside more in fresh air and are not in confined spaces with large groups of people as often as in the winter months.

Of course the reverse is true in the Southern Hemisphere. There, the flu season is just beginning, and the new outbreaks being reported now are in places such as Australia, Chile, and other locations in the Southern Hemisphere.

What we don't know now about this virus is whether it will disappear completely or reappear in the Northern Hemisphere in the fall with the seasonal flu. An influenza virus stops infecting people when it runs out of hosts susceptible to the infection. Once everyone who is going to get it has it, the virus stops because there is no one left to infect. But, of course, viruses have survived throughout the millennia for one reason—adapt or die.

What we also do not know and why we need to remain watchful and prepared is that, if it does come back, will it be the same or will it be more transmissible and/or more virulent than the current circulating virus? At the CDC press briefing on May 26, 2009, the spokesperson said, "We really are on a fast track over the next eight to ten weeks to learn as much as we can as this virus heads to the Southern Hemisphere and to strengthen our planning for the surge of illness that we expect to experience here in the fall."

The CDC and WHO are watching the flu season as it begins in the Southern Hemisphere. They are watching to see how this flu presents itself there, how lethal the virus is, and how it spreads in countries with different types of societies and healthcare systems. They will continue to test flu specimens, watching closely for mutations or recombination with other viruses, and of course they are working on a flu vaccine for the upcoming flu season in the Northern Hemisphere.

They remember the Spanish flu—the first wave of the infection occurred in March 1918 and was mild by comparison to the second wave, which began in August of that year and was more lethal by far then the first wave. The third wave occurred from February to April 1919 and again was mild by comparison to the second wave of the virus.

A conservative estimate is that the Spanish flu killed 550,000 Americans in ten months—that's more than the number of Americans who died in combat in all the wars of that century. An estimated one-third of the world's population (roughly 500 million persons) was infected during the 1918–1919 influenza pandemic. Case-fatality rates were between 2.5 and 4 percent, compared to less than 0.1 percent in other influenza pandemics. Total deaths were estimated at roughly 50 million and were arguably as high as 100 million.

The impact of this pandemic was not limited to 1918 and 1919. All influenza A pandemics since that time, and indeed almost all cases of influenza A worldwide, have been caused by descendants of the 1918 virus, including the "drifted" novel H1N1 virus we are currently experiencing and the reassorted H2N2 and H3N2 viruses from the 1957 and 1968 pandemics.

At the beginning of other "off-season" influenza pandemics, successive distinct waves within a year were not reported before the 1918 pandemic. The 1889 pandemic, for example, began in the late spring of 1889 and took several months to spread throughout the world, peaking in northern Europe and the United States late in 1889 or early in 1890. The second recurrence peaked in late spring 1891 (more than a year after the first pandemic appearance) and the third in early 1892.

As was true for the 1918 pandemic, the second 1891 recurrence produced the most deaths. The three recurrences in 1889 to 1892, however, were spread over more than 3 years, in contrast to 1918 and 1919, when the sequential waves seen in individual countries were typically compressed into roughly eight to nine months. The point of this is that, even if we do not see a second wave this fall, it may come back next spring.

The CDC, WHO, and my pandemic team are using the current flu outbreak as a "pandemic stress test." The results from analyzing this stress test will be used to significantly improve the state of readiness to deal with a more serious outbreak when and if it does occur. We need to remain prepared!

Economic Impacts of a Pandemic

The Asian Development Bank estimated that the economic impact of SARS on the Asian economy was $59 billion in lost business revenue. The economic impact of a global pandemic would be much higher. Impacts would include:

- Severe impact to airlines, tourism, and hospitality industry
- May trigger foreclosures, bankruptcies, and credit restrictions
- Collapse of the housing market
- Healthcare system strained to the breaking point
- Huge increase in medical claims
- Rampant decline in spending, high unemployment
- Flight to gold and other "safe" investments
- Border and port closures
- Environment of less goods and services as movement of goods is impacted
- Shortage of goods resulting in panic buying

PUBLIC HEALTH LAW AND QUARANTINE

An executive order of the president limits quarantine to nine diseases: cholera, diphtheria, infectious tuberculosis, plague, SARS, smallpox, yellow fever, viral hemorrhagic fevers like Ebola, and influenza caused by new strains that could cause pandemic effects.

The Public Health Authority is required during a state of emergency to use every available means to prevent transmission of infectious disease including the following:

- Right to close, direct, evacuate, or decontaminate any facility that is reasonably believed to endanger public health
- Control or limit egress to and from any affected public area, the movement of persons in that area, and the occupancy of the premises
- Perform physical exams or tests as necessary
- Collect specimens from both living and deceased persons
- Treat persons exposed or infected
- Isolate or quarantine individuals or groups of individuals, including those who refuse medical examination, testing, or vaccination

PANDEMIC PLANNING ASSUMPTIONS FROM THE CDC

The Center for Disease Control (CDC) has published a list of pandemic planning assumptions to be used by health officials in preparing for a pandemic illness outbreak. Though these were specifically addressed to the healthcare industry, the assumptions are universal:

- Susceptibility to the pandemic influenza virus will be universal.
- Efficient and sustained person-to-person transmission signals an imminent pandemic.
- The clinical disease attack rate will likely be 30 percent or higher in the overall population during the pandemic. Illness rates will be highest among school-aged children (about 40 percent) and decline with age. Among working adults, an average of 20 percent will become ill during a community outbreak.
- Some persons will become infected but not develop clinically significant symptoms. Asymptomatic or minimally symptomatic individuals can transmit infection and develop immunity to subsequent infection.

- Of those who become ill with influenza, 50 percent will seek out-patient medical care.
- With the availability of effective antiviral drugs for treatment, this proportion may be higher in the next pandemic.
- The number of hospitalizations and deaths will depend on the virulence of the pandemic virus. Estimates differ about tenfold between more and less severe scenarios. Two scenarios are presented based on extrapolation of past pandemic experience. Planning should include the more severe scenario.
- Risk groups for severe and fatal infection cannot be predicted with certainty but are likely to include infants, the elderly, pregnant women, and persons with chronic medical conditions.
- Rates of absenteeism will depend on the severity of the pandemic.
- In a severe pandemic, absenteeism attributable to illness, the need to care for ill family members, and fear of infection may reach 40 percent during the peak weeks of a community outbreak, with lower rates of absenteeism during the weeks before and after the peak.
- Certain public-health measures (closing schools, quarantining household contacts of infected individuals, "snow days") are likely to increase rates of absenteeism.
- The typical incubation period (interval between infection and onset of symptoms) for influenza is approximately 2 days.
- Persons who become ill may shed virus and can transmit infection for up to one day before the onset of illness. Viral shedding and the risk of transmission will be greatest during the first two days of illness. Children usually shed the greatest amount of virus and therefore are likely to post the greatest risk for transmission.
- On average, infected persons will transmit infection to approximately two other people.
- In an affected community, a pandemic outbreak will last about six to eight weeks.
- Multiple waves (periods during which community outbreaks occur across the country) of illness could occur, with each wave lasting two to three months. Historically, the largest waves have occurred in the fall and winter, but the seasonality of a pandemic cannot be predicted with certainty.

WHY IS THIS PLAN DIFFERENT?

Traditional business-continuity and disaster-recovery planning focuses on building a plan that puts us back in business by going from the affected site to an unaffected site and resuming business. The plan assumes that whatever caused the disruption, your business operations will get back to business as usual in 30 days or less either in the repaired primary site or in an expanded alternate site. Neither of these is true in a pandemic. It is not your building or your systems that are unavailable—it is your people.

A pandemic is a workforce-impairment event. In this event, your building is fine, your data center is fine, but your people are not. A pandemic event will impact your organization for an extended period of time, perhaps as much as 18 months. Depending on the severity of the pandemic, up to 40 percent of your workforce may be unable or unwilling to come to work, either because they are sick, their family members are sick, schools or daycare facilities are closed and they need to stay with their children, or they are afraid to come to work because of the fear of infection.

Think about it. If the current "bird flu" mutates and becomes the next influenza pandemic and it remains 60 to 70 percent fatal, are you coming to work? If you are not sick, your children are not sick, and your spouse and extended family are not sick, will you come to work or will you be among the "scared well?"

This type of event will present challenges for the organization that are not experienced in other events. It is important that the organization spend some time working though the issues that this type of event may present so that decisions can be made while the organization is not under stress and all parties are available to make decisions.

As a workforce-impairment event, the primary owner is human resources, which will have the most tasks to perform that are outside the traditional BC/DR plan. HR will need to work closely with the planning team. The scope of this part of the BC/DR project is to develop appropriate contingency plans and implement the necessary capabilities that will allow the firm to maintain its core business functions in the event that its workforce and/or key suppliers are impacted by a pandemic event.

The plans and capabilities to be addressed in this section will encompass the following areas:

1. Development of workforce communications (prior to and during a pandemic) and communication capabilities
2. Development of workforce policies for handling absenteeism, sick

leave, family support, work at home, flexible hours, and mandatory sick leave to be implemented during a pandemic event

3. Development of alternate workforce plans and work access to address workforce shortages.
4. Work-site changes to be implemented in a pandemic event
5. Recommendation for community collaboration.
6. Development of alternate/contingency plans for critical supplies

The plans and capabilities need to be accepted by the executive leadership team.

The implementation phase of the BC/DR project will be undertaken by a core team of individuals from various areas of the company. The core team will be formed with representation from the following areas;

- Human resources
- Facilities
- Legal staff
- Technology
- Corporate communications
- Key business operations
- Finance

When beginning my pandemic planning, I made the following assumptions in developing the plans:

- Rates of absenteeism will depend on the severity of the pandemic, but our planning assumption will be that a workforce and/or supplier absenteeism rate of 30 percent will last for two to three months.
- Not every site will be impacted by the pandemic at the same time with the same severity.
- In a severe pandemic, absenteeism attributable to illness, the need to care for ill family members, and fear of infection may reach 40 percent during the peak weeks of a community outbreak, with lower rates of absenteeism during the weeks before and after the peak.
- In an affected community, a pandemic outbreak will last about six to eight weeks
- The pandemic may last as long as 18 months in three separate waves—the first 3 to 4 months will likely produce the greatest number of deaths and illnesses.

- Critical functions carried out by contractors, consultants, and vendors cannot be guaranteed.
- Delivery and availability of critical supplies such as fuel, paper, and forms will be slowed but will be available.
- No mandated closure or quarantine of business offices will occur.
- Civil-society infrastructure will be stressed but remain functional.
- Civil order will be maintained; there will be no widespread panic or lawlessness.
- Local, regional, and national infrastructure (power, water, telecommunications, banking) will be stressed but remain functional.
- Potential closure of gathering places in the community including schools, churches, events, malls, and daycare may increase absenteeism.
- There will be less than six weeks of warning from the time a pandemic is announced until it reaches the U.S.

Below are sample project tasks that may be considered or used in developing the plans:

1. Identify a pandemic coordinator and planning team with defined roles and responsibilities for preparedness and response planning. Leverage the existing BC/DR program.
2. Identify essential employees and other critical inputs required to maintain business operations by location and function during a pandemic.
3. Determine potential impact of a pandemic on company business financials.
4. Determine potential impact of a pandemic on business-related travel (e.g., quarantines, border closures).
5. Forecast and allow for employee absences during a pandemic due to factors such as personal illness, family-member illness, community containment measures and quarantines, school and/or business closures, and public-transportation closures.
6. Implement guidelines on when and how you would modify the frequency and type of face-to-face contact among employees and between employees and customers.
7. Encourage annual influenza vaccinations for employees.

8. Evaluate employee access to and availability of healthcare services including mental health and social services during a pandemic so information can be made available to employees at need.
9. Identify at-risk employees (pregnant, health issues) and incorporate the requirements of such persons into your preparedness plan.
10. Establish policies for employee compensation and sick-leave absences unique to a pandemic (e.g., nonpunitive, liberal leave), including policies on when a previously ill person is no longer infectious and can return to work after illness.
11. Establish policies for flexible work sites (e.g., telecommuting) and flexible work hours (e.g., staggered shifts) and triggers for implementing.
12. Establish plan for employees who have been exposed to pandemic influenza, are suspected to be ill, or become ill at the work site (e.g. infection-control response, immediate mandatory sick leave).
13. Provide sufficient and accessible infection-control supplies (e.g., hand-hygiene products, tissues, and receptacles for their disposal) in all business locations.
14. Enhance communications and information-technology infrastructures as needed to support employee telecommuting based on business requirements.
15. Ensure availability of medical consultation and advice for emergency response.
16. Develop and disseminate programs and materials covering pandemic fundamentals (e.g., signs and symptoms of influenza, modes of transmission), personal and family protection, and response strategies (e.g., hand hygiene, coughing/sneezing etiquette, contingency plans).
17. Anticipate employee fear and anxiety, rumors, and misinformation and plan communications accordingly.
18. Disseminate information to employees about your company's pandemic preparedness and response plan.
19. Provide information for the at-home care of ill employees and family members.
20. Develop platforms (e.g., contingency information line, BCP website, HR website) for communicating pandemic status and actions to employees, vendors, and customers inside and outside the work site in a consistent and timely way.

21. Collaborate with state and local public-health agencies and/or emergency responders to participate in their planning process-es, share pandemic plans, and understand their capabilities and plans.
22. Communicate with local and/or state public-health agencies and/or emergency responders about the assets and/or services your business could contribute to the community.
23. Perform critical vendor/supplier review and stockpiling of critical resources as needed.

HUMAN-RESOURCES POLICY CHANGES

Human-resource policies that may be impacted by a pandemic event are as follows: Family Medical Leave Act (FMLA), family support, paid sick time, attendance, vacation, floating holidays, alternative work arrangements, short-term disability, and privacy.

Possible options for scenarios where an employee is home sick, caring for a family member, or attending to children whose schools are closed include:

- Extend FMLA eligibility below service/hours minimum re-quirement by law
- Broaden family-support definition
- Allow use of vacation time for additional family-support time
- Advance up to 10 days of next year's unearned vacation time
- Allow paid sick days to supplement family-support time
- Allow and encourage the use of alternative work arrangements
- Apply policies with a delay in formal paperwork (sick leave, long-term disability, FMLA)
- Require medical attention and implement a more formal "return to work" authorization
- Possibly allow unpaid leave of absence for a determined period of time

Possible options for scenarios where an employee is at work and is sick or there is a prior exposure concern:

- Evaluate and send employee home
- Return-to-work authorization required
- Apply sick/absent treatment as in the case of other sick, family-support, or FMLA absences
- Allow and encourage the use of alternative work arrangements

Possible options for scenarios where an employee is afraid to come to work due to fear of being exposed to illness:

- Employee assistance program
- Allow and encourage the use of alternative work arrangements
- Allow the use of other paid-time applications
- No termination for two weeks and work through HR as an ER case to determine action (not contesting unexcused absence and possible benefit continuance)

Possible options for scenarios where an employee does not come to work due to being called to civil-service duty:

- Apply military leave as appropriate
- Extend military-leave provisions to other civil-service situations (EMT, firefighter)

Possible options for scenarios where an employee has travel exposure concerns:

- Evaluate and send home (not allowed in the building)
- Allow and encourage the use of alternative work arrangements
- Use of paid time off (sick, vacation, floating holiday)
- In the case of travel being due to work, consider additional paid sick pay (not workers compensation as the employees may not even be ill but will require quarantine/send home).
- Require employee to seek medical attention

Possible options for office-closure scenario:

- Allow and encourage the use of alternative work arrangements
- Apply some allocation of available paid time

Possible options for lack-of-work scenario:

- Keep on payroll for up to 30 days
- Apply some allocation of available paid time
- Temporary layoffs

16

Life Safety

To recover your business, the most important asset you have is your people. It is important that you validate that the company has solid life-safety procedures established for any type of event where employees may be at risk.

WHAT IS LIFE SAFETY?

Life safety includes the management of physical-security risks that may expose employees to harm and practiced response plans when an event that could cause harm to employees occurs. This chapter will focus less on the management of the physical-security risks and more on the validation of adequate response plans when an event occurs.

Aspects to consider include:

- Floor/fire wardens—trained in evacuation and shelter-in-place procedures.
- Evacuation drills—conducted at least annually in every facility

- Tornado drills—conducted at the beginning of tornado season in locations where tornadoes are prevalent
- Assembly areas—clearly defined and communicated to all employees
- Workplace-violence programs—workplace violence can happen anywhere

Floor/Fire Wardens

The United States has one of the highest fire death rates in the industrialized world.

An average of 4400 Americans lose their lives in fires each year, and another 25,100 are injured annually. America loses on average 100 firefighters a year fighting fires. More than 2 million fires are reported each year, and many others go unreported. Direct property loss is estimated to be $8.6 billion annually.

Each year fires kill more Americans than all natural disasters combined.

Floor/fire wardens are individuals within the organization who have been trained in safe evacuation and shelter-in-place procedures. I recommend that you have at least one warden for every 20 employees and at least two per site (if there are fewer than 20). The reason is that it is really difficult to keep track of more than 20 people—who is in today, who is out, who is traveling, who is on maternity leave, who is on vacation, etc. I also strongly suggest that all line managers, supervisors, and administrative assistants be trained as floor wardens.

In an event where there are life-safety concerns, the employees are naturally going to look to their immediate managers for direction, and the managers and the administrative support staff are most likely to be the people who know the status of employees and can answer the questions above.

Floor wardens should be issued a hat, vest, and/or a flag that identifies them as a floor warden, a flashlight with batteries, and a whistle and should attend a training class that identifies their role and responsibilities as a warden.

The duties and responsibilities of a floor warden *before* an event occurs are as follows:

1. Be familiar with the facility and the emergency exits.
2. Know the location of all disabled personnel in your area of responsibility (such as people confined to wheelchairs, the hearing-

impaired, people with temporary medical injuries requiring casts or crutches, and visually impaired people).

3. Know the primary and secondary evacuation routes and make sure they are posted on every exit.
4. Periodically check to ensure that all exits are open and free of debris that may restrict evacuation.
5. Know the location of your assembly area and area of refuge.
6. Know your local emergency number and the location of pull stations.

The duties and responsibilities of a floor warden during an emergency are as follows:

1. Direct orderly evacuation or shelter in place.
2. Assist with special-needs employees.
3. Remain calm and dispel false information or rumors.
4. Check your assigned area to ensure that all have evacuated.
5. Check rest rooms.
6. Close appropriate doors after the area is evacuated.
7. Report conditions to the fire department and home office.
8. Know and use alternate routes if the primary route is blocked.
9. Keep employees in the assembly area or area of refuge and keep them busy (assign tasks, use the buddy system).
10. Account for all employees following the evacuation.
11. Assist in reentry.

Fires and Evacuation Drills

Most people killed in fires actually die from inhalation of smoke and/or toxic fumes long before the fire reaches them. The materials used in furniture and carpets are composites that release hazardous fumes when ignited. Fire spreads very rapidly given the right conditions. A small trash can fire can become a room-engulfing inferno within three minutes of starting. Most smoke alarms do not activate until 1.5 to 3 minutes after a fire starts.

When an evacuation is needed, the floor wardens need to ensure that all personnel in their area of responsibility are out. Keep stairwells open and keep people moving; this is not the time to chat with others from another floor. The wardens need to check bathrooms, meeting rooms, break rooms, and server rooms to ensure that everyone is out of the space.

The warden is responsible for moving disabled personnel who cannot reasonably be expected to evacuate the building/floor on their own to an area of refuge. An area of refuge is a location away from the fire, behind doors, and with expectations of safety until rescue is effected by trained firefighters. Very few events are smoke and rubble events; in fact, most fire alarms are false alarms. The warden is much more likely to hurt him- or herself or the disabled person by trying to carry the person down the stairs than by putting him or her in an area of refuge until the firefighters can get to them or the all-clear is given. You do not have to leave disabled people alone. You can have someone stay with them until help arrives.

The very first thing the fire department does when it arrives, before the firefighters attach any hoses, is to ask if someone is still inside. The very first thing the firefighters do if someone is reported to be inside the building is to execute search and rescue. I am sure you have noticed at every elevator a sign that says, "In an emergency, use the stairs; do not use the elevator." In fact, if the fire alarms are going off, elevators, by fire code, have to drop to the first floor and lock. You cannot use the elevator even if you wanted to. But the firefighters can.

The firefighters have a special key that unlocks the elevator so they can use it for search and rescue. If the problem is actually in or near the elevator, making that impractical, the fire-fighters have rescue chairs and are trained to bring people down the stairs; you are not.

Notify firefighting personnel immediately upon arrival of the exact location of all disabled persons.

Doors, even non-fire-rated doors, slow the movement of fire and are especially helpful in slowing toxic smoke fumes. Ensure that all doors are closed as personnel exit the room or area. Close hallway doors when you know all personnel have evacuated the immediate area. Close stairwell doors to prevent smoke from traveling upward.

Once evacuation is complete, ensure that personnel do not reenter the building and account for all personnel in your area. Notify the fire department of any missing personnel. Do not reenter the building until told that it is safe to do so by the local fire department.

Assembly Areas

Assemble employees in designated assembly areas and try to keep them calm. Accounting for all employees following an evacuation is critical. Confusion in the assembly areas can lead to delays in rescuing anyone trapped in the building or unnecessary and dangerous search-and-rescue operations. Every floor warden needs to specify for their staff where to assemble once outside the building. It is important that every single employee check in with the floor warden following the evacuation in the assigned assembly area. Even if employees are at the other end of the building and have to walk all the way around the perimeter to get to their floor warden and assembly area, they must be told to do that.

I find it helpful for floor wardens to have a visible location to reference for employees to find them once outside and to keep the names of the employees they need to account for in their floor-warden hat so they do not have to remember when they are in the middle of a crisis. In one building, we put up numbers at various intervals around the parking lot for employees to assemble. I do not recommend a sign that says "assembly area." If someone wanted to inflict the most human damage in an event, that person could call in a credible bomb threat, watch the evacuation, and set off the bomb in the assembly area. (I am the gloom and doom queen!)

Once assembled in your assembly area, wait for further instructions from the management team or responding authorities. If the assembly area becomes unsafe for some reason, move employees as a group to an alternate assembly area, but try to keep the group together.

Using Fire Extinguishers—Why I Don't

I make a conscious choice not to train my floor wardens in the use of fire-fighting equipment. I do not want them to fight the fire. I can replace almost everything in our buildings, but I cannot replace any of the employees for their families. If you want to train staff in firefighting, then you must follow the regulations concerning frequency and type of training.

Unless you are a trained firefighter or have been specifically trained to do so, the only time you should ever fight a fire, whether at work or at home, is when the fire is between you and the way out. Then fight with everything you can. When faced with a fire, you have to make some split-second decisions under duress. Unless you have been trained to make those decisions, you may not be able to make them quickly enough. Remember, a small trash can fire can become a room-engulfing fire in three minutes. You need to quickly ascertain:

- Do environmental conditions indicate that fighting this type of fire would endanger others or me?
- Is the extinguisher the proper type for this type of fire?

149

- Are the capabilities of this extinguisher sufficient for the size of the fire?
- Does the fuel source make the fire too hazardous for this extinguisher?
- Is there a safe way to turn off or remove the fuel source?

Fight the fire only if:

- It is small—wastebasket size or smaller.
- It is contained in one area.
- You *know how* to use the firefighting equipment. The average hand portable extinguisher will only operate for 30 seconds—there is *no time* to learn during an actual emergency.
- The extinguisher is capable of putting out the fire. *You have 30 seconds.*
- And, most importantly, you have an escape route whether it works or not!

It is *reckless for you or anyone else* to fight the fire unless *all* of these conditions exist. Instead, leave the building, closing the doors behind you to slow the spreading of the fire and smoke. *Evacuation is always the best option!*

How Often to Conduct Drills

Evacuation drills should be conducted at least annually in every building. If you lease space and the landlord does not conduct drills, conduct your own. Have your floor wardens blow their whistles to announce the evacuation and have the employees go through the process.

In a recent evacuation drill, we found problems that we were so glad to find in a drill instead of a real event. In one building the sirens were not functioning on one entire floor. In another, the entire leadership team got stuck behind a door that would not open. The door was only to be used in an emergency, so it rarely got opened. The building had settled, and the door got stuck in the jam. How much more tragic that could have been if this had been a real emergency.

Once outside, have the floor wardens go through the practice of accounting for the employees and giving instructions on what would happen if this were real. If I am present for the evacuation drill, I ask the assembled employees how many of them brought their wallets, purses, and car keys with them. I explain that if this were a real event, they may not be able to get back into the building and that if their car keys and wallets were inside, they may never see them again.

I tell the story about how the building in New York on September 11, 2001, had motion-sensitive security cameras in the space. After the last person evacuated the building, the very next thing the cameras turned on was the vibrations from the first tower coming down and all the dust and debris coming into the building. Then the cameras turned on when the second tower came down. The third thing on the camera was looters. Several men with backpacks came into the space and picked up people's wallets, purses, cell phones—anything that was left behind.

Don't ever go back for something, but if you are at your desk, bring it with you. I always carry my car key, my driver's license, and a credit card with me wherever I am in the building.

Shelter in Place

Shelter-in-place orders are rare occurrences for events other than tornados, which we will discuss separately, but they do happen and I always talk to my floor wardens about the possibility. In all the years I have been involved in this industry, I have had them happen twice in my professional career and once in my personal life. One was a bomb threat; one was an ammonia cloud from an overturned tractor-trailer truck; and one was a police action. (They were chasing several people who had run into my yard.)

What I tell the floor wardens is that in some types of emergencies, a decision to shelter employees in place rather than evacuate them will be made. These situations include tornado warnings, bomb threats, police activity, chemical spills, gas leaks, and release of biological agents.

When one of these events happens, the local authorities may or may not immediately be able to provide information on what is happening and what you should do. This is a time to use common sense and all available information to assess the situation. If you see large amounts of debris in the air or if local authorities say the air is badly contaminated, you may want to shelter in place.

If there are customers, clients, or visitors in the building, provide for their safety by asking them to stay as well. When authorities provide directions to shelter in place, they want everyone to take those steps immediately. Do not drive or walk outdoors.

Unless there is an imminent threat, ask employees, customers, clients, and visitors to call their emergency contact to let them know where they are and that they are safe. (An imminent threat would be seeing a funnel cloud heading in your direction.) Because shelter-in place-orders are rare,

151

they may quickly become a news item, at least in the local market. By calling family members, you can at last let them know that at the start of the event you were fine, that you were sheltering from danger, and that you will call them when it is over.

I encourage this because when these events hit the news, if you have not called family members, they are going to try to call you. You will not be at your desk because your are in your shelter area. Cell phones can be forgotten and cell lines can be clogged during an emergency. Everyone is trying to use them and the bandwidth is not there to support that much simultaneous traffic.

Again, if you have time, quickly lock exterior doors and close windows and, if necessary, air vents. Reroute 800 phone numbers and/or change any recordings including voice mail to indicate that the business is closed due to an emergency and that staff and visitors are remaining in the building until authorities advise that it is safe to leave. You should watch TV, listen to the radio, or check the internet often for information or official instruction as it becomes available. If you're specifically told to seek shelter, evacuate, or seek medical treatment, do so immediately.

At shelter-in-place locations, you should select interior room(s) with the fewest windows or vents. The room(s) should have adequate space for everyone to be able to sit because you may be there for a while. Avoid overcrowding by selecting several rooms if necessary. Large storage closets, utility rooms, pantries, rest rooms, copy facilities, and conference rooms without exterior windows will work well. Even interior hallways with no windows will be fine.

If there is something in the air outside that you don't want to be exposed to, you should try to avoid selecting rooms with mechanical equipment such as ventilation blowers or pipes, because it may be difficult for this equipment to be sealed from the outdoors. If possible, have the building management turn off any mechanical system that brings in external air, such as air conditioning.

If there is a danger of explosion or breaking windows, as with a bomb threat or a tornado, close curtains or blinds in the building. It will not keep the windows from breaking, but it will keep the glass from flying around the room as much when they do break. If air contamination is a risk, close or tape off vents in the room. Gather essential disaster supplies, such as first-aid kits, nonperishable food, bottled water, battery-powered radios, first-aid supplies, flashlights, batteries, duct tape, plastic sheeting, and plastic garbage bags.

If possible, have a hard-wired telephone in the room(s) you select to call emergency contacts, and have the phone available if you need to report a life-threatening condition. Cellular-telephone equipment may be overwhelmed or damaged during an emergency. If your cell phone cannot get a circuit to place a phone call, you may want to try text messaging on the cell phone. Three things that worked more consistently than anything else during September 11 and Katrina were two-way pagers, phones with walkie-talkie capabilities, and text messaging. If you don't know how to text-message on your cell phone, ask teenagers, who would be happy to help you. That is, after they stop laughing.

Take your emergency supplies and go into the room you have designated. Seal all windows, doors, and vents with plastic sheeting, duct tape, or anything else you have on hand. You could consider precutting plastic sheeting (heavier than food wrap) to seal windows, doors, and air vents in the rooms you shelter in. I have several offices that, because of their proximity to local highways, have chosen to do this. Each piece should be several inches larger than the space you want to cover so that it lies flat against the wall.

Listen to the radio, watch television, or use the internet for further instructions until you are told all is safe or to evacuate. Local officials may call for evacuation in specific areas at greatest risk in your community.

Tornados and Tornado Drills

Tornados are the most common threat that causes a shelter-in-place order to be issued. Tornados can happen anywhere in the world, but they are more common in the central and southern states. When doing safety training, I always include tornado training even in areas that generally don't experience them, because they can happen anywhere.

A tornado watch is issued when conditions are favorable for formation of a tornado. A warning is issued when the event is happening or detected. Someone has reported a funnel-cloud sighting or seen a hook on radar.

- **Thunderstorm Watch**—conditions are favorable for the formation of thunderstorms.
- **Thunderstorm Warning**—a thunderstorm has developed and is in progress.
- **Tornado Watch**—conditions are favorable for the formation of tornadoes.
- **Tornado Warning**—a tornado has been detected/sighted.

153

Danger signs of a tornado include:

- Large hail—tornadoes frequently emerge from the hail-producing portion of the storm.
- Calm before the storm —before a tornado hits, the wind may die down and the air may become very still.
- Clouds of debris—an approaching cloud of debris can mark the location of a tornado, even though the funnel may not be visible.
- Greenish clouds—one or more clouds around a tornado may appear green, a phenomenon caused by hail.
- Roaring noise—the high winds of a tornado can cause a roar that is often compared to the sound of a freight train.

If a watch is issued for your area, monitor local radio and TV stations for weather updates. Stay alert for the danger signs of a tornado. If danger signs are observed or a tornado warning is issued for your area, immediately go to your safe area.

Remember, unless you are really high up or really far away with nothing else in your line of sight, a tornado is not going to look like that video you saw on the weather station of the funnel cloud in the Kansas corn field. It is going to look like a cloud of debris. If you look at it and it does not appear to be moving to the left or the right, it means it is moving toward you and it is time to take cover!

If you are caught in your car with an approaching tornado, do not try to outrun it. They move very fast and are unpredictable in their movements. The safest thing to do is get out of your car, get to the lowest point possible, make yourself as small a target as possible, and cover your head with anything you have, with your arms if you have nothing else. Do *not* stay in your car. I have seen too many videos of tornados picking up cars and throwing them around like they are matchbox cars.

At work, unlike many homes, the construction of most commercial buildings offers at least some protection. The buildings have a steel-beam construction that supports the building and walls. If the roof becomes damaged, the walls should not collapse, as they will in most homes. The largest danger at work will be from flying debris and glass.

Safe areas include:

- Stairwells
- Restrooms
- Service levels or basements
- Interior rooms or hallways without windows

Areas to avoid include:

- Auditoriums, gymnasiums, or areas with large spans
- Atriums and rotundas
- Areas with exterior glass windows

If a tornado is in the area, *do* remain calm, *do* follow directions from local authorities, *do* seek shelter in a safe area, *do not* go outside, and *do not* pull fire-alarm stations.

After a tornado has been through your area, be careful! Watch for fallen power lines, unsafe structures, broken gas lines, etc. Make sure everyone is safe and attend to those needing first aid. Use flashlights. Do not use candles or open flames at any time. Listen to the radio for instructions and information on damages and what you should do.

In any event where there has been local damage such as a tornado or earthquake, some employees are going to want to leave right away to check on their homes, their kids, their parents, etc. Try to discourage them from leaving a safe place to head into potential danger. Encourage them to check the internet, the media, and any other resources to make sure they know what they are going into when they leave. Check for road closures and downed trees or power lines that may make their travel dangerous.

The company I work for at this writing has offices in the Midwest. In one of our larger sites, we own the facilities our business operations are located in and we installed tornado sirens. The company had not conducted tornado drills in quite a few years. When a tornado touched down in the town but not near the office, it raised awareness among the employees and we began to do tornado drills again. The first one we conducted, some of the employees did not recognize the tornado siren and evacuated instead. Not what you want to happen in a tornado. This again showed the importance of doing drills.

In critical emergencies and evacuations it is possible that some employees may become frightened to the point of panic. The floor wardens must not only be able to recognize this dangerous condition but be taught some tools for appropriately dealing with it.

Employees who are panicked could react by making an unreasonable effort to evacuate the area, such as running or pushing others out of the way. Such panic may lead an employee to cause injury to him- or herself or others. An employee may panic into a flurry of activity that may appear to be productive but actually does little to assist with the situation, and sometimes when someone is really frightened he or she becomes numb or

155

appears to be in a dreamlike trance. In this circumstance, the employee has become so overwhelmed by the situation that he or she is shutting it out.

One of the ways to avoid panic when there is a real event is by conducting periodic drills. One of the things that makes people panic is when they think that no one knows what is going on or what to do. I tell my floor wardens that they are chosen because they are the calm ones. They always laugh or roll their eyes when I first say that, but then I explain that when they go back to their desk they will most likely get teased about their hat, flashlight, and whistle but when and if an event happens for real, their coworkers are going to look for that hat because they have been trained and know what to do in an emergency.

If you have someone who is just about to lose it, who is just on the verge of full-fledged panic, give that person something to do. It does not have to be anything important. I tell the person to count how many people come out of a particular door, how many men vs. women they see, or how many words beginning with the letter "r" he or she can think of. The point is that if you give the person something to do, he or she now has something to think about other than being scared.

Another tool is the buddy system. Yes, just like in kindergarten—it makes two people responsible for each other. To stay together, help each other, whatever. They may still both be scared, but just knowing that someone has your back and you have his or hers can provide a level of comfort in a crisis.

If you have someone who has just lost it and cannot control him- or herself, you need to separate that person from the others if possible, because panic is contagious. If you are sheltering in place and one person in the room is saying, "We are all going to die, I just know it, we are all going to die!" one of two things is going to happen: someone is going to go after the person physically to shut up or everyone in the room is going to start to agree. Separate the person from the others.

Workplace Violence

Never, ever deprive another human being of personal dignity, respect, or hope nor allow anyone else under your control to do so. Once someone has lost those, he or she is capable of anything.

I tell that to all my floor wardens when I introduce the topic of workplace violence. I am not going to arm my floor wardens with handcuffs and guns any more than I trained them to fight fires, but I do teach them a little bit about the management of aggressive behavior and dealing with the potentially violent person. What does this have to do with business continuity, you ask? Nothing, unless it happens. I would much rather prevent an event than recover from it. I never want to recover from a workplace-violence event. I have known several people who have, and they are very difficult and emotional events to recover from.

Workplace violence can happen anywhere. Certain types of jobs are more subject to industry-specific threats, such as police officers, convenience-store clerks, bank tellers, hospital emergency-room workers, and prison guards. But workplace violence can happen anywhere. It can be a current or former employee, a termination gone bad, a husband/wife situation that has spilled into the workplace, or a random act of violence.

A spouse or partner who has come to the office with a gun in hand intent upon killing his or her spouse has already passed the point of no return, and you need to call 911 and shelter as far from this person as you can. But sometimes, the person who is behaving or talking in a threatening way just does not think he or she has been heard. I will tell you that most people are a lot scarier over the phone than they are in person. People will make threats on the phone in the heat of the moment that they never intend to act on. That does not mean that you should just take the abuse or that you should not report it.

I remember when I first started talking about this at my current company, one of the branch-office leaders told a story. Just the week prior to my starting work, a customer had come to the office in a rage. He walked in the door, walked up to the first person he found, and started screaming, shaking his fist, and behaving in a threatening way. The manager happened to be in the office that day—he was often on the road—and heard the commotion. He came out of his office, went right up to the guy, looked him in the eye, stuck out his hand to shake, and said, "Hi, my name is John Smith and I am the RVP here in this office. I am so sorry to hear you are this upset with something we have done. Why don't you come into my office, sit down, and tell me what is going on? I am sure we can find a solution." This defused him immediately. What do you think this angry man's reaction would have been if "John" came out of his office and said, "You know, you are really behaving like a jerk; get out of here before I call the police!"

Another man told me a story of something that happened to him at a previous job. The company had been granted a judgment against a man for money owed and had placed a lien on his checking account for $2000.

157

The man whom the judgment was against had my colleague's name from the filing, came to the office, and asked for him by name. He was put in a conference room, and my colleague came to meet him there. When he walked in, the guy took the briefcase he had with him, put it up on the conference table in front of him, and folded his arms on top if it. Feeling a bit uncomfortable and not recognizing this man, my colleague asked, "So, what's in the briefcase?" The man replied, "It's a gun, just in case we don't settle this the way I want."

No one deserves to die over $2000. I tell my people that if they are confronted by a potentially violent person, do whatever it takes to satisfy him or her and get him or her out of the space. I am not saying that you should not dial 911 while this is happening but that if the intruder wants the money, give him the money, write him a check, do whatever it takes to stay safe, and get him out of the space. We will worry about the rest later.

In response to workplace-violence threats, you need to establish a process for reporting them and for responding to them once reported. In my company, we have established and trained a threat-assessment team to address threats of violence in the workplace. The threat-assessment team's purpose is to determine the credibility of a threat and the appropriate response to the threat.

The purpose and objective of a threat-assessment team is to ensure that the company has a defined process and identified resources that can quickly and effectively respond to threats or potential threats and take appropriate actions to ensure the safety of the workplace.

The goal of threat assessment is to place a threat somewhere on a hierarchy of credibility or danger and on that basis determine an appropriate intervention. Any workplace violence strategy must include measures to detect, assess, and manage threats and potentially violent behavior.

Threat assessment has two parts:

- An evaluation of the threat itself—that is, an assessment of the capability and credibility of the threat
- An evaluation of the person making the threat

Together, these evaluations can help lead to an informed judgment on whether someone who has made a threat is likely to carry it out—a determination that has been described as "differentiating when someone is making a threat versus posing a threat." The assessment can also help management decide what will be an appropriate intervention:

- If a threat is immediate, specific, and critical ("I've got a gun in my car and I'm going to wait for that S.O.B. and blow him away the minute he steps on the parking lot"), the obvious response is to call the police right away.

- A threat that is veiled or less specific and does not appear to presage immediate violence may call for less urgent measures— referral for psychological evaluation and counseling, for example.
- Many threats will turn out to be harmless blowing off steam and require nothing more than a formal admonition to the employee that his or her language or conduct was not appropriate and violates company policy.

The purpose and role of the threat-assessment team is to:

- Immediately respond to threats and issues related to threats
- Evaluate any issue of violence and provide a plan of action
- Provide consulting help to line managers and HR
- Quickly problem-solve and plan appropriate responses
- Bring consistency and expertise to the process

The threat-assessment team includes:

- Human resources
- Security
- Legal
- Manager (if employee-related)
- Medical, EAP, others (as needed)

The role of each threat-assessment-team group can be summarized as follows.

Human resources:

- May be first point of contact
- Leads the threat-assessment team
- Partners with security, legal, and others on investigations
- Provides knowledge of employees and business issues
- Advises on disciplinary action if needed

Security:

- Primary responsibility for security and facility-related aspects
- Partners with HR on investigations
- Provides timely reporting and trend analysis of incidents

Site security—first responder/protect employees in the workplace/ liaison to local agencies (i.e., police) as needed, provide safety/security information to employees.

Legal:

- Provides guidance on matters in which the company may have legal exposure, such as rights of the different individuals, legal issues involved in investigations, legal risks to the company based on proposed courses of action, and advice on disciplinary action

Manager:

- May be the first point of contact
- Responsible for managing employees and responding to issues
- Take disciplinary action as appropriate
- Create a positive general work environment in the group
- Address any issues that contribute to a harassing or otherwise unwelcome environment

EAP (employee-assistance program):

- Provide counseling, guidance, and resources to employees and family members on issues
- Provide counseling support to managers and HR on difficult issues

Human Resources will take the lead role in coordination by immediately pulling in security, legal, and the manager (if an employee) as the minimum core threat-assessment team. Involvement of others may occur immediately or as needed.

The general procedure to be followed in the event of a threat include:

1. Threat awareness occurs and is reported to HR.
2. HR gains initial understanding of the situation and contacts security and legal support and the manager if employee-related.
3. This initial TAT assesses the situation and makes an initial threat evaluation.
4. The team determines immediate steps to be taken.
5. The team conducts further investigations as needed.
6. The team involves and informs others as appropriate from initial investigation.
7. The team determines action steps, precautionary measures, etc., to be taken (immediate as well as longer-term).
8. The team follows up as necessary.
9. The team concludes that the situation has been fully addressed and that no further action or follow-up is needed (closes the case).

Various tools and support pieces need to be developed to assist with a consistent and thorough process for handling workplace-violence cases and to help proactively address them through awareness, including:

- Detailed outline of the overall process
- Threat-assessment team investigation worksheet
- Workplace-violence policy
- Workplace-violence awareness training for all employees and managers

Threats or even rumors of possible threats need to be taken seriously. Conducting an investigation and threat assessment will derive the best outcome from the threat. To accomplish this, employees, managers, and in particular the threat-assessment team need to:

- Treat all threats seriously.
- Investigate the incident promptly and efficiently.
- Utilize support staff and external resources to evaluate the threat.
- Involve and utilize local agencies/authorities.
- Take appropriate disciplinary and criminal-enforcement steps.
- Document the threats and actions taken.
- Enhance security measures, as appropriate, to ensure the safety of all employees, visitors, and facilities.

Depending on the situation and the facts uncovered during an investigation, the range of responses will be narrowed from the many possible responses below to the most appropriate given the circumstances:

- Do nothing—threat is not deemed credible
- Employee coaching
- EAP referral
- Disciplinary actions
- Termination
- Reporting to authorities
- Requesting authorities' involvement
- Legal action

A problem that sometimes occurs in threat management is what to do when someone is evaluated as dangerous but has not committed any serious crime. In those cases, managers will need legal and often law-enforcement attention. Managers may sometimes want to terminate an employee on-the-spot after a threat or other incident—in effect, kicking the problem out the door. Termination may indeed be appropriate, but doing so in the heat of the moment without any time for evaluation or preparation may be exactly the wrong thing to do. Removing the potentially dangerous person from where he or she can be observed and the reaction to the termination by the employee may possibly bring on a violent act instead of preventing one. Although quick action is needed, acting hastily without anticipating or preparing can be as bad as or even worse than moving too slowly.

Once the TAT is confident that the investigation and assessment are complete and that an action plan has been established, it is important to implement the plan, follow up as needed, and document the investigation, conclusion, results, and action(s) taken. A TAT worksheet should be developed as an *in-the-moment* worksheet and process guide as well as a tool to capture a summary of key pieces of the investigation and assessment. The worksheet is not intended to capture every detail. Individual interviews with witnesses, for example, would be captured separately in detail and attached as part of the case/incident file.

The incident files are retained by human resources per defined HR record-retention-schedule guidelines.

17

Transitioning from Project to Program

Chapter Objectives

- The Project Ends, the Program Begins—How to Make the Transition
- Defining Program Requirements

At the conclusion of the "project" to build a business-continuity and disaster-recovery plan for your business, you need to transition from a project to a program. Business continuity is a process, not a product, and developing and implementing a plan do not end the project. Life happens and things change. You need to implement a program for the ongoing support and maintenance of the viability of the business-continuity and disaster-recovery plans you have built.

The contingency-planning program is an ongoing process. All of the tasks required to build the program originally need to be repeated on a regular basis to ensure that the plan stays current with the business and technology environment of the company. The program needs to be reviewed annually in order to retain the state of readiness.

Like any other phase of this process, without leadership support this program will fail. Leadership needs to understand that this is not a once-and-done process. As the program matures, the work needed to maintain it becomes easier because you are not creating something that does not exist; you are updating something that already exists. Nonetheless, it still takes resources and commitments from each and every business line, senior leader, and technology group.

THE COMPONENTS OF THE CONTINGENCY-PLANNING PROGRAM

The contingency-planning program is designed to serve as an aid in developing and maintaining viable business function as well as disaster recovery for the technology that supports the business.

The program's goal is to ensure a state of readiness to respond to any event that either already has or may have the potential to cause a significant business impact to any location where the company conducts its business. In order to be ready to respond to and provide management direction during significant emergency situations, ongoing work with management and employees should be performed to ensure that at time of disaster well-trained employees and support personnel respond immediately to:

- Maintain safety of all individuals in occupied space
- Minimize damage to buildings and equipment
- Coordinate response and communication with senior management, employees, media, and customers
- Provide support for recovery of time-sensitive business functions
- Maintain public image
- Maintain positive customer relations
- Minimize and contain physical and electronic breaches of corporate assets
- Comply with legal requirements
- Avoid costly penalties and fines

The following assumptions are made as part of the business-continuity and disaster-recovery program:

1. The cause of an event (water damage, loss of power, civil unrest, natural disaster, terrorist attack, chemical spill, etc.) and the impact of the event will vary significantly. The specific categories planned for concern include facility, technology, information-security, and workforce-impairment events.

2. Each division has implemented and tested procedures for recovery of the critical business functions performed by that division based on the loss of a single site.
3. The technology-services division has implemented and tested procedures for the recovery of critical platforms and applications required to support the business operations.
4. Defined alternate sites will be available at the time of need.
5. To ensure the viability of the plan, adequate testing of the plan components is conducted and adequate training is given in the use of the plan to all team members.
6. Documented plans, related procedures, and all vital records are stored in a secure offsite location and not only survive the event but are accessible immediately following an event.

ANNUAL PROGRAM BUSINESS REQUIREMENTS

In support of the continuing viability of the program, annual program requirements need to be established and delivered to the team. Similar to the project phase, the requirements are a series of tasks that must be performed to keep the recovery of the business and the technology that supports it up to date with changes in the business environment.

The first requirement is that senior managers of each operating area understand that they have the responsibility for ensuring the company's survival. They need to appoint a business-contingency planner (BCP) to coordinate the maintenance of the contingency plan for that area.

The annual program requirements that I use and that appear on the program status report (Exhibit 17.1) begins with foundation-level requirements: The level of management and BCP engagement in the contingency-planning program is usually revealed in the overall status ratings, but I include a foundation section and define it as follows:

1. Management engagement is made up of three components. The business-unit senior executive must appoint a BCP, ensure that the BCP's responsibilities are incorporated into the annual employee-review process, and arrange for or allow the BCP to meet with the business unit's senior management at least once every 12 months. To get credit on the status report, the BCP must provide to the corporate planner, whether or not BCP responsibilities are a part of their formal review, the date of the last presentation to senior management.

For Business Line _____   Status as of xx/xx/xxxx

BCP Name _____

Tasks are shown as either complete (checked) or incomplete (unchecked).

Foundation Tasks:	
Management Engagement	☑
BCP Engagement	☑
Employee Awareness:	
Quarterly Awareness campaign	☐
Recovery Tools:	
Pagers or cells phone for key employees	☑
ENL	☑
Conference bridge procedures	☐
Vital records program	☑
Business Impact Analysis:	
Classify Business Function:s	☑
Resource Requirements	☑
Technology Review	☐
Interdependencies defined	☐
Recovery Strategies:	
Documented Strategies/Procedures for loss of primary site	☑
Documented Strategies/Procedures for loss of technology	☐
Alternate site defined	☑
Published plan with sign off	☑
Recovery Exercises:	
Alternate site exercise	☑
Walkthrough exercise	☑
Call notification exercise	☑
Compact exercise	☐

Exhibit 17.1   Contingency Planning Program Status Report.

2. BCP engagement is made up two components. The BCP must attend the monthly BCP meetings and attend training while acting as a BCP. Training includes the courses offered by the company or external sources of certification from the DRII or BCI. To get credit on the status report, attendance is taken at every BCP meeting, and the BCP needs to provide a record of any outside training or certification in contingency planning.

There are five basic recovery tools that are invaluable to every business unit whenever a business interruption occurs:

1. Pagers and or text-enabled cell phones for key employees: Key employees include the BCP, the senior executive, the senior technical person in your business unit, and anyone else you may need to notify immediately in the event of an interruption. While pagers do not guarantee that you can reach your key employees, they greatly increase the likelihood of it. To get credit on the status report, the BCP must submit a copy of their ENL including pager numbers/cell-phone numbers.
2. Published ENL: All employees whom you may need to contact during a business interruption should be in your emergency-notification list along with their relevant phone numbers (work, home, pager, cell phone, vacation home, etc.) This list should be verified, updated, and distributed at least quarterly. For many business units, it is critical that this list be updated monthly. To get credit on the status report, a dated copy of the ENL should be submitted each quarter.
3. Conference-bridge procedures: Include a paragraph or two in your plan or ENL that explains which conference-bridge system your business unit uses, how to set up a bridge, and how participants can access it. This information can save hours during the critical first stages of a recovery. To get credit on the status report, a copy of the ENL or plan containing the procedures should be submitted.
4. Using the automated notification system: Contingency notification systems automate call testing and ENL maintenance and can increase the speed and accuracy of the information provided during an emergency. To get credit on the status report, the BCP must confirm that employees have updated their contact information.
5. Vital-records program in place: This helps ensure that critical information stored on electronic and physical media is backed up in a safe location such as an offsite vendor or your alternate site.

A vital-records program includes documented processes for storing and retrieving both electronic and physical media as well as a process for ensuring that all critical data is included in the program. To get credit on the status report, the BCP needs to provide the documented process for storing and retrieving both electronic and physical media that is in compliance with the records-retention schedule.

There are four steps in a business-impact analysis; they document the time sensitivity of each part of the business unit and all of its inputs. The BCP generally needs to meet with many different people in the business unit to complete these steps. They result in a clear knowledge of what can cause a business interruption for you and thus what you need to plan for.

Validating business functions and their recovery-time requirements is the basis of your contingency plan. A business-function listing should include the following:

a. Function name
b. Location
c. Alternate site location (if there is one)
d. Number of people who staff the function normally
e. Minimum number of people required to staff the function
f. Recovery time

Defining resource requirements involves making a list of all the supplies, equipment, and connectivity that are needed to perform that function. This is not an inventory but a list of those resources that are critical to that function.

A technology review is an inventory of all the systems and technologies that each function requires.

Defining interdependencies is a process of documenting all inputs to the business function, including where they come from and where they go to.

To get credit on the status report, all the information in the business-impact analysis needs to be validated twice a year and a dated list provided.

Contingency planners are asked to plan for two types of outages: loss of primary site (something wrong with your building) and loss of applications (the building is fine but the systems are down). Five recovery strategies help the BCP document timely recovery from either of these categories. All of these steps need to be performed/updated at least once every

12 months and can be submitted in any combination or all together as part of the contingency-plan document:

1. A documented strategy for the site is a high-level plan of what each business function is going to do if it loses its primary operating site. The general strategy should list where each function is going to recover and in what order. It might include information such as what percentage of the normal employee base will be relocated to the alternate site and how ready the alternate site is to accommodate them.
2. A documented strategy for systems is a plan of how each business function is going to continue to operate if it loses its critical systems. The function may revert to manual processes, switch to a completely separate second system that is still available, or postpone business until the systems are available again.
3. A documented list of the alternate sites in place to support the business operation should be provided.
4. Procedures for loss of systems are the manual procedures or alternate methods of performing a business function without its critical systems for the period of time it takes for the system or application to be recovered.
5. The published plan with sign-off contains the business-impact-analysis and recovery-strategies deliverables along with details about the vital-records program and a copy of the ENL. The plan also includes detailed procedures for recovering from a loss of site.

Procedures for loss of each site the business unit occupies must include:

- Recovery procedures for any business-owned technologies that are co-located with the business function
- Disaster-declaration procedures
- Travel procedures for employees to the alternate site
- Recovery management
- A method of tracking and paying for recovery expenses
- Problem-management procedures
- Notification procedures
- Recovery communications to employees, vendors, customers, etc.
- Instructions for preparing the alternate sites for business functions

- Command-center locations
- Human-resources issues

The business unit's senior executive must also sign off on the plan. To get credit on the status report, a signed, dated copy of the plan must be provided with all components and distribution list.

Contingency plans for every business function need to be tested on a regular basis. The type of testing and the frequency of each test are as follows:

1. Call tests: Each business unit must perform two call tests every 12 months in order to verify that you have the correct contact numbers for everyone on your ENL and provide an estimate of how long it takes to contact everyone.
2. Walkthrough test: The walkthrough test must be performed at least once every 12 months. This involves a meeting in a conference room or on a conference bridge in which a test scenario is presented and all the participants in the meeting walk through the plan and discuss how they would respond to the test scenario using the plan.
3. Each business function must be involved in an alternate-site test at least once every 12 months. This test involves moving a small group of employees to the alternate site and verifying that they can actually perform their business function(s) in that space. This may include having them log onto systems, receive inbound calls, process real or test transactions, or any other tasks that should be tested. Depending on the business functions involved, you may move one person for a few minutes or dozens of people for an entire workday.
4. A systems-loss test must be performed at least once every 12 months. Validate that each business function can continue to operate without its critical systems.

To get credit on the status report, the BCP must provide dates and results for each test.

Some basic parts of your plan should be made known to all of your business unit's employees. Employee-awareness activities can involve almost anything that communicates a contingency-related message to all or some of your business unit's employees. Each business unit must perform two employee-awareness activities every 12 months. To get credit on the status report, the BCP must provide copies of the awareness materials. A status report showing compliance with the program by each business line and by site should be produced quarterly and distributed to the operating committee.

ANNUAL TECHNOLOGY-PROGRAM REQUIREMENTS

The technology recovery must be maintained in a state of readiness as well. In order to achieve this, technology-recovery strategies must stay in synch with the current technology environment. To ensure this, the technology planner must work closely with change management so that any significant changes to the production environment or the addition of new technologies are reflected in the technology-recovery plan.

I use the same status report for my reports to the operating committee on technology recovery as I do for reporting the results to leadership of a technology-recovery exercise. The data-center exercise report contains the all the information the operating committee may need on the status of our recovery capabilities. For each platform and application recovered the following is reported:

- The name of the technology or application restored
- The RTO for the application
- The date last tested
- Whether the application was recovered in the RTO during the test
- Whether the application recovered at all even if it did not meet the RTO
- Whether current documented repeatable processes for recovery execution are stored offsite
- If the application had a batch cycle, was it run and was it successful?
- Application owner
- Business-unit validation

ANNUAL CRISIS LEADERSHIP PROGRAM REQUIREMENTS

In addition to program compliance within the business units and technology areas, a state of readiness must be maintained with your crisis-leadership teams. This requires that the emergency management plan be updated and the teams maintained. Quarterly updates with the leadership team on the overall status of the program should be conducted and at least semi-annual drills.

The leadership teams include representatives from real estate, physical security, business leadership, technology, human resources, corporate communications, legal, risk management, and contingency planning. Each of these groups has specific responsibilities in the event of an emergency, including:

- Responding to incidents and emergencies
- Determining the extent of the impending or actual emergency situation
- Establishing and maintaining communication with senior management
- Communicating with employees and customers
- Managing media communications, security, systems, facilities
- Coordinating and integrating with business-contingency planners

When I meet with my crisis-leadership team, we spend some time on the state of readiness across the firm, specific risks I want to raise their awareness of, and finally a drill of some type to get them thinking again and working as a team.

EMERGENCY OPERATIONS CENTER

The corporate emergency operations center (EOC), which was established to provide a location equipped with all of the necessary resources to manage the business-resumption process whenever activated, must also be maintained in a state of readiness.

PROGRAM ROLES AND RESPONSIBILITIES

Corporate Contingency Planning

The corporate contingency-planning group develops, implements, and maintains a corporate-wide business-contingency-planning program for the company. This group provides leadership and guidance in maintaining integrated continuity of critical business functions, and assists management in achieving timely recovery of business operations in the event of interruption.

The roles and responsibilities of the group are:

- Setting strategic direction and planning for all business units to ensure business continuity and effective emergency management

- Integrating the contingency-planning process across business units when the nature of the business requires it
- Providing consulting services and direction to senior-level contingency planners
- Coordinating and integrating the activation of emergency-response organizations within the business units
- Providing periodic management reporting and status updates
- Ensuring executive management compliance with the contingency-planning program
- Ensuring the identification and maintenance of all critical business functions and requirements
- Procuring and managing the alternate sites used to support recovery of the operations of the company, whether technical or business
- Developing, implementing, and maintaining policy and guidelines for all business units to follow
- Developing and maintaining testing and maintenance programs for all contingency-planning organizations
- Providing training, maintenance, and support for approved contingency-planning tools

Business-Continuity Planners

The business-contingency planners act as a focal point for the company in any situation involving contingency planning or emergency response. The BCPs plan the integration of a series of tasks, procedures, and information that direct actions at the time of a business interruption in order to reduce confusion, improve communications, and achieve a timely continuation/resumption of business. The roles and responsibilities of the BCP include:

- Provide primary contact for the functional area to handle coordination response during a business interruption
- Act as a resource for contingency-planning efforts within the area of responsibility
- Secure appointment, training, and backup of all contingency-planning and response teams
- Assist in the design and maintenance of alternate sites
- Maintain currency of all contingency-planning documentation including all deliverables listed in Exhibit 17.2

Current BCP Deliverable	Description/Specifics	Due Date
1. Management engagement	• Appoint BCP • Established goal for BCP • Present to President	On going
2. BCP engagement	• Attend Monthly BCP meetings • Participates in training\conferences • Actively work BCP deliverables list	On going
3. Pagers/cell phones for key employees	• ID who really needs to be contacted • Maintains event management listings	On going
4. Published ENL	• Publish and distribute emergency notification listings to key personnel	Quarterly
5. Conference bridge procedures	• Establish and distribute Emergency Conference Call number and call in procedure to key personnel	Annual
6. Using call notification systems	• Provide corporate planning team with call scenarios of critical contingency teams within your organization	On going
7. Identify business functions and criticality's	• ID all functions the group performs • ID on core or mission critical function although the rating may be below A	Twice per year
8. Resource requirements defined	• Document systems and personnel needed to perform functions	Twice per year
9. Perform technology review	• Inventory and assess hardware and software used by business function	Annually
10. Interdependencies defined	• ID any internal or external dependencies	Annually
11. Document strategy for loss of site	• Document high level strategy	Annually
12. Document strategy for systems	• Document high level strategy	Annually
13. Define alternate site	• Work with corporate planning team to determine a viable alternate location to perform your critical functionality	Annually

Exhibit 17.2 Annual Program Requirements for the Business Continuity Program.

Current BCP Deliverable	Description/Specifics	Due Date
14. Document procedures for loss of systems	• Document viable recovery procedures • Document media backup procedures • Document manual procedures	Annually
15. Publish hardcopy plan with executive signoff	• Publish and distribute document strategies for recovery • Submit copy to corporate planning team	Annually
16. Plan and conduct contingency call testing	• Perform call out of critical employees • Capture action items • Submit results to corporate planning team	Twice per year
17. Plan and conduct contingency walk-through exercise—Y2K related	• Perform table top exercise discussing business interruption recovery • Submit results to corporate planning team • Follow-up on action items	Annually
18. Plan and conduct contingency alternate site exercise	• Perform actual exercise • Submit results to corporate planning team • Follow-up on action items	Annually
19. Plan and conduct contingency testing—systems	• Participate in systems exercises • Capture action items • Submit results to corporate planning team	Annually
20. Plan and conduct awareness campaigns	• Publish and distribute educational materials dealing with various aspects of recovery, specifically everyone's roles in contingency. • Test employee knowledge via call exercise • Submit results to corporate planning team	Quarterly

Exhibit 17.2 *(Continued).*

The Leadership Team

The emergency management plan is a preestablished document to aid in management decision making in the face of physical or electronic threats, promote effective utilization of resources, and support compliance with notification procedures. The initial procedures deal primarily with notification of first responders, addressing any life-safety issues caused by the event, and securing the scene. Once those issues are resolved, the focus turns to business resumption or recovery.

KEY LEADERSHIP-TEAM RESPONSIBILITIES

Contingency Planning

Contingency planning acts as the crisis-management team leader for all events regardless of event type to ensure that a consistent approach is used in the management of events. Contingency planning is responsible for the notification to all business-contingency planners and event-management teams. Working with the business-contingency planners from the site and those impacted by the site incident, they will assist in identifying the impact of the disaster, the implementation and execution of individual business contingency/resumption plans, the coordination of response to business needs from corporate real estate, the activation, and equipping of alternate sites, and the escalation of issues to the event-management team. The contingency staff will provide ongoing support to the business-contingency planners throughout the recovery effort.

The corporate contingency representative in the EOC (emergency-operations center) is responsible for coordinating the response to the incident as it relates to the recovery and restoration of the critical business functions impacted by the incident. Contingency staff will provide ongoing status updates to the EOC on the recovery efforts of the impacted business and regular status updates to the event-management team.

Information Security

The information-security incident team is an organization that is assembled to assess and respond to major information-security incidents across business units. The team's role is to perform functions in direct support of the incident. The team reports to the executive management team through the information-security incident team leader. The leader is responsible for defining and coordinating an integrated response to information-security incidents across business units. When a potential incident is identified, the leader decides whether to activate the assessment team or respond to the incident with routine procedures. The subordinate teams may be broken into subteams, each with its own leader to facilitate team responsibilities.

The assessment team consists of individuals throughout the organization who possess special skills applicable to the incident. They are responsible for the assessment of the situation and the development of responses specific to the incident. The members who participate will vary from incident to incident and are likely to come from multiple business units. They will not be members of the response team.

The response team consists of members from business units throughout the business who are responsible for managing technology that may be involved in an information-security incident. Their responsibilities are to support the coordinated response efforts and to execute the procedures defined by the assessment team. In order to maximize the effectiveness of a response technique, cooperation across all business units is essential. Each business unit will be led by an individual who can coordinate activities across the business unit and ensure that all requested actions can be completed in a timely manner.

The support team is a collection of teams that provides support to the response efforts. This team is activated on a case-by-case basis as needed for the specific incident. Team members come from functions throughout the business that normally provide the required support. Responsibilities and support plans are documented in the plan.

The information-security incident team fits into the existing structure, reporting to the executive management team. The team leader is not the same person as the event-management team leader, since both teams may be active at the same time. The decision to activate the information-security incident team is made by the team leader or the executive emergency-management team.

The information-security incident team is composed, as noted above, of two major teams, an assessment team and a response team. Support is provided by the emergency-management support teams. The information-security incident team leader must have the critical skills to effectively communicate with the executive emergency-management team and all of the subordinate teams. Subordinate teams are made up of employees who possess critical skills. In several cases, team membership probably will be cross-functional across organizational boundaries. Subordinate teams may be collections of individual members or of teams.

Human Resources

Human resources' role in the management team is to provide the corporate response to human-resource issues that may arise as a result of the incident. It is the event owner of any workforce-impairment event such as a pandemic but also has responsibility to manage the human impact of any event type.

Responsibilities may include issues such as employee injuries or fatalities resulting from the incident, posttraumatic stress or grief counseling to employees, reassignment of staff to support the recovery effort, hiring of additional temporary help or contractors to support recovery, as well as responding to family issues that may arise as a result of the demands placed on the emergency-management teams.

Human resources will establish as needed a corporate response towards issues such as these and will work closely with the human-resources representatives from each of the impacted areas.

Corporate Communications

Corporate communications' role on the leadership team is to assist the event-management team members and company leadership with all communications regarding the incident.

All internal/external communications will be handled by the corporate communications staff. A media briefing center will be established, and a representative from corporate communications will be at the scene of the impacted site at all times during the incident if the media is present.

Corporate communications will assist senior management, serving as spokesperson during the incident and will also keep employees apprised of any public announcements regarding the incident. Corporate Communications will work with the appropriate business leaders to develop talking points.

Security Services

A security employee will often be the first responder to the site when an incident occurs. Security is responsible for responding to all life-safety issues that may arise from the incident, coordinating with outside emergency-management services such as fire, police, and EMS, as well as physical security for the employees being evacuated and the site itself.

The senior onsite security-staff member at the scene is responsible for establishing an incident-command post to coordinate the response at the scene. In addition, the senior member is responsible for providing updates at least every 10 minutes during the incident, more frequently if significant events occur or important information becomes available. Security will act as the incident commander for the incident until such time as all life-safety issues have been resolved. At that time, the incident command will be turned over to the real-estate manager.

If there are any injuries or fatalities at the scene, the security staff must notify the leadership team immediately and provide as much information as possible so that the human-resources representative can respond.

The security member of the management team is responsible for coordinating the response to all life-safety or physical-security issues arising from the incident. This includes but is not limited to directing the response of the security command center, providing support and direction to the on-scene staff, reassigning staff to support building security while regular staff responds to incident events, and coordinating with the outside emergency-response teams.

Technology Services

Technology services has several representatives on the team. Data-center-operations members are responsible for the data-center infrastructure and delivery of applications. They are contacted directly and are normally one of the first responders to any event that impacts the data center or its applications. If the event has data-center impact, the data-center-operations team leader becomes the event owner; and, once the crisis-management plan has been activated, he or she is responsible for reporting status to the EOC on impacts and recovery of the data-center infrastructure.

The data-center-operations response-team members include mainframe, midrange, and client-server platform support, application teams, network and voice teams, and desktop support. They are responsible for the recovery of the platform infrastructure and applications.

The technology leader is located in the EOC and is responsible for overall coordination of the technology response to the event. This includes but is not limited to escalation and communication within the technology group, ensuring that voice and data networks are appropriately managed, providing resources to equip alternate sites as needed, working with equipment vendors to restore or replace damaged equipment, and communicating the status to the leadership team in the EOC.

Corporate Real Estate/Facilities

Corporate real estate is responsible for the management of the physical building asset as well as fire-suppression technology and mechanical, and electrical technology in owned buildings. Corporate real estate will have a responder at the scene as well as a representative on the EOC.

In an owned facility, the corporate real-estate/facilities team member at the site should report to the incident command post upon arrival for an update on the situation. The member may be requested to identify alternate power sources and their locations in that building. He or she is responsible for coordinating with the security staff and the outside emergency-management organizations such as police and fire to support the management of the incident. He or she is also responsible for communications to the corporate real-estate management team representative in the EOC concerning any pertinent information as it becomes available. Once the life-safety issues have been resolved, the corporate real-estate manager assumes the role of incident commander at the scene.

The corporate real-estate representative in the EOC is responsible for the management of overall response to the situation including but not limited to working with risk management to provide information on losses for insurance purposes, coordinating the cleanup and repair or rebuild of the primary site, identifying and locating additional space for displaced employees if the building will be closed for more than 24 hours or recovery teams that will be deployed, coordinating with building management in leased spaces, coordinating with state and local agencies to deal with air quality or physical infrastructure safety issues, and providing continuous updates to the team in the EOC.

Corporate Risk and Insurance

The corporate-insurance representative is responsible for coordinating with all the recovery teams and collecting of information related to any recoverable losses sustained either during or as a result of any significant incident.

The insurance and risk-management team member coordinates with the affected individuals or business units and various insurance carriers to obtain details and manage the claims.

Losses may include but are not limited to:

1. Injuries resulting from the incident to employees, customers, or tenants

2. Property and equipment that is destroyed, damaged, or rendered unusable for a period of time
3. The cost of business function, including in some cases transportation, lodging, and use of contingent sites or services

Note: In the case of any fatalities or multiple injuries in any given event, there are certain reports that must be completed within eight hours, as per federal Department of Labor standards. The insurance and risk-management representative must be informed of any such occurrences as soon as possible and work with human resources to file the necessary reports.

Corporate Legal/Compliance

The corporate legal team member in the EOC is responsible for reviewing the decisions being made regarding recovery for adherence or deviation to regulatory compliance and for coordinating with the legal department to contact the necessary regulatory agencies in the event that the company needs to enact emergency procedures. In the event that the incident is a deliberate act of sabotage directed at the company, legal is responsible for working with the investigations staff and in determining the course of action to be taken, including prosecution, as well as reviewing customer impact to determine if restitution to customers financially or otherwise impacted by the event is necessary.

Logistics

The logistics team is comprised of members from desktop, network services, finance, travel, procurement, information security, the mailroom, facilities, and claims. The team is responsible for logistical support for any event where staff will be deployed to alternate sites. Team members are prepared to support the procurement and deployment of office space, supplies, rental cars, airline tickets, hotel rooms, equipment, cash, credit, etc., as needed to support the recovery efforts.

The logistics team is responsible for providing logistical support to the event and consists of the following groups:

- Real estate—responsible for providing office space to responding teams
- Finance—responsible for cash and credit availability
- Travel—responsible for providing lodging, rental cars, flights, and other travel-related services

- Desktop—responsible for providing desktop hardware and software to responding teams
- Network—responsible for providing network connectivity to responding teams
- Mailroom—responsible for redirecting mail from impacted site to alternate site(s)
- Procurement—responsible for procuring supplies needed by responding teams
- Information security—responsible for providing logical access to responding teams

Business

The business team leader becomes the crisis leadership team leader and is responsible for managing the business response to the event. He or she works with the crisis-management team to assign the event level based on the impact of the event, determine the communications response, assign business resources to respond as needed, and manage all communications to the executive emergency team.

The business contingency planner from each organization is responsible for identifying the impact and coordinating the business response to the incident. Each BCP impacted by the event will implement all or a portion of the business-continuity/resumption plan for the organization. BCPs are responsible for communications related to the incident within their organization and with other organizations impacted by their loss. BCPs will work with corporate contingency planning to identify open issues related to the recovery of the critical business functions of their company. They will ensure that inbound 800 numbers and critical administrative phones at the impacted site have been properly identified and rerouted to the alternate sites. They will coordinate the activation of their alternate site from day one for their critical business functions and facilitate the recovery of those business functions by their recovery teams. They will provide updates on a regular basis on the status of the recovery efforts to contingency planning.

Administrative Support

During the recovery effort an administrative-support team will be required to support the recovery efforts. This team will be located in the EOC. It is each team leader's responsibility to determine the staff's food, lodging, and transportation needs during an emergency situation and to communicate them to the administrative-support representative. Consolidating the requests for these services during an emergency will help ensure the quickest possible response while eliminating redundancy.

The administrative-support representative is responsible for ordering food for the recovery locations, facilitating lodging, and facilitating transportation, particularly where normal methods of transportation are unavailable. Travel arrangements through the ongoing recovery efforts will generally be made by the administrative-support team working with the travel team. All travel arrangements will be made through corporate travel agents.

18

Industry Certifications and Professionalization

Chapter Objectives

- The Importance of Being Certified
- Certification Programs

Fifteen years ago, very few employers knew that there was a certification process for this industry, but that is not true today. Even though many prospective employers still do not understand what the certification means, most job openings for business-continuity or disaster-recovery positions request certification as one of the criteria for employment. In a recent survey conducted by BC Management, a recruitment firm specializing in this field, the majority of open positions in the field required the applicant to have some type of certification, and having a certification also meant an increase in salary. The higher the certification level a practitioner had, the greater the compensation received.

As of this writing, two certifications are the most highly recognized in the field of business continuity and disaster recovery. There are other certification bodies, but the most respected are DRII and BCI. Both have differing levels of certification based on the experience the applicant can demonstrate in the field.

Ten professional practices in business continuity were originally jointly developed by DRII and BCI. BCI has since moved on, and the practice list is wholly owned by DRII.

DRII—THE INSTITUTE FOR CONTINUITY MANAGEMENT

DRI International (www.DRII.org) provides five levels of active professional certifications. The DRII certification is well respected and recognized worldwide. The certifications offered by DRII are quickly becoming the "standard of excellence" in business-continuity management, and the various levels of certification acknowledge an individual's effort to achieve a professional level of competence in the industry.

The certifications offered by DRII are: ABCP (Associate Business Continuity Professional), CBCV (Certified Business Continuity Vendor), CFCP (Certified Functional Continuity Professional), CBCP (Certified Business Continuity Professional), and MBCP (Master Business Continuity Professional). The organization also offers a retired category for the CFCP, CBCP,, and MBCP levels. The ABCP certification supports entry-level proficiency in professional practice for someone with less than two years' experience in the field. To obtain this entry-level certification, you must pass a certification exam. To progress to a higher level, you must complete an application for certification. An additional exam is not needed.

The CBCV designation is the newest offering by DRII to recognize business-continuity vendors. To obtain this certification, the applicant must pass the DRII certification exam and submit an application demonstrating more then two years' experience as a vendor in the field.

The CFCP designation is reserved for individuals who specialize in a specific functional area such as call-center recovery or technology recovery rather than enterprise-wide recovery. The applicant must pass the certification exam and demonstrate knowledge and working experience of greater then two years. The applicant must be able to demonstrate practical experience in three areas of the professional practice.

The CBCP designation is reserved for individuals who have demonstrated knowledge and working experience of greater then two years. The applicant must pass the certification exam and be able to demonstrate practical experience in five areas of professional practice. The MBCP designation is the highest, reserved for individuals who have demonstrated knowledge and working experience of greater then five years. The applicant must pass the certification exam and demonstrate knowledge and practical experience in seven areas of professional practices Maintaining your DRII certification carries requirements for all levels. The levels of CFCP, CBCP, and MBCP require payment of an annual maintenance fee, accumulation of continuing-education activity points (CEAPs), and involvement in the BC community every two calendar years. Individuals certified at the ABCP, CBCV, and retired (RET.) level simply need to remit an annual certification-maintenance fee.

The 10 professional practices that are the basis for all the DRII certifications are as follows:

1. Program initiation and management: Establish the need for a business-continuity management (BCM) program, including resilience strategies, recovery objectives, business continuity, operational risk management, and crisis management. The prerequisites within this effort include obtaining management support and organizing and managing the formulation of the functions or processes required to construct the BCM framework.

2. Risk evaluation and control: Determine the risks (events or surroundings) that can adversely affect the organization and its resources (example(s) include people, facilities, technologies) due to business interruption; the potential loss such events can cause, and the controls needed to avoid or mitigate the effects of those risks. As an outcome of the above, a cost-benefit analysis will be required to justify the investment in controls.

3. Business-impact analysis: Identify the impacts resulting from business interruptions that can affect the organization and techniques that can be used to quantify and qualify such impacts. Identify time-critical functions, their recovery priorities, and interdependencies so that recovery-time objectives can be established and approved.

4. Business-continuity strategies: Leverage the outcome of the BIA and risk evaluation to develop and recommend business-continuity strategies. The basis for these strategies is both the recovery time and point objectives in support of the organization's critical functions.

5. Emergency response and operations: Identify an organization's readiness to respond to an emergency in a coordinated, timely, and effective manner. Develop and implement procedures for initial response and stabilization of situations until the arrival of authorities having jurisdiction (if/when needed).

6. Business-continuity plans: Design, develop, and implement business-continuity plans that provide continuity and/or recovery as identified by the organization's requirements.

7. Awareness and training programs: Prepare a program to create and maintain corporate awareness and enhance the skills required to develop and implement business-continuity management.

8. Business-continuity-plan exercise, audit, and maintenance: Establish an exercise/testing program that documents plan exercise requirements including planning, scheduling, facilitation, communications, auditing, and post-exercise review documentation. Establish maintenance program to keep plans current and relevant. Establish an audit process that will validate compliance with standards, review solutions, verify appropriate levels of maintenance and exercise activities, and validate that the plans are current, accurate, and complete.

9. Crisis Communications: Develop and document action plans to facilitate communication of critical continuity information. Coordinate an exercise with stakeholders and the media to ensure clarity during crisis communications.

10. Coordination with External Agencies: Establish applicable procedures and policies for coordinating continuity and restoration activities with external agencies (local, regional, national, emergency responders, defense, etc.) while ensuring compliance with applicable statutes and regulations.

BCI—THE BUSINESS CONTINUITY INSTITUTE

BCI certification levels and requirements can be found at www.thebci.org. The BCI Professional Recognition Program provides an international structure for the certification of business-continuity practitioners. It has created a benchmark for the assessment of best practices and encouraged the enhancement and further development of related skills. The certification is based on a set of standards known as the Certification Standards for Business Continuity Professionals, which has been accepted internationally and was developed and published in cooperation with the DRII. Each element links with the other elements to form the continuum of business-continuity management.

Historically the skills required to achieve certification and ultimately professional membership in the Business Continuity Institute have been presented as a list of 10 required subject areas. To maintain consistency with the continuum of business-continuity management as illustrated by the BCM lifecycle, the BCI has taken the decision to map these fundamental required skills against stages of the lifecycle, presenting these mandatory requirements in six distinct sections as detailed on pages 189 and 190. The Business Continuity Institute's good practice guidelines are published in six chapters that correspond to these sections.

Candidates who successfully pass the BCI Certificate will be entitled to use the post-nominal credential CBCI. Holding the BCI Certificate is an essential requirement of professional BCI membership, along with proven practical experience and competence in BCM and an undertaking to subscribe to BCI's Code of Ethics. The levels of BCI certification are: FBCI (Fellow), MBCI (Member), SBCI (Specialist in one of the BCI's faculties), and AMBCI (Associate).

The six subject areas listed below cover the competencies required by a professional practitioner in order to deliver effective business-continuity management:

- Establishing the need for a business-continuity-management (BCM) process, including: resilience strategies, recovery objectives, business-continuity and incident-management plans, obtaining management support for such a process; organizing and managing the formulation of the function or process either in collaboration with or as a key component of an integrated risk-management initiative; developing, coordinating, evaluating, and creating plans and procedures to communicate with external stakeholders, including the media, during incidents.

- Understanding the organization, including business-impact analysis (BIA); identifying the impacts resulting from disruptions and disaster scenarios that can affect the organization, and developing techniques that can be used to quantify and qualify such impacts; establishing critical functions, their recovery priorities, and interdependencies so that recovery time objectives can be set; risk evaluation and control; determining the events and environmental surroundings that can adversely affect the organization and its facilities with disruption and/or disaster, and understanding the damage such events can cause; establishing the controls needed to prevent or minimize the effects of potential loss; providing cost-benefit analysis to justify investment in controls to mitigate risks.

- Determining business-continuity management strategies, including determining and guiding the selection of alternative business-recovery operating strategies for continuation of business within recovery time and/or recovery point objectives, while maintaining the organization's critical functions; delivering solutions for continuation of business within the recovery time and/or recovery point objectives, while maintaining the organization's critical functions; developing, coordinating, evaluating, and creating plans and procedures to communicate with internal stakeholders during incidents; provision of post-incident support and guidance for employees and their families.

- Developing and implementing a BCM response, including developing and implementing emergency-response procedures for responding to and stabilizing the situation following an incident or event; establishing and managing an emergency operations center to be used as a command center during the emergency; practical experience in handling incidents/emergencies; designing, developing, and implementing business-continuity and incident-management plans that provide continuity within recovery-time and/or recovery-point objectives.

- Exercising, maintenance, and review, including preplanning and coordinating plan walkthroughs/exercises; evaluating, updating, improving, and documenting the results of exercises; developing processes to maintain the currency of continuity capabilities, business-continuity and incident-management plans in accordance with the organization's strategic direction; establishing appropriate policies and procedures for coordinating incidents, continuity, and restoration activities with external agencies while ensuring compliance with applicable statutes and/or regulations; practical experience in dealing with external agencies.

- Embedding business-continuity management within the organization's culture, including designing a program to create and maintain corporate awareness and enhance the skills required to develop and implement the business-continuity-management program or process and its supporting activities.

Until 2007, certification for professional grades of membership had been done exclusively through scored assessment based on understanding and experience within the previously defined certification skills of business-continuity management. As of 2008, all applicants for professional certified grades are required to pass the BCI Certificate (CBCI). The BCI Certificate will examine knowledge of the BCI's good practice guidelines, which are consistent with the certification standards as outlined above. In addition to holding the CBCI, applicants for the senior grade of MBCI will continue to have their knowledge and experience score-assessed.

19

Disaster Planning at Home

Chapter Objectives

- Why you Need to be Ready at Home Too

BE READY WHEN DISASTER STRIKES YOU PERSONALLY

Disasters do not have any respect for people. They know no social class, no income bracket, no education level. It is difficult for you or your team to respond to the needs of your company disaster plan if your own homes or your families are at risk from an event. Just as at work, you cannot prevent or predict everything that may happen to you, but some basic preparations at home will help you be ready to keep your family safe in an emergency.

Regional disasters can be caused by natural, man-made, or techno-logical means. During one of these disasters you can find yourself isolated from the world, in need of help, and on a long waiting list to receive assistance from responding authorities. During a smaller disaster you too may find yourself isolated from the world and in need of help, with the only difference being that there is less assistance available for these less devastating, less visible disasters. In either case, personal preparedness measures made well in advance can provide you comfort while living through a bad situation, and, yes, it can happen to you—just ask the thousands who thought it couldn't happen to them.

FAMILY EMERGENCY PLAN

In a widespread disaster, the initial hours after it occurs are yours to weather on your own. There are preparations you can make to ensure that this waiting period is as pleasant as possible. Consideration should be given to the preparation of a family-emergency kit for each person in your household to ensure that you have necessary items to not only survive but thrive after a calamity strikes. These items should be packed so they are easily mobilized and taken with you during evacuation. They can also be used to sustain you when returning home to start damage assessment and repair after the event has occurred. Here are some procedures to follow:

1. Have a family evacuation plan and practice it. Just as you perform evacuation drills at the office, you want your family to practice evacuating from your home. You want to make certain that everyone knows how to get out of the house from any room they may be in. If you have only one stairwell from upper floors, make certain that you have emergency ladders or a fire escape from the upper floors. Teach everyone in your family how to evacuate; even children as young as three can understand the basics. Teach family members to keep low if there is smoke present. Teach them to go in the bathroom, to seal around the door with wet towels, and to hold a towel up to their face. Teach them not to hide under beds or in closets. Teach them to go to a window and signal for help. Teach them to dial 911.

2. Make sure you have properly working smoke detectors on every floor of your home and a carbon-monoxide detector. If you only have one carbon-monoxide detector, put it near the bedrooms. Check these detectors periodically to make certain they are working properly. Make sure everyone is familiar with what they sound like when they go off and what to do when they hear the sound.

3. Have a designated assembly area outside your home, one that is close by, across the street from your home, and one that is farther away but still within walking distance.

4. Have a relative or someone who lives outside your area act as an "I am OK" contact when family members get separated. Make sure everyone knows who that is and the contact information including full address.

5. When severe weather is expected, make sure that you have sufficient amounts of any prescription medicines needed by family members available in your home. In addition, if you are in area that is subject

to natural hazards that do not give any warning, you should always keep on hand the following:

a. A first-aid kit and a first-aid handbook. The kit should include sterile gloves, sterile dressings, cleansing agent, antibiotic ointment, burn ointment, adhesive bandages, eye-wash solution, thermometer, prescribed medical supplies such as glucose or blood-pressure monitoring, scissors, tweezers, petroleum jelly, aspirin and non-aspirin pain relievers, anti-diarrhea medicine, antacid, and laxative.

b. Consider the needs of any chronically ill, disabled, or special-needs person in your home. Have sufficient supplies on hand of items such as oxygen, wheelchairs, hearing aids, eyeglasses.

c. Have available sufficient nonperishable foods to feed everyone in the house, including pets, for a week.

d. Have sufficient potable water for everyone in the home, including pets, for a week—one gallon per person and pet per day.

e. Have at least two working flashlights with extra batteries.

f. Have a hand-operated can opener.

g. Keep a battery-powered radio and extra batteries.

h. Keep matches in a plastic bag to keep them dry.

i. Keep on hand moist towelettes, garbage bags, and plastic ties.

j. Have local maps available.

k. Don't forget dust masks, duct tape, and plastic sheeting.

l. If you have young children, have infant formula and diapers available.

m. Don't forget cash or traveler's checks and change.

6. In your car, keep a safety kit that includes a basic first-aid kit, road flares, Fix-A-Flat® can, emergency blanket, flashlight and batteries, jumper cables, small shovel, tow rope, and bungee cords.

7. Take pictures of every room in your home and of any items of significant value in your home for insurance-claim purposes. After a loss, you must prove the contents of your home to receive payment on your claim.

8. Have a waterproof grab-and-go bag that includes your important papers such as medical-insurance documents, house-insurance documents, doctors' numbers, estate-planning papers, passports, birth certificates, car titles, checks, negotiable instruments, etc.—anything that you would need following a disaster. Make duplicates of all of these papers and store them somewhere offsite.

20

The Regulatory Environment

Chapter Objectives

• Understanding the Regulatory Environment

I am going to briefly cover the regulations that exist in today's environment, but I warn you that regulations are constantly changing. To be honest, many companies still choose not to take them seriously. After September 11, 2001, my company began to receive many more requests from organizations that we did business with for information about our contingency plan. Despite all the regulations that have been introduced on this topic in a free-market economy, private business began to take real notice because their customers started to ask about them. More companies find that external parties have demanded proof of their readiness, and more often than not it was not just a government or industry regulator that demanded the proof but their customers as well.

Readiness may become critical to your profitability and longevity as a company if you have a disaster, but whether or not you have a plan that will work in the event of a disaster also affects the profitability and wellbeing of your employees, partners, and customers. Since they are dependent on you being there when they need you, before the contract gets signed or the customer signs on the dotted line, you may need to provide proof of your company's readiness.

LEGAL AND REGULATORY REQUIREMENTS

The legal and regulatory requirements that the organization is subject to are very industry-specific, and the number of regulations in this area have increased substantially since the events of September 11, 2001. I am not a lawyer, and the extent to which these laws impact your organization is for your legal staff to decide. Two of the most recent regulations introduced are Title IX of the Private Sector Preparedness Act Implementing the 9/11 Commission Recommendations Act of 2007 and British Standard BS25999.

Title IX (Public Law 110-53) addresses a variety of national-security issues as well. It was signed into law on August 3, 2007. The intent of the law is to implement the findings of the 9/11 Commission Report. The law recommends that private-sector organizations validate their readiness to recover by comparing their programs against an as yet unnamed standard. NFPA 1600 was recommended by the 9/11 Commission, but the law does not specify that standard as the only standard to be used. The DRII Professional Practices are the basis for business-continuity planning (BCP) in NFPA 1600. Will it become a standard? That is unknown as of this writing. Today, it is voluntary.

BS25999, Part 1, is an extension of PAS56, which provides guidance and is non-performance-based. Part 2 has a certification body and specific requirements and is auditable. The intention is to create the ability to demonstrate compliance with the standard. Stage 1 is an audit including a desktop review that must be completed before moving to stage 2. Stage 2 is a conformance and certification audit according to which the planner must demonstrate implementation. If the company fails, it requires corrective action, which must be agreed upon, and that failure is discoverable in court. If the planner successfully completes stages 1 and 2, the company can then apply for BS25999 certification.

REGULATIONS FOR FINANCIAL INSTITUTIONS

The *Federal Financial Institutions Examination Council BCP Handbook* specifies among other things that business-continuity planning is about maintaining, resuming, and recovering the business, not just the technology, and that the planning process should be conducted on an enterprise-wide basis. It also stipulates that a thorough business-impact analysis and risk assessment are the foundation of an effective BCP, that the effectiveness can be validated only through testing or practical application, and that the BCP and test results should be subjected to an independent audit and reviewed by the board of directors. In addition, Appendix D of the FFIEC states that a company should be aware of third-party providers, key suppliers, and business partner's BCP plans. When a company outsources information, transaction processing, and/or settlement activities, the company should review and understand service providers' business-continuity plans and ensure that critical services can be restored within acceptable time frames based upon the needs of the institution. If possible, it recommends that the institution consider participating in the provider's testing process.

NASD Rule 3510 requires a business-continuity plan that addresses, at a minimum, that data backup and recovery (hard copy and electronic) exist for mission-critical systems, that financial and operational assessments are performed, and that alternate communications between customers and the firm and employees and the firm have been identified and implemented. It also requires that business-constituent, bank, and counter-party impact are documented and that regulatory reporting and communications with regulators would continue in an event.

NYSE Rule 446 requires a written business-continuity plan and yearly review.

The Australian Prudential Standard, April 2005, states: "Business continuity management (BCM) describes a whole of business approach to ensure critical business functions can be maintained, or restored in a timely fashion."

Monetary Authority of Singapore, June 2003, states: "Business Continuity Management (BCM) is an over-arching framework that aims to minimize the impact to businesses due to operational disruptions. It not only addresses the restoration of information technology (IT) infrastructure, but also focuses on the rapid recovery and resumption of critical business functions for the fulfillment of business obligations."

Standard for Business Continuity/Disaster Recovery Service Providers (SS507), developed in Singapore, is the first standard and certification program for BC/DR service providers. Developed by the Infocomm Development Authority of Singapore and the IT Standards Committee (ITSC), the standard specifies stringent requirements for BC/DR service providers. These requirements benchmark against the top practices in the region and stipulate the operating, monitoring, and upkeep of BC/DR services offered.

197

Technical Reference 19 aims to help Singapore-based enterprises build competence, capacity, resilience, and readiness to respond to and recover from events that threaten to disrupt normal business operations.

HIPAA requires a data-backup plan, a disaster-recovery plan, and an emergency-mode operations plan as well as more familiar components regarding privacy and portability of health insurance.

Many people make the case that there is a business continuity component in Sarbanes Oxley – SEC. 404 Management assessment of internal controls but the PCAOB (Public Accounting Oversight Board) disagrees stating that a company's business continuity or continuity planning is not part of internal control over financial reporting.

Sarbanes Oxley—Section 404
Management Assessment of Internal Controls

Many people try to make the case that there is a business continuity component in Sarbanes Oxley. The PCAOB (Public Company Accounting Oversight Board) made this statement about Sarbanes Oxley. "Furthermore, management's plans that could potentially affect financial reporting in future periods are not controls. For example, a company's business continuity or contingency planning has no effect on the company's current abilities to initiate, authorize, record, process, or report financial data. Therefore, a company's business continuity or contingency planning is not part of internal control over financial reporting." No, there is not but many will make the other case.

Additional regulations for financial firms include but are not limited to:

- National Association of Insurance Commissioners (NAIC)
- National Futures Association Compliance Rule 2-38
- Electronic Funds Transfer Act—"reasonable" standard of care (the care that a reasonable person would exercise under the circumstances; the standard for determining legal duty)
- Basel Committee—banks should have in place contingency and business continuity plans
- NYS Circular Letter 7

LEGAL STANDARDS

Legal standards to be considered include liability of corporations, liability of corporate executives, liability to outside parties, standard of negligence, standard of care, prudent-man doctrine, and informed business judgment versus gross negligence.

In criminal law, corporate liability determines the extent to which a corporation, as a fictitious person, can be liable for the acts and omissions of the people it employs.

The corporate form of business organization is intended to protect shareholders from personal liability for the civil debts of the corporation. Executives, directors, and other officers and employees of the corporation enjoy no immunity from either criminal or quasi-criminal liability. Such persons are legally accountable for any misconduct of their own and for any misconduct by others to which they are a party, whether done on behalf of the corporation or otherwise.

The negligence standard is ordinarily defined in terms of how a reasonably prudent person would have acted under the same circumstances.

In tort law, the standard of care is the degree of prudence and caution required of an individual who is under a duty of care. The requirements of the standard are closely dependent on circumstances. Whether the standard of care has been breached is determined by the tryer of fact and is usually phrased in terms of a reasonable person. It was famously described in *Vaughn v. Menlove* (1837) as whether the individual "proceed[ed] with such reasonable caution as a prudent man would have exercised under such circumstances."

The prudent-man rule is based on common law stemming from the 1830 Massachusetts court decision, *Harvard College v. Armory*. It directs trustees "to observe how men of prudence, discretion and intelligence manage their own affairs, not in regard to speculation, but in regard to the permanent disposition of their funds, considering the probable income, as well as the probable safety of the capital to be invested."

Informed business judgment presumes that "in making business decisions not involving direct self-interest or self-dealing, corporate directors act on an informed basis, in good faith, and in the honest belief that their actions are in the corporation's best interest."

Gross negligence is a conscious and voluntary disregard of the need to use reasonable care, which is likely to cause foreseeable grave injury or harm to persons, property, or both.

21

Tools, Software, Recovery Contracts, Consultants and Other Matters

COMMUNICATION TOOLS

When planning for communications to use in a disaster event, you have to remember that many of the tools you use every day among staff and team members, such as email and internal phone systems, may be not be immediately available following a disaster. Part of your plan must be a plan for communications that are external to your environment and would therefore survive an event that disabled your facility.

COMMUNICATION METHODS

I have worn a pager since the 1980s because I have been in roles that required me to be "electronically leashed," meaning that I needed to be available to respond any time of day or night. Early pagers were numeric only, and so the person who needed you would call a phone number and enter a phone number for you to call back. Alphanumeric pagers are now available that receive text messages and that can convey enough information for someone to understand a situation and begin a response. Since pagers use satellites to relay the information, they work when other devices may not. In fact, they were one of the few devices that worked consistently on both Septermber 11 and during Katrina when a lot of the infrastructure for other communications was damaged.

Most cell phones can receive both voice calls and text messages. Your cell phone is hosted externally from your environment and would therefore be available in an event if the cell-phone towers are not impacted by the same event. Text messaging may be available on a cell phone even when voice communications are not, as was the case during Katrina.

During the planning for Y2K, satellite phones became available as a source of communications that was not dependent on cell towers and land lines. The technology continues to improve, but they still work much better in flat terrain than in cities or mountainous areas, due to line-of-sight issues.

Paging service providers offer software tools that allow you to build teams and page a group of people instead of one person at a time.

Notification systems are offered by an increasing number of vendors. These software applications are designed for rapid, high-volume communications to any voice- and text-enabled device. That means that they can call you at any number you give them, send a text message to your cell phone or pager, or send an email. Some support a limited amount of bi-directional communications such as the ability to press 1 if you if you are able to report to the alternate site or 2 if you are not able to report to the alternate site. Most if not all of them give you the capability to build teams either by selecting certain individuals or by specifying criteria to include in a team—for example, send this communication to everyone whose location equals Boston. They provide a variety of reports that tell you whom you have reached, when you reached them, where you reached them, and whom you did not reach. The capability of these systems to send a communication to hundreds or even thousands of people nearly simultaneously and the fact that everyone they reach hears exactly the same message make them an invaluable tool in your communication arsenal.

Conference bridges and virtual meetings are used by most companies today, so they are not as unknown as when I first began using them for event management. Most voice-communication providers offer conference-bridge capabilities. The range of services you should contract for is dependent on the size of your company and what you would use this tool to do. I recommend that you look for a service that can handle on-demand meetings so that each meeting does not have to be scheduled in advance and that can provide you with a standing conference-call number to be used in your plan document and in your emergency-notification list.

Most conference-call services have a variety of options including the ability to record the meeting, announce participants as they join and leave the call, and provide a roll call. Be careful which ones you select to use during an event. It is a good security practice to have participants give their name and be announced during a call, but it can be very disruptive if people tend to come to the call late or leave early.

You must teach and enforce conference-call etiquette particularly in a disaster event, otherwise conference calls can become disasters themselves. There needs to be one facilitator of the call who has the ability to manage the call and all the participants. For example, in a status call that is held during an ongoing event the facilitator would be responsible for announcing the beginning of a call, welcoming the participants, conducting a roll call as needed, asking the event owner to provide an updated status, opening the floor for questions, reviewing open action items, establishing the need for the next call, and gaining agreement on the timing of the next update call.

Rules for effective conference calls:

1. Participants need to arrive on time. Anyone arriving late needs to wait until the end of the call, then get the information they missed so that it does not need to be repeated with every late-comer.
2. Any participant who is not speaking should have their phone muted.
3. The facilitator should be the first person on the call; he or she should welcome participants as they join and discourage or delay any discussions until everyone who needs to be there is on the call.
4. In an audio-only call, every time someone speaks he or she should identify who he or she is. Voices are not always recognizable.
5. The facilitator needs to defer items that are not part of the agenda to later discussions.
6. The facilitator needs to open the call with a stated agenda followed by a brief description of the event that precipitated the meeting.

7. Individuals providing a status update on the event need to adhere to the "facts only" rule. No guesses on root causes or when things will be recovered; facts only. If we don't know yet, then say we do not know but will attempt to find an answer and report when known.
8. The facilitator needs to close the call by repeating the understanding of the event, decisions that were made or need to be made, ownership of any actions items, and the agreed-upon time for the next update.

Meetings can also be held with video where participants in multiple locations can not only hear each other but can see each other as well. There are also tools for sharing documents and dashboards throughout the call. My husband works as an instructor at a company that has "virtual academies," where the instructor-led course is taught entirely over the internet with people from all over the country or even the world learning together.

Whether you are doing voice-only conferencing or more sophisticated means of communication, these tools can help you manage communications about the event to your recovery teams, your leadership, and your employee base.

PLANNING TOOLS

There are many planning tools available today with a wide range of costs from nothing to thousands of dollars. None of them will actually write a plan for your organization (you still have to do that), but they do offer tools to collect and store the data you need to build and maintain your plan.

If you are interested in software tools, the best advice I can give is the same advice I would give if you were planning on buying a car, a house, or anything else. Do your homework. Make sure you understand the problem you are trying to solve before you go out and buy a solution. You don't want to end up with a sports car if what you need is a station wagon.

Collecting all the data you need to build your plan once is difficult and time-consuming, but if you do not have a simple and logical way to sort it and update it to keep it current, then you will have to redo the whole process every time you need to update the plan, rather than being able to have the previous data validated. The software tools on the market today are generally databases that allow you to query and to view the data you have collected in different ways. For example, you can ask it to tell you all the business functions that operate in this site or all the business functions that use this application.

Many of the current tools have a BIA (business-impact analysis) component that allows you to send questionnaires to your planning team to help quantify business-recovery priorities using the same set of criteria for more consistent results.

As you evaluate software tools against the needs you have, consider the following:

- Cost—how much of your budget will this take?
- Maintenance—is there a annual maintenance fee?
- Hardware requirements—what type of system does this software run on?
- License requirements—is there a cost per desktop the software is installed on, a cost per site, a cost per user?
- Ease of use—how easy is this system to use?
- Reporting—what types of reports can the system generate and can you build other reports?
- Training—how hard is it to train your planning team to use the software?
- Database—what is the hierarchy of the data being stored?
- Data collection—how is the data collected for input to the system?
- Enterprise class—is this an enterprise-class software that can be loaded on a server and accessed by multiple users simultaneously?

THIRD-PARTY RECOVERY SITES

Many companies elect to contract with third parties to provide recovery services for their technology and/or business environments. Generally speaking, it is less expensive to contract for these services than to build out dedicated solutions because vendors are able to achieve economies of scale. Not every company that contracts for third-party services will suffer a disaster simultaneously, so the same technology can be utilized for multiple companies.

The obvious disadvantage of contracting for these services is that overselling of available resources could result in shortages in the event of a widespread outage impacting multiple companies that have contracts with the vendor. When a declaration of disaster occurs, the vendor provides the service on a first-come, first-serve basis. Most of the recovery facilities are very large and have the ability to support multiple declarations. However, if multiple subscribers declare into the same alternate site and resources become constrained, then any additional declarations may need to be moved to other facilities.

Another challenge that I have experienced is an issue with hardware incompatibility between my home environment and the vendor environment. The vendor selects the hardware it keeps on the floor, and it is obviously going to keep the most commonly required hardware. This could result in the need to maintain dedicated hardware at the vendor site or to pay additional costs to have that hardware available at the vendor location.

There are also advantages of using a recovery-service provider beyond cost reduction. Most if not all of the companies I am familiar with provide not just the systems and real estate to do your recovery but also consulting services. The vendor you select to provide your recovery services has been through more recoveries than you ever will (hopefully!) and can therefore be very helpful in building your program.

Company leadership generally finds it difficult to perceive any value in having a collection of expensive technology sitting on the floor waiting for the "big" one or 150 business-recovery seats set up unoccupied except for tests with PCs and phones for business recovery. The technologies used to support internal strategies are often older equipment, whereas the technology provided by a vendor tends to be newer and refreshed more often, as the vendor must meet the requirements of their most advanced customers.

In internal-recovery environments, the "extra" equipment for recovery or end-user space tends to get swallowed up to support growth or to reduce costs in struggling financial times, and adding onto an internal-recovery environment can be cost-prohibitive. Because testing can happen anytime in an internal environment, it tends not to happen or to get postponed by other pressing production needs. In an external environment test, time is built into the contract costs and is expensive, so tests rarely get canceled.

When contracting for a recovery-services provider, the most important aspects to consider are as follows:

- Costs—how are costs for the service charged?
- Changes—how easy will it be to change recovery components as your production environment changes?
- Declaration fees—how much will it cost you to declare a disaster (usually called a declaration fee), and how much will it cost for you to stay at the site (usually called daily usage fee)?

- Test time—how much test time will you receive, and how far in advance must it be scheduled?
- Location of other subscribers—how many other companies subscribe to the same space, and how many of those are located within 10 miles of your primary facility?
- Compatibility of your environment to the vendor environment—what are your hardware requirements, and how do they match up to what the vendor can provide?

As with any vendor you do business with, it is important that you do due diligence for the financial viability of the vendor, sign confidentiality agreements, check out the physical security practices, and ask for referrals to other customers who would be willing to share their experiences with the vendor.

USING CONSULTANTS

If you can afford to do so, using consultants to help you build your program can give it the kick start it needs to get moving forward on the right track. For some reason, I have found that if I say something to the leadership team members, they may or may not accept it, but if a consultant tells them something is true, then it is gospel. Knowing this to be the case, using consultants during the early phase of the program to sell leadership on the need to do it and to get the commitment of resources to support it can be very helpful.

Consultants can also provide you with tools to perform an effective and efficient BIA with your planning team and help you to organize the results. They are familiar with different recovery strategies and their pros and cons, have worked with many of the different vendors and software tools, and will be a great resource to you in these matters.

What you should never have the consultant do (and if you are a consultant, I apologize!) is write the plan for you. They can help; they can provide a structure or a template; but do not let them write the plan. The people who have to execute the plan when an event happens for real need to write the plan. They have to own it. If the consultants write it, then they are the only ones who will know what is in the plan—and they won't be there on the scene to help you recover.

22

Summary and Lessons Learned from Real Events

Chapter Objectives

- What It Is Like When It Happens for Real
- It's All About the People
- Summary of the Tasks to Get to a Plan

LESSONS LEARNED FROM REAL RECOVERIES

The two biggest lessons I learned from every recovery I have been a part of are the following:

1. Technology recovery is easy—it either works or it doesn't, and how well it works and how quickly you recover are entirely dependent on how much money you spent to build out your recovery and how often you test.
2. Recovery of the business operations and the people who perform them is much, *much* harder.

September 11, 2000

On September 11, 2000, a water-main break occurred that impacted three buildings my company did business in, affecting about 1600 employees.

When there is a large water-main break like this one, it takes some time to repair; take my word for it. Even if the Board of Health or the local fire chief doesn't close the building, you do not want to occupy buildings with 1600 other people and no working toilets. We declared into our alternate site.

We had been testing in this site for three years or so, four times a year. We tested twice a year with just the technical folks and a few business partners and twice a year with a full complement of business partners. We had transferred calls, processed real work, printed, faxed, etc., and we believed we were ready. For the most part, we were.

The desktop build went very well. The transportation plan worked well. The site had limited parking, so we had car pools to bring people to the site, a parking lot at an abandoned super-market, and a van that we used to shuttle people to and from the site. The vendor actually commented that he had never seen a group come into the site in a real event and just sit down and work. We could do that because most of the people who came for the recovery had been to the site before. They knew how to get there, where to park, where the restrooms were, where the food would be, and how the desktop would look, so it was a lot less scary because it was familiar. We still learned a few things.

Lessons learned—the good:

- Event-management process worked very well
- Communication is the key to event management; if you don't communicate well, nothing else works well.
- Having one crisis manager and one lead responder to provide updates worked well.
- Relationships with city officials paid off. We knew whom to talk to, and they knew us.
- Testing paid off (EMO and alternate-site).
- Having preexisting relationships between responders and business partners was important in establishing trust and understanding roles.
- Regional communications quickly crafted and approved a message for dissemination before employees left for the day.

Lessons learned—the bad:

- Not everyone had directions to the alternate site.
- Not everyone had card access to their alternate site.
- One group had one of the other impacted buildings as the alternate site.

- Due to scheduled maintenance that happened to occur during the event of our mass-communications system, individuals had to be paged through the paging software if they had a pager or called individually if they did not.
- Business units should have aggressively tested six new T1s in the alternate site. The new T1s, which were installed to handle call volume, were not installed correctly and therefore some inbound calls to the rerouted 800 numbers rang busy for the early part of the recovery until this was corrected.
- It is important to provide for multiple shift coverage for key roles. We had multiple shifts working but had not planned to have key roles staffed to support them. Some individuals had to work long hours to support recovery.

Lessons learned—the ugly:

- Order enough food, or you will have a second disaster on your hands.

One of the business planners whose group was impacted by the water-main break wrote this list of the top 10 things to do in a contingency event. As you can see, we shared the number-one issue:

10. Be sure the batteries in your mobile phone and pager are fresh.
9. Be sure you can read your own hastily scribbled notes.
8. Don't get caught wishing you had updated the emergency-notification list last week.
7. Make sure your senior management team, systems-support team, and onsite recovery team are working off the same plan.
6. Stick to your disaster-recovery plan; don't let managers start winging it.
5. Pictures and diagrams of the disaster-recovery rooms help a lot— they are better than written descriptions.
4. Have a hard-card map and directions to the alternate site available to give to every employee as they leave the building.
3. Delegate recovery tasks; you'll be surprised at how willing people are to help with *anything*.
2. Have a parking plan at the alternate site and appoint someone to monitor the parking situation, especially as people arrive at the alternate site.
1. Order enough lunches, or you will have a second disaster on your hands.

September 11, 2001

On September 11, 2001, my company had 850 people in a building across the street from the towers. Our people worked on floors 4, 5, 26, and 27. When the first tower was hit, the folks on the fourth floor decided that an evacuation was necessary despite the fact that no building alarm had occurred. They picked up a copy of the plan and declared with the alternate-site vendor nine minutes after the first plane struck. When they got to the lobby, the security staff for the building told them to go back inside. They ignored the advice and continued to evacuate. The rest of the building did not evacuate until after the second plane struck.

The assembly area designated for the building was too close to the event, so each group improvised. The fourth floor decided to go south because that was the fastest way to the water; this fairly large group of employees stayed together. When the rest of building evacuated, these employees decided that north was a better direction because the debris was falling and blowing in a southerly direction—they used pagers and cell phones to instruct the first group to reverse direction. The first tower collapse dispersed all the employees in different directions; they eventually met up at recovery sites or just went home.

In fact, that first day most people went home. Their first priority was getting home, making sure their families were safe and that their families knew that they were safe. They did not have the advantage of those of us who were watching from a distance to know what was happening. All they knew was what they could see. What they could see was terrifying. They could not reach their families easily because cell lines were completely clogged. Cell-phone towers were lost along with the buildings, and two telephone-company central offices were also impacted by the events, which meant that long-distance calls were easier to make than local ones.

Getting home was not easy. Every subway, bus, and train was shut down. Every bridge and tunnel was closed to traffic. If you lived in the city itself, you had to walk home. If you lived outside the city, you had to walk across bridges and get picked up on the other side of the river to get home.

I was in my car driving to the hospital to pick up my sister, who was being released that day after a week in the hospital. (She is disabled and lives with me and my family.) I was listening to talk radio when they interrupted for a special news report that a plane had struck one of the twin towers in New York. Like most people, my first thought was that a small plane must have lost control. Before I had even reached the hospital, the second plane struck, and it was clear that America was under attack. On the way home from the hospital, the Pentagon was hit, and there were reports of the plane that had crashed in the field in Pennsylvania. I packed a bag as soon as I got home, got back in the car, and drove to the alternate site in New Jersey.

I drove from Massachusetts to New Jersey listening to talk radio and having conference calls with various groups as we put into motion the necessary recovery plans. We declared into no less than 10 alternate sites across the country, a combination of both internal and external sites. If you remember that day, no one knew what was going to be next, so owners of tall buildings in cities across the country were proactively closing their buildings, not willing to take the risk of being sued if they left the buildings open under these circumstances.

I reached the alternate site at 3:00 in the afternoon of September 11, went to our recovery space, and found two people from the New York office at the site. One was one of the technical staff who had supported testing in this site. He had the entire environment built out before I got there. The day 1 requirements were 164 desktops, printers, fax machines, phones transferred, network up. The other person who was there was the president of the New York operations. I was impressed that he could find the site, as they guys do not often come to the tests. We came to an agreement that day that he ran the business and I ran the recovery.

No employee who was actually in the New York office at the time of the event made it to the alternate site until about 6:00 that evening. At that point these 12 or so people were sent to hotels with money for clean clothes and toiletries because they were covered in soot and dust.

By the end of the day on September 11, this is what we reported from the alternate site in New Jersey:

1. Declaration to Carlstadt site at 9:03 a.m.
2. Network up at 11:00 a.m.
3. 164 desktops imaged at 1:00 p.m.
4. Phones rerouted
5. 12 Printers, 6 faxes, 12 modems available 1:00 p.m.
6. Reports printing in MRK and shipped
7. Managers contacting employees
8. Settled trades through pay phone enroute to site
9. Small group of employees arrive at site via Boston Coach
10. Addressed transportation and hotel for 12 +/- onsite employees

On Wednesday, September 12, the entire senior team was onsite, and a decision was made to prep space for long-term recovery based on information from real estate on the status of the building. We had motion-sensitive security cameras in the space that stayed up until the generator ran out of fuel. We could see inside the building that extensive damage had occurred and that we would be in the alternate site for the foreseeable future. We had no idea at the time how long that would actually be.

We also had a problem we needed to sort out. Some of the recovery staff was supposed to go to the internal recovery facility in New Hampshire. We had made a conscious choice to recover certain areas in an internal facility because it had what we considered to be nontransportable applications. These applications were delivered through a direct point-to-point circuit between our company and a vendor service. We did not want to put point-to-point circuits into a first-come, first-serve environment. We tested in New Hampshire four times a year as well. The employees knew that was where the recovery facility was. However, when managers started discussing travel plans with employees going to NH, the vast majority of them said,"Fire me if you want to, but I am not leaving my family."

The other problem was the senior staff. We had planned each of the seats, 164 on day 1 for specific departments. We had a floor plan of where each area sat in the alternate site. But on September 11, when the president arrived at the site, he took a seat. When the rest of the senior staff arrived on September 12, each took a seat. We had not planned seats for them. We had a conference room for them with connections for their laptops, their own printer, conference phone, fax machine, etc. They wanted to use the conference room, but they each wanted a seat as well. Since they had a seat, of course, each one of the administrative assistants also had to have a seat. (I talked them into only two.) We had planned the seats for people who do real work.

We had to find a way not only to accommodate the staff that did not go to New Hampshire, but we also had to add more seats for the leadership team.

We implemented the transportation program we had designed for the site. We had built this plan, but it had never been tested. Most people who work in the city do not drive there every day. They take public transportation. Parking in the city is difficult and expensive. Those who live in the city often do not even own cars; a few did not have driver's licenses. Now we were going to be running our business from New Jersey where public transportation was not available on the scale that it is in New York. Our plan was to pick employees up from gathering places such as subway stations, train stations, and bus terminals in contracted buses and bring them to and from the site each day. We needed to implement this quickly and communicate it to the employees who had seats at the site by updating the contingency line with instructions.

Managers continued contacting all employees to ensure they were safe and to provide further instructions. It took us until the end of week 1 to find our last employee. We had 12 new hires starting that Monday. We were lucky if they remembered their manager's name, much less where the alternate site was. We actually had to send one of our security staff to their homes and knock on the door to determine if they were ok.

We made arrangements for counselors to be available onsite, both in group and individual sessions, so that employees could schedule time with a counselor to help them deal with the stress of the situation and the grief they may be experiencing from loss of family or friends. We established a daily run for supplies from Staples® for immediate needs while we waited for the delivery of ongoing supplies.

We worked with our mailroom to establish a mail zone for the alternate site and to have mail that was being held forwarded to the site, and we worked with our alternate-site vendor to provide mail support until we could establish a mailroom at the alternate site. They provided things like postage metering, Airborne® accounts, etc.

The report at the end of the day on Wednesday confirmed the following:

- 60 employees onsite and fully operational
- Two controllers with terminals and SNA network installed, one to support local mainframe print and backup for workstation and one for Loanet® connections and print, as group will recover in Carlstadt instead of Merrimack
- 164 workstations configured
- Additional 250 IP addresses created
- First print reports from Merrimack delivered
- Day's activity reports to be delivered at 8:00 in the evening
- Two servers and backup devices received
- Building servers up at alternate site
- Mailroom contingency plan initiated at Pitney Bowes®
- Money-market funds opened

Though the full market stayed closed, money-market funds were opened, allowing customers access to cash. Elsewhere in the organization, the communications staff prepared talking points for customer-service reps and anyone else who had regular contact with external parties. The decision was made not to "go public" but to reach out to specific customers and be prepared to respond to customers' questions and concerns.

By Thursday, September 13, we had 200 employees at the alternate site and working. The bond market opened that day, and we installed four televisions in the alternate site so employees could keep up with the news and the markets. We continued to play musical chairs to accommodate employees who we supposed to travel to alternate sites in other states who flat-out refused to go.

By September 14, additional support staff arrived, and we began to prep the space for a long-term recovery. We ordered high-speed fax machines and printers to replace the smaller ones provided by the alternate site. We brought an additional 39 PCs out of our own storage as well as renting another 75 from the vendor and installed them in preparation for additional staff that would arrive for the full market open on Monday. We also brought in a 1000-pound safe to act as a vault for securities and other negotiable instruments held at the site.

We ordered receptacles for proprietary waste and worked with our vendor to provide shredding services; we brought in file cabinets for storage and began to look for real estate for the interim recovery. Our international funds opened that day as well.

By September 15 we had 285 PC desktops plus an additional two controllers' worth of dumb terminals set up. The high-speed printers and fax machines arrived and were installed over the weekend. We had people so densely packed in the space that everyone literally had no more room than a keyboard to work. The head of facilities came up to the space, shook his finger in my face and said, "Kelley, you cannot plug one more thing in this room!"

Exhibit 22.1 is a picture I took on September 17 in the recovery facility.

On September 17, the first day of full market open, we had 310 employees onsite and fully operational and what happened? The NIMDA virus struck that day. My company was shutting down external ports that were not active to reduce the threat of the virus and inadvertently shut down the port we were using at the alternate site. Our network between the alternate site location, and it ran on a single LAN bridge from the facility to our network node. When the technicians shut down that port off the node, they took the network down for the whole site in the middle of a very volatile trading day.

Exhibit 22.1 September 17 in the Recovery Facility.

Beginning September 18 and beyond, we built out a mainframe print room nearby, because waiting for the reports to arrive from our print facility in New Hampshire was just not working in the long term. The print facility began operations on September 19. We also added a redundant port to the LAN bridge between North Bergen and Carlstadt and designed for a more robust network, which eventually eliminated this SPOF. We moved servers from the business-contingency site to the network room due to temperature; anyone who sat near them was very warm. We signed a contract for a build-out of 9000 square feet of dedicated space within the alternate site. The space was completed, and staff was moved into it on November 3. This was the first time since the recovery began that people had drawers to put stuff in. The night before the move, I saw all these employees going to the supply cabinet and getting supplies to put into the drawers. We also signed a contract and began build-out of additional interim space for remaining employees. The last employees left New Hampshire the weekend before Thanksgiving, which is when I also went home to Massachusetts.

What was different about this disaster? Some of the accepted disaster-recovery assumptions didn't hold:

- We assumed that only one disaster strikes at a time. We lost access to our building in New York and simultaneously lost access to key buildings in Boston and other cities that were evacuated as a precaution. This led to multiple disaster declarations in diverse locations that had to be staffed at the same time by multiple support groups.

- We assumed that the infrastructure required for recovery was in place, but telecommunications, power, and transportation were all impacted. No one had ever imagined a scenario where all the planes in the country would be unavailable.

- We assumed our disaster-recovery team and the rest of the corporation would survive the attack. My organization was unaffected by this, but other New York-based corporations lost entire recovery teams and the documentation required to recover. I personally witnessed other corporations struggling to do required day-to-day business functions because those responsible died in the event and because materials for the position were stored in the building

- We assumed the ability to get required equipment from our vendors very quickly. This did not impact my firm directly, but the drop in the economy at that time left many vendors with little or no inventory. The ability to obtain required equipment quickly was hampered.

- The disaster recovery plan was built for a short interruption in business, not a long-term disaster. This type of planning assumption led many business units to assume that plans only needed to be done for very small numbers of employees. This led to scrambling during a disaster, not necessarily the best recovery plan for the employees involved.

Some of the good news from this event:

- We personally experienced no loss of life in New York, and injuries were not serious. All the required personnel were available.

- The market remained closed, allowing initial recovery efforts to be augmented and the business to prepare to conduct business for a long period of time in the alternate sites

- The time and money invested during Y2K to document the business-recovery plans and since that time to acquire/build alternate recovery sites and to test on a regular basis proved invaluable.

- We had up-to-date plans and contact lists.

- We had business and technical people familiar with the testing/ recovery process.
- We had appropriate crisis-management skills.
- Two-way pagers worked consistently when other forms of communication were either busy or completely unavailable.
- Build-out of all of the alternate sites occurred very quickly to allow critical business functions to resume.
- All of the people involved exhibited teamwork, flexibility, availability, and an excellent attitude. Many volunteered to work longer hours and additional shifts to get the job done.
- We had the ability to build networks on the fly to get New York back in business and to use alternate network resources to provide redundancy for network lines running in backup mode.
- We had the ability to leverage business relationships to aid the recovery process.
- Vendors called to assist in the recovery—not looking for money, just trying to help. There was outstanding turnaround time on all requests.

Some of the bad news from this event:

- Plans assumed a short-term outage rather than a long-term scenario. This led to a shortage of space, networks, and equipment that had to be built on the fly.
- Requiring New York-based employees to move to New Hampshire to recover their portion of the business placed on the individuals and their families and had a negative effect.
- Following the set procedure to declare a disaster with the vendor is cumbersome if you manage to get in at all. The vendor received this complaint from numerous customers and is revamping the process.
- The restoration of the network node at the alternate site had problems. Some technology changes made in production were not replicated in the room, causing the recovery process to be elongated.
- Transportation of employees to the alternate sites had never been tested and took a few days to be implemented.
- Reciprocal backup plans called for teams to fly from the affected location to an internal area that would give up seats in the event of a disaster. Flights were not available, and the seats had to be rebuilt because of changes made to the image by other users.

219

- Some contingency plans had insufficient amounts of workstations, network, and equipment; requirements had never received budget approval
- Some key information, both paper and tape, was located only in WFC.

Some key lessons learned during the recovery:

- Testing was the key to the success of the recovery—we tested four times a year and it paid off.
- Critical operations in a single site are bad business. If we had been unfortunate enough to have lost employees like other companies, our recovery would have been much more difficult. This operation was unique in its skills, and though the plans were in place to split them between two geographical operations in the summer of 2002, in the fall of 2001 they were all at one site and we were very lucky that we did not lose them.
- We don't have problems by business; we have problems by building. Our planning up to this point had been done by business operation. We had not built plans at the building level; to execute the logistics of the recovery, we needed to look at three different plans.
- Transportation was a major issue in the first few days.
- Incomplete/inaccurate inventories made the insurance claim difficult. We were lucky we could get back into the space and document losses for our insurance carrier.
- People do not want to travel away from their families. This message came out loud and clear and is repeated by every company I talked to. People want to stay near their families if they perceive them to be at risk in any way. Plans must take families, even pets, into consideration.
- Very few business operations stand alone. Even though it was just our New York offices that were ultimately impacted by this event, the impact rippled through the rest of the firm, clearly showing interdependencies that had not been documented before.
- Voice is harder than data to recover. It's not getting the calls there, it is getting the right calls to the right desk. I can put the exact desktop image on every single desk. It may have more applications than any one user may need, but everything they need

can be there. But the phone is very specific to the person who sits in that desk. Since we had a number of people who were supposed to go to New Hampshire in New Jersey instead, and because the leadership team took desks that had been assigned to specific teams, our alternate-site floor plan became useless very quickly. It was days before we could publish a phone directory that did not change a minute after we published it.

- Some of our vendors were in trouble too. Check your vendor plans and test with them if you can.
- The devil is in the details. Small details like not having a mail zone set up for internally routing mail, not having an Airborne® or FedEx® account set up for the site, not having the site recognized by our office-supplies firm, not having the right size and type of printers and fax machines in the alternate site—all of these created issues during the recovery.

Things we changed or reinforced after the recovery:

- Continuation of aggressive testing of recovery plans with emphasis on testing by site rather than by individual business units. This would allow for the creation of realistic support models that could be utilized at time of disaster.
- Assume the worst-case scenario when developing the disaster-recovery plan and size the solution to fit in terms of seats, network, equipment required, etc.
- Alter plans to allow for alternate sites near the homes of the affected employees. A recovery situation is stressful enough without adding personal stress to the mix.
- Require two-way pagers or text-enabled cell phones for key individuals.
- Develop a turnkey solution for the recovery of the network node; require quarterly testing of the production network into the node.
- Formalize the required corporate functions (HR, finance, real estate, contracts, and security) into swat teams assigned to each alternate site. Document their role and test with the business units.
- Review all sites to determine the risk faced by having key personnel in the same building.

Additional things to consider that others shared with me about their experiences during the 9/11 recovery:

- Implement your plan and associated vendor services with urgency:
  - Our recovery vendor received 14 declarations in 30 minutes, 24 within an hour, and 19 in the second hour on September 11. If it is not just your company that has a problem, declare quickly, as you will be in competition with other businesses for services and manufacturers.
  - Quickly establish damage assessment and need for services and implement.
- Undersubscription or additional needs remains an issue:
  - Many businesses requested additional needs ATOD from the vendor. This puts recovery and business continuity at risk due to the extended recovery timeline. Contract for what you need.
- Personnel and intellectual property are the keys to recovery:
  - Methodologies, ideas, and documented plans will be utilized.
  - You absolutely must have documented, repeatable processes for recovery of technology.
  - Assign backup roles and succession planning in advance.
  - Provide for intellectual capital and personnel in alternate locations.
  - Consider the use of professional organizations to augment staff.
- Reluctance to travel is a repeated theme:
  - End users generally won't travel far from home.
  - Ensure that adequate end-user facilities are available nearby (within 50 miles).
- Air travel may be unavailable:
  - Allow for delayed delivery of offsite-stored media to recovery location.
  - Identify alternate means of transportation.
  - Assess need for electronic journaling of data to alternate location.
  - Expect that staff will be unable to travel.
  - Identify options for local access by staff to remote alternate systems (and possibly home systems).
  - Assess value of "turnkey" services with vendors.

- Offsite storage is critical:
  - Evaluate for frequency and completeness.
  - Paper records and transactions may be totally lost.
  - Ask if your offsite storage is far enough away to avoid the effects of the disaster.
  - Evaluate the need/value of electronic journaling.
- Advanced recovery solutions can be highly successful:
  - Consider electronic journaling, database Mirroring, SRDF, etc.
  - Data requiring physical transport may be delayed.
- Active testers will be more successful:
  - Those who test frequently were more successful at meeting RTO/RPO.
  - Frequent testers had a more realistic understanding of application performance in recovery.
  - Active testers had fewer problems.
- Plan on very high demand for voice recovery:
  - Realistically evaluate needs, such as line trunking, extensions, call recording, voicemail, and call forwarding to avoid customers receiving a fast busy signal, no answer, or a message stating,"I'm sorry, this number is not in service at this time."
- Logistics will be important:
  - Travel restriction had an impact during 9/11 recovery; you may need to use ground travel for many shipments.
  - Parking, busing, catering, and hotel rooms need to be lined up quickly.
- Getting restoration media to the alternate site may pose a challenge:
  - Transportation may be canceled.
  - Complete set should be available and labeled.
  - Missing or unavailable documentation can be a problem.
  - Prepare start-up scripts in advance.
  - Run instructions should be easily accessible.
- There is value in preplanning staff placement within rooms:
  - Evaluate end-user priorities and usage.
  - Know end-user equipment requirements to avoid setting up more than once.
- It is critically important to have a team leader for each shift.
- Integration of recovery requirements into change control is important:
  - Know the number and positions of PCs.

- Know the network capabilities.
- Know processor, disk, and tape capabilities.
- Know the number and type of printers and fax machines you need.
- Know PBX features and functionality.
- Keep track of platform technology upgrades, changes, and maintenance.
- Quick assessment and implementation of the plan is critical.
- A solid backup-records program is key:
  - Tape, electronic, and paper records are the foundation of recovery.
  - Evaluate the right balance for your company.
  - Document and label records so vendor(s) can assist.
  - Have scripts shipped with restoration media or stored at the alternate location.
  - Back up frequently.
  - Be aware of offsite location and transportation dependencies.
  - Examine the benefit of electronic transmission of offsite storage data, as it can significantly improve recovery time and reduce data loss.
- Evaluate Shared vs. dedicated resources:
  - Dedicated resources guarantee access for the most critical requirements.
  - Complement with shared resources.
- A PC image-restoration tool can be effective:
  - Use Ghost® or a similar technology.
- Basics are fundamental:
  - Establish personnel roles and assign backup.
  - Document methodologies, ideas, business plans, and recovery plans.
  - Review, update, and follow established procedures.
  - Test the way you would recover; recover the way you test.
  - It is worthwhile to review how home procedures apply in alternate-site production mode.
- Revisit your plan and recovery requirements for business and technology often.

The Recovery from Hurricane Katrina

I only had a small office with 40 or so employees in New Orleans, so the recovery from that event was not to the scale of the other two recoveries mentioned here, but there were still some valuable lessons learned.

Fortunately, unlike many other disasters, you can see hurricanes coming, so we began our preparations the week before. A conference call was held with the leadership team for the site, and we discussed preparations the office should make as the hurricane approached—things like making sure that all employees brought their laptops home, covering equipment in the office with waterproof sheeting, validating that all critical files were offsite, communications to employees reminding them of how to determine if the office was open, etc.

On the Saturday morning before the storm was due the following Monday, we agreed that, regardless of the path it took, we would proactively close the office on Monday and allow employees in harm's way to evacuate if they felt the need to do so without worrying about whether the office was going to be open. We made plans for the leadership team to meet again on Monday night after the storm would have passed and then again on Tuesday morning at specific times and on specific phone numbers. When Katrina came through initially, though the storm caused great damage, we felt we had dodged a bullet—until later when the levees broke.

Sometimes 800 numbers do not work following a natural disaster, so the conference bridge number provided could not be used by those who stayed in New Orleans, nor could the contingency information number. That infrastructure was impacted by the storm. We learned to publish the 800 *and* the direct-dial numbers.

If you lease space, it is up to the building owner to decide when you can go back in the building, not you. Our space was near the airport and had little flooding and no significant damage; however, the building management was so worried about mold and lawsuits that they kept the building closed for two months.

Separate the business issues from the people ones. We initially held conference calls with the staff in New Orleans to talk about the office and its contingency plan for the staff, but the claims organization (we are an insurance company) wanted to talk with the local team about cat deployment (a catastrophe response to support the insureds we held policies for). The folks in New Orleans wanted to talk about their homes and their families for the first 15 minutes of the call:—"Did you find your cat yet" "Have you been back to your house yet?" "Do you have power yet?" "How's your mother holding up?"—but the folks from the home office wanted to talk about the claims office, and binding restrictions, and agent communications. Both are very important, but they needed to be separate calls.

Home disaster planning is very important. If people are needed at home, they cannot be at work doing a recovery. The more prepared we are at home, the sooner we will be able to help recover at work.

225

Learn to text-message on your cell phone. If you do not know how, ask any teenager.

Cash is king when ATMs don't work and connections are down to validate credit. If you want to rent a hotel room, lease office space, or buy goods or services, you had better have cash on hand, because if you are standing there with a credit cad and someone else is standing there with cash, even if you agree to pay more the vendor is going to take the cash.

You need a way for employees to reach into the company, not just for the company to reach out to the employees. We had employees who needed help, and we quickly had to convert our contingency information line to an to an "I'm OK" or "I need help" line so that if employees at risk from an event needed help, they could reach into us 24/7.

The mobile unit we contracted to recover this office was ineffective in this event, not because it could not be brought to New Orleans and made operational but because the people scattered. They were all over the place—northern Louisiana, Texas, Arkansas, Alabama, and Georgia. There was no place to bring the unit that had a significant number of employees able to get to it.

It's All About the People

Just before the events of September 11, 2001, occurred, I had accepted a job in another division of the company I was working for. I had not even had a chance to tell my current boss that I was leaving the corporate group to go into a business line in a broader risk-management role when I found myself in a car on the way to New Jersey for what turned out to be nine weeks. I let the other division know that I had to do what was in the best interest of the company, and at that time, it was best that I stayed in New Jersey to support the recovery.

What I observed during those nine weeks was an amazing group of people coming together to accomplish the recovery under extremely stressful and tragic circumstances. Yes, all the work we did planning for a recovery of business operations and all the testing we did gave them a greater chance of being successful, but it was the people—those from New York, those from other areas of the organization who came to support them, and the people who worked for the vendor—who made it happen.

An important factor in this success was taking care of the people. An organization has to demonstrate that it cares about the recovery staff in meaningful ways. Having crisis counselors available, addressing the additional costs people had coming to the facility in New Jersey, keeping them well supplied with food and drinks, regular support from senior leadership, enforcing no more than 12 hours a shift, encouraging the taking of frequent breaks, sharing successes, allowing time off for wakes and funerals, accommodating the need to stay close to their family and not go to New Hampshire—all of these things made a difference to the people. They made them want to be a part of making it through this event as a team, as a company.

Recovery from disasters requires that the management team be prepared to take care of the humans. Abraham Maslow identified the hierarchy of human needs starting with food, clothing, and shelter and noted that, until those needs are met, a human cannot address the needs of the social structure around them. The same is true of humans in a disaster: unless they feel confident that they and their families are safe and have their basic needs met, they will not come to work.

As devastating as September 11 was to the people who lived and worked in lower Manhattan and to the country as a whole, Katrina was a whole different kind of human event. Whole communities were destroyed. People lost loved ones or pets. They lost their cars, their homes, and their sense of security. They had no place to go. They had to pack up their belongings and leave behind everything, with no guarantee as to when they could come back or whether there would be anything to come back to. We did not have a physical alternate site for the New Orleans office to recover to. Because of the size of the office, we contracted for a mobile unit with 50 seats in it. We contemplated declaring, but the problem was that the people scattered. There was no central location where the employees of that office were located to move the trailer to, so we did not use it. Instead, we accommodated those we could in other offices near where the employees and their families evacuated to.

A few of our employees lost everything. A few had only minor damage, and most fell somewhere in between, but everyone, every single one of those people, was impacted. If their home survived Katrina, they had relatives or friends who lost everything living with them, sometimes for months. I don't care how much you love your parents or your siblings and their children, cramming two or three families into a house designed for one family and having them not there just for a visit but for months— it is stressful.

Have a plan for supporting your employees. Have a plan for recognizing their efforts during the recovery and acknowledging the personal impacts the event has had on them. The events of September 11 and Katrina faded from the minds of those not directly impacted as other news and other worries took their place. Not so for those who were there. Not for a long time. When the building in New York was finally repaired and ready to be reoccupied after 15 months in interim sites, we gave up two of the floors. Beautiful views, but no one wanted to be that high again. Some employees resigned or moved to other divisions so they would not have to go back to the city. They never wanted to go to the city again, much less work there every day. The scars from Katrina are still visible everyday in many parts of New Orleans.

Employees and customers remember what you did and did not do for them when they needed you. When I finally left New Jersey, I was part of their family, and years later I still hear from some of them. It has been a few years since Katrina, but every time I go to the office in New Orleans I am greeted as one of them because I was there for them when they needed it most.

Take care of the people. Without them, you cannot do anything. With them, amazing things are possible.

CONCLUSION

It's all about being ready. This is not rocket science. You can make this very complicated if you like, and you can, as I have said, "what-if "yourself to death, but it is really very simple if you take it one step at a time.

One Step at a Time

In summary, the business-continuity and disaster-recovery domain is comprised of the process for determining risks, adopting countermeasures to mitigate those risks, and developing real, tested, and executable plans for continuing the business if the disaster occurs. Contingency plans are what we implement when all other mitigating factors fail.

If you "what-if" yourself to death, the task before you can seem so overwhelming and so complex that you don't event know where to start. So let's go back to the basics for this review:

- Step 1: Convince leadership of the need for a plan. Without leadership support this project will fail. Managers have to commit to the project and allow you to have the resources you need to get it done.
- Step 2: Identify your team. You need at least one person from every functional area of the company to participate in building the plan.

- Step 3: Identify your vital records and make certain they are offsite. Make sure you consider both legal information and operational information. You will need both to continue your business.
- Step 4: Identify your business functions. Have your planning team identify everything your company does and then classify each of those functions based on its time sensitivity in a recovery. Assess what needs to be recovered and when.
- Step 5: Identify all the resources needed to recover. This includes both technology resources such as PCs, applications, telephones, fax machines, and printers as well as human resources—how many people with which skill sets?
- Step 6: Identify your possible recovery strategies. This includes both internal and external recovery options. Identify pros and cons of each solution and perform a cost-benefit analysis to prove whether the risk justifies the cost of the recommended strategy.
- Step 7: Select and implement approved recovery strategies. This includes alternate site selection and build-out.
- Step 8: Document recovery plans. This includes documented, repeatable processes for recovery of both technology and business operations in every site where you do business.
- Step 9: Build a crisis/event-management plan and make it part of the fabric of your business. Events happen every day. Practice your event-management process every day.
- Step 10: Test, test, test.
- Step 11: Maintain and update.
- Step 12: Test again, then again, then again.

When I first started working with the folks who ended up in the recovery after September 11, 2001, they drove me crazy. They asked. "What if it is the whole city of New York, what if all the telecommunications infrastructure is down, what if …?" Finally, frustrated with their "what-ifs," I asked them, "So tell me, what do you have right now?" The answer was, "Well … nothing, I guess." I said, "Let's make a deal. You have nothing, and I am offering you something. It's not perfect, and, yes, you can probably invent a dozen scenarios where this 'something' I am offering you will not work. But for now we are going to figure out how to do the most important pieces of what you do in this building in this other building I am calling an alternate site. Once we figure out how to do it at all, then you can ask me all the 'what-ifs' you want, and we will figure out a way to address them."

What-if is an excuse to do nothing, because nothing you do will ever address every possible scenario an active imagination can invent. *But* you have to start somewhere. Figure out how to do it at all. Start with the support of leadership; find your team, and go. I wish you all the best. Good luck!

The Future of Business Continuity

Business continuity and disaster recovery continue to evolve, but the basic principles remain the same. We have changed the way we recover through the years. The world had changed its expectations of how available we should be. Have you ever heard the term "banker's hours?" Banks used to be open from Monday through Friday from 9 a.m. to 3 p.m. at the latest. If you needed cash, you had to get to the bank and see an actual teller to withdraw money from your account. Everything except churches used to be closed on Sundays. If you needed directions, you bought a map. TV used to be free, but you only got three channels.

Expectations have changed and the business of recovery will continue to evolve, but the reasons we need to be recoverable remain the same—to continue the business. The more competitive an industry, the more recoverability may matter. More companies have built recovery programs because their customers required it. You can write all the regulations in the world, but business takes things seriously when having a plan vs. not having one is a competitive advantage. As the demand for availability grows, as customers demand proof of recovery capabilities before signing the contract, the more the demand for qualified, experienced planners will grow.

The way we recover will continue to evolve. Technology recovery is moving from a recovery strategy to a restart strategy where you never really recover in the way we do today but instead have backup technology in place that simply picks up where the primary center stopped. The introduction of "cloud computing," where we have technology on demand the same as we have utilities on demand, if it ever comes to full maturity, will change the face of the technology environment as we know it. But remember the first two things I said very early in the book that I learned about recovery. Technology recovery is easy. It either works or it doesn't, and how well it works and how fast you recover are entirely dependent on how much you are willing to spend on your recovery. People recovery is *much, much* harder, because people have emotions and needs and fears and families and pets and all kinds of other things that you cannot mitigate against.

Hopefully, now you have your deck chairs open. :)

Appendices

All documents in the Appendix can be downloaded from the following website: www.kelleyokolita.com.

A

Sample Business-Resumption Plan

A copy of the sample plan document included here can be downloaded from the following website: www.kelleyokolita.com.

Sample Business-Resumption Plan

Company Name

Comments or Revisions Please Contact:
John Smith, BCP
Mary Jones, BCP

INTRODUCTION

This sample business-resumption plan is intended as a guide for business-contingency planners to the type of information you would expect to find in a working plan. This sample plan has been produced as one document with a comprehensive table of contents; however, depending on the complexity of your plan, it may be too elaborate for your needs. The plan may be adjusted by adding or deleting sections as needed to match your recovery requirements.

The plan is not intended to be a fill-in-the-blank plan, It is a sample, which you can duplicate or borrow from as appropriate for your business.

Business-recovery planning is a process, not a product. As long as the business continues, technology and business functions change; the plan you develop will need to be continually modified and repeatedly tested.

The plan is organized in sections. Each section includes the type of information that may appear in that section if this were an actual plan. A brief description of each section is listed below:

1. Purpose, objectives, and assumptions: This section defines the purpose of the plan document, the objectives to be accomplished, and the assumptions used in the plan.
2. Recovery strategies: This section briefly describes the strategies the company has developed to respond to an emergency situation.
3. Recovery management: This section describes the organizational structure of the recovery teams and the roles of the management team members.
4. Human-resource management: This section describes how the company will manage the various human-resource issues that may arise during the recovery effort—providing for temporary or contractor help, financial assistance to employees, and help in dealing with family issues.
5. Administrative support: This section describes how administrative functions such as food, travel, and lodging for recovery staff will be managed.
6. Finance issues: This section identifies how finance issues, such as procedures for ordering of equipment or supplies, expense reports, and identification of the cost center for recovery expenses, will be handled during the recovery.
7. Recovery communications: This section identifies how communications will be handled during the recovery process. This includes communication to other employees and business units, communication of the status of the recovery, problem management, and external communications.
8. Plan activation: This section begins by describing the normal process by which an emergency situation is communicated, how the damage assessment is performed, and how a decision to activate the plan is made and by whom. Once the plan is activated, it describes the establishment of the command centers and the emergency-notification process to the recovery teams.
9. Site-recovery plan: This section details the recovery process and the actions that will be executed by the recovery teams as the result

of losing the physical site where business is performed. This section includes a checklist for each recovery-team member during the recovery effort.

10. Business-application recovery plan: This section details the recovery process and the actions that will be executed by the recovery teams as the result of losing the business applications required by the critical functions. This section includes a checklist for each recovery-team member during the recovery effort.

11. Appendices: These sections provide additional information and procedures referred to in the main document.

12. Sample recovery procedures: A sample of a detailed recovery procedure for a site outage and an application outage.

The sample plan makes the assumption that the business being recovered is a large multi-level management organization. If your company is small, you may delete teams or team members to more accurately reflect the size of your organization.

The detailed recovery procedures included in this sample plan document are intended to provide a format for detailing the actual steps to recover a function, whether it is a business function, a server recovery, or a system-application recovery. You may include these as part of the plan or keep them as separate documents referred to in the plan. They are the step-by-step procedures that need to be developed for each critical function performed by your business.

Each critical function must plan how it will recover from a site outage and how it will recover from an application outage.

A *site outage* assumes that the entire building and all of its contents are unavailable and that you must perform the function at another location. If the function must be recovered the same day (AAA, AA, and A functions), then there must be identified in the recovery procedures a contracted alternate site with all necessary facilities to support the function. That means desks, chairs, paper, pencils, calculators, terminals, or PCs with connectivity to all required applications, printers, phones, and other tools. These *must* be in place before a disaster occurs.

An *application outage* assumes that the facility you are in is intact but that you do not have access to the applications required to perform the function. For example, if the data center were to experience an outage, you must plan for a minimum of 24 hours before those applications are returned to you and potentially as much as 72 hours. When the application becomes available, it will be current only to the latest backup taken before the disaster occurred. You must plan how you will perform your critical business function without the application and how you will "catch up" once the application has been made available to you.

For current recovery timeframes for your dependent applications, contact the application-support manager for the application.

QUICK REFERENCE INFORMATION IN AN EMERGENCY

When an emergency happens, you need to know what to do next: gather, assess, decide, mobilize, communicate, and recover:

Gather

In an event where the building the plan is designed for is available, the responding teams will meet in the EOC (emergency-operations center).

Emergency-operations-center locations:

Primary EOC	Conference Room B
Secondary EOC	Conference Room A
Tertiary EOC	Training Center
Virtual EOC	Conference Call
	1-800-555-5555

If an evacuation of the site occurs:

The executive leadership team at the site will initially meet outside following emergency evacuation of the building **at front of the Main Street Building under the Bus Shelter**. If that location becomes unsafe, they will proceed directly to the _____ Hotel at 10 Lincoln Street in Anytown, USA.

If it is clear that we are not getting back into the building, the ERO team will assemble at _____ Hotel, 10 Lincoln Street, Anytown, USA. The first parties there will negotiate for rooms, call into the conference bridge, send necessary communications to responding teams through the notification system to alert them of the location and the conference bridge number for event management.

Assess

Things to consider:

1. Has anyone been hurt?
2. Should staff be sent home?

3. What has been impacted?
4. From initial assessment, how long will we be unable to operate normally if at all?
5. Who owns the problem?
6. Who else needs to know?
7. Who else needs to help?

Decide

Things to consider:

1. If it is just our company, wait to declare as long as necessary, but if other companies are impacted, declare immediately.
2. Once we move the data center, it is a *long* process to come back, but we can start to recover at the alternate site while still trying to recover the primary.
3. Business operations are comparatively easy and inexpensive to move—don't wait on this.

Mobilize

Things to consider:

1. Once you have decided on the initial response, you need to mobilize the appropriate responding teams and put contingency plans in action.
2. Business teams in each business unit in each site must have at least one planner who has built a response plan for the business operations. Once activated, planners will begin to assemble their teams to execute the business recovery based on their plans.
3. Technical teams need to execute their plans based on the site impacted, the type of event, and the technology impacted and on their plans for recovery of that site. Steps could include:
   a. Rerouting phones
   b. Activating voicemail recovery
   c. Retrieving data from offsite storage vendor for recovery of technology
   d. Building desktops in the alternate site
   e. Rerouting networks
   f. Traveling to the data-center alternate site to execute data-center recovery
   g. Activating email recovery

4. Logistics team needs to provide logistical support for recovery teams, such as travel arrangements, rental cars, hotel rooms. GPS devices, alternate-site supplies, laptops, printers, and cell phones, as requested by the responding teams.

Communicate

We need to communicate to our employees, our vendors, our customers, and possibly the media about this event and how we are managing:

1. Employees need to know what to do, where to go, what has happened, and, later, do they still have a job, will they get paid, is everyone else ok, and what about their benefits?
2. Customers need to know what services will be unavailable and for how long and how they can reach us if they need something.
3. Vendors need to know where to send supplies and what we need from them.
4. The media needs a story; if we are going to give them one, let's make it a positive one. One spokesperson, one message, talking points to all who might be asked.

Recover

Business as usual is the goal.

Contingency information line: 800-555-7207 or 555-555-7207	Can be used to record messages for employees to hear or can be reached on "I'm ok" line for employees to reach into the company depending on the event
Alternate site: 200 Center Street, Anytown USA	Contracted for recovery seats for business operations
Alternate-site phone number: 555-555-4500	Main phone number in the alternate site
BCP website: http://bcp.your company.com	General information for all sites/employees on our program
Remote email: http://mail. yourcompany.com	To access email from *any* web connection
Gathering location—XXXXX Hotel, 10 Lincoln Street, Anytown, USA	If you cannot get back into the buildings, meet the EURO team here

238

Report problems or trigger ERO: 555-555-4444	If you want to trigger *any* type of ERO event, call this number
Event conference bridge: 1-800-888-5555 passcode 5082779—does *not* need a leader passcode for all to join	
Notification Website: http://www. notification.com/your_company/	All ERO teams start with ERO (i.e., ERO Crisis management team)—emergency login info: login ID XXXXXX Case-sensitive password ABABA
Remote Access: https://apps. yourcompany.com/	To get to all published CITRIX applications or to remote into your desktop at the office

We have contracted alternate-site service with _____ vendor for the following services:

1. Data-center recovery—hot-site contract in _____ for recovery of the data center
2. Email recovery services—for recovery of our email post office in the event of a outage
3. Alternate site for business operations—in main offices in physical alternate sites
4. A mobile unit with 50 seats for small-office recovery

To declare a disaster with the vendor, use the procedure in Appendix A.

EXECUTIVE OVERVIEW

The goal of the emergency-response organization (ERO) is to respond to and provide management direction during significant emergency situations. ERO will work with management and employees to ensure that at a time of disaster, well-trained employees and support personnel respond immediately to:

- Maintain safety of all individuals in company-occupied space
- Minimize damage to buildings and equipment
- Coordinate response and communication with senior management, employees, media, and customers
- Provide support for recovery of time-sensitive business functions
- Maintain public image

- Maintain positive customer relations
- Minimize and contain physical and electronic breaches to corporate assets
- Comply with legal requirements
- Avoid costly penalties and fines

The emergency management plan is a preestablished document to aid in management decision making in the face of physical or electronic threats, promote effective utilization of resources, and support compliance with notification procedures. The initial procedures deal primarily with notification of first responders, addressing any life-safety issues caused by the event, and securing the scene. Once those issues are resolved, the focus turns to business resumption or recovery. The following assumptions are made as part of the ERO plan:

1. The cause of an event (water damage, loss of power, civil unrest, natural disaster, terrorist attack, chemical spill, etc.) and the impact of the event will vary significantly. The specific events we have planned for are as follows:
   a. Facility event
   b. Technology event
2. For each division the company has implemented and tested procedures for recovery of the critical business functions performed by that division based on the loss of a single site.
3. The technology-services division has implemented and tested procedures for the recovery of critical platforms and applications required to support the business operations.
4. Defined alternate sites will be available at the time of need.
5. To ensure the viability of the plan, adequate testing of the plan components is conducted; and adequate training is given in the use of the plan to all ERO team members.
6. This document, related procedures, and all vital records are stored in a secure offsite location and will not only survive an event but are accessible immediately following an event.

EXECUTIVE SIGNOFF

Note: The company has a policy that requires the senior leader of a business area to be responsible for having a plan and for the contents of the plan document itself; this is where that leader signs off on the plan documentation.

The following business-resumption plan and all related procedures are approved by the President and senior management of _____ Company effective the date below.

Signed by	MM/DD/YY

PLAN MAINTENANCE HISTORY

Note: This information provides an audit trail of the changes made to the plan, when they were made, and the type of change

Original Issue Date   MM/DD/YY

Maintenance Date	Type of Maintenance

SAMPLE PURPOSE, OBJECTIVES, AND ASSUMPTIONS

Purpose of the Plan

The purpose of this plan is to define the recovery process developed to recover this company's critical business functions. The plan components will detail the procedures for responding to an emergency situation that affects the company's ability to provide services to its customers or its ability to meet legal or regulatory requirements.

The plan is organized in sections for easy reference. Each major section deals with a component of the plan beginning with plan activation through restoration of normal operations. The appendices contain information such as forms that may be required during the recovery process, business-application priorities by platform, vendor lists, and other elements.

Objectives of the Plan

Note: These are common business-continuity objectives. You should add the objectives specific to the actual plan document, such as what business it is for or what site it is for:

- Facilitate timely recovery of business functions
- Minimize loss of revenue/customers
- Maintain public image and reputation
- Minimize loss of data
- Minimize the critical decisions to be made in a time of crisis

Plan Overview

The business-resumption plan is organized in the following sections:

1. Purpose, objectives, and assumptions: This section defines the purpose of the plan document, the objectives to be accomplished, and the assumptions used in the plan.
2. Recovery strategies: This section briefly describes the strategies the company has developed to respond to an emergency situation.
3. Recovery management: This section describes the organizational structure of the recovery teams and the roles of the management team members.
4. Human-resource management: This section describes how the company will manage the various human-resource issues that may arise during the recovery effort; providing for temporary or contractor help, financial assistance to employees, and help in dealing with family issues.
5. Administrative support: This section describes how administrative functions such as food, travel, and lodging for recovery staff will be managed.
6. Finance issues: This section identifies how finance issues, such as procedures for ordering of equipment or supplies, expense reports, identification of the cost center for recovery expenses, will be handled during the recovery.
7. Recovery communications: This section identifies how communications will be handled during the recovery process. This includes communication to other employees and business units, communication of the status of the recovery, problem management, and external communications.
8. Plan activation: This section begins by describing the normal process by which an emergency situation is communicated, how the damage assessment is performed, and how a decision to activate the plan is made and by whom. Once the plan is activated,

it describes the establishment of the command centers and the emergency-notification process to the recovery teams.

9. Site-recovery plan: This section details the recovery process and the actions that will be executed by the recovery teams as the result of losing the physical site where business is performed. This section includes a checklist for each recovery-team member during the recovery effort.

10. Business-application recovery plan: This section details the recovery process and the actions that will be executed by the recovery teams as the result of losing the business applications required by the critical functions. This section includes a checklist for each recovery-team member during the recovery effort.

11. Appendices: These sections provide additional information and procedures referred to in the main document.

Assumptions

Note: These are common assumptions you are making about the plan in general. You need to add specific assumptions that you made during the planning process, such as: Are you going to assume that telephones work so you can use them to contact your team? Are you assuming that the staff survives the event and is available to support the recovery? What were your planning assumptions?

This section identifies the assumptions made by the business-resumption plan:

1. The type of disaster (fire, civil unrest, natural disaster, terrorist attack, chemical spill) and the impact of a disaster will vary significantly.

2. Only one building in one geographical location (i.e., Boston, Dallas, Salt Lake, and Cincinnati) will be impacted by a single disastrous event.

3. Contracted alternate sites will be available to the company at the time of need.

4. Adequate training is given in the use of the plan, and all employees are made aware of its existence and their roles within the plan.

5. The plan is tested and reviewed on a regular basis.

6. This document, related procedures, and all vital records are stored in a secure offsite location and not only survive the disaster but are accessible immediately following it.

RECOVERY STRATEGIES

This section describes the recovery strategies identified for company equipment and services.

General recovery strategies:

- Recovery will focus on time-sensitive business processes and applications before other processes will be considered.
- Business functions will be recovered in priority sequence based upon the classification of the function. Changes to priorities will not be made without leadership agreement.
- Communications concerning the recovery status will be coordinated through the command center so that those executing the recovery will not be interrupted repeatedly for status reports.
- Purchase and acquisition of equipment and supplies needed for the recovery effort will be coordinated through the command center as per the instructions in this document.
- The contingency-planning infrastructure detailed in this document will provide for coordination of travel arrangements, food, and accommodations for individuals supporting the recovery effort.
- Noncritical functions such as development and test environments will be cleared without backup as necessary to support the recovery efforts.
- Personnel from other sites may be called in to support the recovery efforts.

Critical-function recovery strategies are shown in the tables below:

Functions by Site

Function	Site(s) where function is performed	Recovery strategy
1. Call center	Boston and Dallas	Surviving site then contracted alternate site
2. Application development	Boston	Work from home
3.		
4.		
5.		

Function by Application Dependencies

Application	Functions that use application and the function time-sensitivity rating	Recovery strategy
1. General ledger	Finance payable/receivable D	Recover from tape ATOD
2.		
3.		
4.		
5.		
6.		
7.		
8.		
9.		
10.		
11.		
12.		

RECOVERY MANAGEMENT

An organization chart appears on the next page. Refer to current emergency-notification list.

(Insert your organization's chart here)

This *is not* the company organization chart. This is the recovery organization chart.

It identifies the recovery-team members by title.

Executive Emergency-Management Team

This team consists of the senior executives who have an overall responsibility for the recovery of the company's business and services. As needed during the emergency, these individuals will participate in the command centers established for the recovery efforts and in EMO (emergency-management organization), a company-wide organization formed to provide both a formal integrated response process for management and onsite coverage/support in emergency situations. The emergency-management team leader has overall responsibility for communications with the executive team.

The executive team does not directly manage the day-to-day operations of the organization under normal circumstances and is not expected to have day-to-day responsibilities in an emergency situation. However, the team will respond to assist in the resolution of issues that may occur as a result of an emergency situation.

Emergency-Management Team for Each Site

These individuals would report directly to the command center and have responsibility to oversee the recovery and restoration process being executed by the emergency-response teams. They are responsible for communicating the recovery status to the executive management team and making the necessary management decisions to support the recovery efforts. The emergency-management team leader has overall responsibility for the recovery team and communications with the executive management team.

The objectives and the functions of this team are:

1. Make a preliminary assessment of the damage.
2. Notify senior management on current status, impact to business, and plan of action.
3. Declare the disaster if necessary.
4. Initiate the plan during the emergency situation.
5. Organize the command centers as a central point of control of the recovery efforts.
6. Organize and provide administrative support to the recovery effort.
7. Administer and direct the problem-management function.

Response Teams for Each Site

These individuals are responsible for executing the recovery processes necessary for the continuity or recovery of critical business functions in that site. These individuals report to the alternate sites for their critical functions to execute the recovery process. They report to the emergency-management team through emergency-response team leaders, who have overall responsibility for the response teams' efforts in those locations.

The response teams may be broken into subteams, each with its own leader to facilitate the recovery effort.

The primary responsibilities of the members of these teams are as follows:

1. Retrieve offsite site records and recover information from offsite site storage
2. Report to the alternate site identified in their procedures
3. Execute the business-recovery procedures for their area of responsibilities in the order of priority identified
4. Communicate the status of the recovery to the command centers as needed
5. Identify issues or problems to be escalated to the management team for resolution
6. Establish shifts for recovery-team members to support the recovery effort 24/7
7. Establish liaison with alternate-site personnel if needed
8. Support efforts to return to normal operations
9. Reestablish support operations affected by the disaster
10. Identify replacement equipment/software needed for recovery effort and to return to normal operations

Command Centers

Command centers are set up as a central location for communications and decision making during an emergency situation. They will be set up in response to the disaster and will be equipped with a copy of the plan document and other resources that may be needed in a disaster.

Command-Center Sites

SITE 1	Primary Command Center	xxx-xxx-xxxx Primary
	Secondary Command Center	xxx-xxx-xxxx Secondary
	Tertiary Command Center	xxx-xxx-xxxx Tertiary
SITE 2	Primary Command Center	xxx-xxx-xxxx Primary
	Secondary Command Center	xxx-xxx-xxxx Secondary
	Tertiary Command Center	xxx-xxx-xxxx Tertiary

HUMAN-RESOURCE MANAGEMENT

Note: Disasters are human events, and human resources plays a critical role in the recovery of an organization's people. If we do not take care of the people, we cannot expect them to take care of business. Give this section to your HR team members and ask them to edit it and make it their own.

Injury to Employee

If an employee is injured as a result of a declared emergency or during the recovery process, the first step is to seek medical attention for the injured employee as quickly as possible. All employees should be made familiar with the emergency numbers in their local area for contacting police, fire, or ambulance services, or the security staff may be contacted to notify the necessary medical assistance.

Once medical attention has been provided for the injured employee, it is important to notify the human-resource representative on the management team as soon as reasonably possible so that appropriate family notifications and paperwork can be completed. Initial information to be provided is as follows:

- Employee name
- Employee company
- Location at time of injury
- Nature of injury (if known)
- Time injury occurred
- Brief description of circumstances under which injury occurred

A form in Appendix P can be used to assist you in preparing this information. This may be faxed to the command center.

Employee Fatalities

In the event that an emergency situation results in the death of one or more employees, it is imperative that the information be communicated to the human-resource representative on the management team as quickly as is reasonably possible. Human-resources staff has been trained to respond to a tragedy such as this so that communication can be made to family members as quickly and compassionately as possible under the circumstances. HR members also have the ability to provide support services to the family if needed as well as to begin the process required to provide financial assistance to the family from insurance or other company benefits.

A phone call to the command center or human-resource representative should be made as soon as possible. Initial information to be provided is as follows:

- Employee name
- Employee company
- Location at time of death
- Time death occurred
- Brief description of circumstances under which death occurred
- Where deceased has been taken (if known)

Temporary Help/Contractors

If you require the support of additional staff during the recovery effort, complete the form in Appendix O and forward via fax to the command center. Every effort will be made to provide any additional help needed to support the recovery effort.

Employees Under Stress

If a disaster has occurred, it is common for employees to exhibit signs of stress. Stress may take the form of headaches, irritability, inability to focus, crying, panic attacks, and many other forms. Human resources will provide support services to employees as needed based on the event to address specific issues or concerns an employee or a manager of an employee may have. In addition, as appropriate, counseling services provided by the company's EAP provider may be made available to staff on an individual or group level.

Family Issues

The company understands that in a disaster situation it must recognize the hardships placed on the families of its response team. To be able to give their best to the company at the time when it is needed most, employees need to have a level of comfort that their family members are safe and that the employees' absence during the recovery effort will not place undue hardship on them.

The level of support to team members will clearly be defined by the nature of the disaster itself. In the case of a natural disaster, where the employee's family may be at risk, the company may provide for temporary relocation of family members or allow the family to accompany the employee to the recovery site. Support may range from facilitating dependent-care services, company-paid travel for employees to return home for a visit or for family members to travel to recovery locations, or cash advances to provide for family needs.

Family issues should be brought to the attention of the human-resources representative as soon as feasible.

ADMINISTRATIVE SUPPORT

Note: We do not often think of our admin support staff as being critical in an emergency, but it is wonderful to have them available in a recovery because they have time to do things that no one else does.

During the recovery effort, administrative-support teams will be deployed to support the recovery efforts as required. The primary team will be located in the command center. Additional teams may be located at recovery sites to provide support such as answering phones, keeping timelines etc.

The primary responsibilities of the administrative-support team are as follows:

1. Answering phones
2. Making pager pages as requested to communicate to recovery staff
3. Making travel arrangements for recovery staff
4. Providing food at recovery locations
5. Keeping minutes of status meetings
6. Distributing information as requested
7. Making copies
8. Arranging courier service
9. Keeping track of the locations of employees
10. Setting up conference bridges

Food, Travel, Lodging

It is each team leader's responsibility to determine the staff's food, lodging, and transportation needs during an emergency situation and to communicate them to the administrative-support representative. Consolidating the requests for these services during an emergency will help ensure the quickest possible response while eliminating redundancy.

The administrative-support representative is responsible for ordering food for the recovery locations and facilitating lodging and transportation, particularly where normal methods of transportation are unavailable.

To order food, complete the information on the form in Appendix G and forward via fax to the command center or contact the admin rep directly and provide the following information:

- Identify the number of meals needed, the times needed, and the locations to which they are to be delivered as well as any special dietary requirements.

For lodging and transportation, complete the form in Appendix H and forward via fax to the command center or contact the Admin rep directly and provide the information.

Travel by Team Members/Travel Arrangements

Travel arrangements through the ongoing recovery efforts will generally be made by the administrative-support team. However, travel arrangements can be made by individual team members, by their management staff, or by the administrative-support staff. All travel arrangements will be made through the company's corporate travel agents, _____ Travel. The number for the travel office in your area, as well as the 24-hour emergency number, is listed in the emergency-notification list.

_____ Travel will make travel, hote,l and rental-car reservations for you. Your tickets may be picked up at the airport or delivered to a the company location at your request.

If you have any difficulty with your travel arrangements, contact ____ _____ Travel directly to resolve. Refer to Appendix E for a list of hotels in the area where a recovery may occur.

Finance Issues

Note: Finance needs to be part of your management team to approve purchases, track recovery costs, etc. Give your finance representative this sheet and ask him or her to modify it.

The cost center and cost pool to be used for all travel, lodging, meals, equipment, cash advances, or any other type of expense related to the recovery effort is _____ (cost center) and _____ (cost pool). This cost center is only effective in a declared disaster. It is imperative that this cost center be used so that all expenses can be tracked for insurance purposes.

Equipment Purchases

General requests for items such as PCs, fax machines, modems, office supplies, PC software, etc., should be requested on the form in Appendix M and faxed to the finance representative of the emergency-management team. Requests will be combined for volume discounts where possible and completed as quickly as possible through existing vendor relationships or if necessary through other vendors.

Purchases may be made directly by recovery-team members using the corporate credit card or through a direct-billing arrangement with the vendor. Existing vendor relationships should be used wherever feasible to facilitate billing and payment for services.

Expense Reports

The normal procedures for submitting expenses reports will continue during the recovery effort. All disaster-related expenses should reference cost center ____. Every effort will be made to reimburse the employee for out-of-pocket expenses as expeditiously as possible.

Cash Advances

Recovery personnel who do not have corporate credit cards can receive cash advances immediately in the event of a declared disaster. To obtain a cash advance, complete the form in Appendix N and forward via fax to the command center. Cash advances will not be issued without this form. It is important that we track expenses related to the recovery effort for insurance purposes. Cash advances will be paid out to the employee within 24 hours of the request.

RECOVERY COMMUNICATIONS
Employee Notification

Employees who are members of the emergency-notification list will be contacted directly in the event of an emergency situation by the responsible management-team member. Employees who are not contacted directly can call the contingency information line at 1-xxx-xxx-xxxx for instructions on where and when to report for work and to receive status reports on the situation.

Internal Business-Unit Communications

Internal communications to the other business units on the status of the recovery will be managed by the emergency-management team member responsible for customer communications and through normal support services.

Communications to the board of directors and senior leadership throughout the firm will be handled by the emergency-management team.

External Communications—Media

External communications will be handled by the corporate communications staff. Any and all press inquiries must be directed to the corporate communications team identified on the emergency-notification list. *Under no circumstances are company employees to provide information to any media representative.* If employees are approached by the media, they should direct them to the communications team.

External Communications—Customers/Clients

Employees who talk with customers and or clients as a part of their normal business day will be provided with a statement or list of statements regarding the recovery effort. *It is important that everyone tell the same story.* Any customer not satisfied with the response provided will be referred to management.

Recovery Status Updates

Recovery status updates will be communicated to the command center by the recovery-team leaders at regular intervals. Recovery status and information on when and where employees are to report to work will be updated to the contingency information line as needed using the procedures in Appendix K.

Problem Management

If a problem is encountered that cannot be resolved by the recovery team and will result in a delay in the recovery of any time-sensitive functions, a special meeting of the impacted recovery-team leader, the emergency-management team, and if needed the executive emergency-management team will be held to determine a course of action to resolve the issue.

Problems will be reported on problem tickets and given to the problem-resolution group for triage, tracking, and coordination of resources.

Communications with Recovery Team
Conference Bridges

During the course of the recovery efforts it may be helpful to establish conference bridges to communicate recovery issues and to coordinate communications between the different recovery locations. To establish a conference bridge, you must do the following:

(Insert your conference-bridge procedures here)

Contingency Notification System

The corporate contingency-planning notification software may be utilized to contact recovery personnel:

(Insert your notification-system procedures here)

Site Recovery

This scenario assumes that the site where you normally perform your business operations or technology services is unavailable to you for some period of time.

If a problem has been identified at a business site, the following steps will be taken by the appropriate teams:

1. Management team follows plan-activation procedures.
2. Authorized management-team member declares a disaster.
3. Any incoming 800 service is redirected as defined in the plan.
4. Management team notifies the alternate site of declaration.
5. Management-team members notify site-response team that a disaster has been declared.
6. Critical-function response teams report to the alternate site to begin recovery.
7. Contact vendor to return offsite records to the recovery site.
8. Facilities team reports to begin damage assessment, repair, and restoration of facility.
9. Management team reports to command-center locations.
10. Client-management team leader provides a statement for all employees to use when talking to customers or clients.

Loss of Site Plan-Activation Checklist

Action	By whom	Comments	Check when done
1. Receive communication on emergency situation	EMT eader	log time	
2. Contact management team and ____ site BCP response team leader	EMT leader	log time	
3. Contact alternate site and alert that disaster may be declared	EMT leader	log time	
4. Assess damage	EMT leader and management team	Network Equipment Building Employees	
5. Estimate	EMT leader and management team	< 1 Hour > 1 Hour–< 2 hours > 2 hours–<12 hours >12 hours–<24 hours >24 hours–<48 hours >48 hours Unknown	
6. Estimate business risk	EMT leader and management team		
7. Make decision; if no declaration, then contact alternate site and inform them alert is over; if decision is to declare, proceed to step 8.	EMT leader		
8. Declare disaster; notify executive team immediately; declare disaster at alternate site as per procedure in Appendix A	EMT leader and management team	log time	

(continued on next page)

255

Loss of Site Plan-Activation Checklist *(Continued)*

Action	By whom	Comments	Check when done
9. Notify EMT leader identified in emergency-notification list using procedure in Appendix C	Management-team leader	log time	
10. Activate command center	EMT leader	log time	
11. Report to command center at ____ site	EMT leader and management team	log time	

PLAN-ACTIVATION PROCEDURES
Emergency Alert

In the event that a situation or disaster occurs, the security staff would contact corporate contingency planning. Corporate contingency planning contacts the business contingency planner for the impacted area. That individual is responsible for contacting the management team and assessing the emergency situation. An alert will be sent to all recovery-team members. A conference bridge may be set up by the BCP response team leader during the damage-assessment phase for team members to contact for status of the alert.

Damage Assessment

During the damage-assessment phase, the management team will identify specifically whom and what has been affected by the disaster. The team leaders will evaluate the event that has occurred and determine which recovery teams will be required to respond to the situation. The decision to activate the disaster-recovery plan for the affected areas may be made at this point or after notification of and review by the executive team.

As part of the damage-assessment process, the risk assessment to the business will be evaluated. If the situation at the ____ site could in any way require recovery at an alternate site, the management-team leader will contact the alternate site and notify it of the disaster alert.

If after assessment it is determined that activation of the recovery plan is required, notification to the executive team will be made. An authorized individual will immediately notify the alternate site that the disaster has been declared using the procedures in Appendix A.

Notification Procedures

Once the disaster has been declared and the decision has been made to activate the business-resumption plan, the emergency-management team will notify the response-team leader. The response-team leader will send another page to the response team to contact the conference bridge. Initial instructions to the response team will be sent through the conference bridge. It is the responsibility of the response-team leaders to coordinate appropriate notification procedures using the emergency-notification list. Initially, only employees who are part of the identified recovery teams will be contacted.

The notification script located in Appendix C should be used when contacting team members, particularly in the event of catastrophic circumstances. The nature and scope of the disaster may not be clearly defined at the time the decision to implement disaster recovery is made. It is important not to cause unnecessary panic among the families of team members. For this reason, as well as to prevent disclosure of the nature and scope of the problem to those outside of the company, it is imperative that information about the disaster be communicated to the team member only. If the team member is not at home, leave a message for him/her to call the phone number at the command center and do not provide any further details.

Command-Center Activation

Once a disaster has been declared, the command centers will be activated. The emergency-management team leader will instruct the management teams from each location to report to the command center. The command center will be equipped with a copy of the plan document and other resources that may be needed in the event of a disaster. It is the management-team leader's responsibility to make certain that the command center is equipped properly and to coordinate any additional resources as needed.

Command-Center Locations

SITE I	Primary Command Center	xxx-xxx-xxxx Primary
	Secondary Command Center	xxx-xxx-xxxx Secondary
	Tertiary Command Center	xxx-xxx-xxxx Tertiary

(continued on next page)

Command-Center Locations *(Continued)*

SITE 2	Primary Command Center	xxx-xxx-xxxx Primary
	Secondary Command Center	xxx-xxx-xxxx Secondary
	Tertiary Command Center	xxx-xxx-xxxx Tertiary

The command centers will become the focal point for management of the recovery process.

SAMPLE CHECKLISTS FOR MANAGEMENT TEAM AND RESPONSE TEAM

Executive Emergency-Management Team Procedures

Note: Customize this checklist to represent your management-team structure. You need one checklist for each team member. The reason for checklists is that no one reads text in a disaster. A checklist is a way to document the steps; if further information is needed or a specific procedure is executed in that step, then you can refer to the procedure and its location. The checklist should be written or at least reviewed and edited by the team member who will be responsible for performing that task. Key roles should have primaries and alternates assigned.

Actions	By whom	Comments
Notification of disaster: declare disaster with recovery EMT leader	Executive EMT leader	
Resume normal activities: you will receive regular status updates as per normal escalation procedures	Executive EMT	
Report to command center for recovery effort as requested by EMT leader [insert command center location]	Executive EMT	
Report to FEMO as requested: 22 floor, 100 Summer Street, provide update on recovery status	Executive EMT leader or member	

Emergency-Management Team Procedures/
Emergency-Management Team Leader

Actions	Comments
1. Receive communication on emergency situation at site	log time
2. Contact site-management team leader in emergency-notification list	log time
3. Notify response-team leader of alert	log time
4. Contact alternate site and notify of disaster alert using procedures in Appendix A	log time
5. Assess damage with team leader	Network facilities Building Employees
6. Estimate length of outage with team leader	Length of outage
7. Estimate business risk	
8. Make decision: If decision is to declare: • Contact executive team immediately • Notify site BCP-response team that disaster has been declared • Have site-management team leader declare disaster with alternate site using procedures in Appendix A • Continue to Step 9 If decision is not to declare: • Have site-management team leader notify alternate site • Notify response-team leader that alert has been withdrawn without declaration	log time
9. Activate command center	log time
10. Report to command center [insert command center location]	log time
11. Direct activities of the management team to facilitate the recovery effort for the site	

(continued on next page)

259

Actions	Comments
12. Communicate status of the recovery on a regular basis to the executive team	
13. Facilitate problem resolution/escalation and coordination between the recovery teams	
14. Establish schedule for management coverage in the command center as needed throughout the recovery effort	
15. Coordinate and chair status meetings with site command center	
16. Maintain timeline of recovery effort in the command center	
17. Facilitate efforts to repair and return to primary site	

Emergency-Management Team Procedure/ Site-Management Team Leader

Action	Comments
1. Receive communication on emergency situation at site from the recovery-team leader	log time
2. With recovery-team leader, assess damage	Computer equipment Network facilities Building Employees
3. With recovery-team leader, estimate length of outage	
4. With recovery-team leader, estimate business risk	
5. With recovery-team leader, make decision: If decision is to declare: • Have recovery-team leader contact executive team immediatel. • Have recovery-team leader notify the response team that the disaster has been declared • Declare disaster with alternate site using procedures in Appendix A	

Action	Comments
• Continue to Step 6 If decision is not to declare: • Notify alternate site • Have recovery-team leader, notify response-team leader that alert has been withdrawn without declaration	
6. Report to the command center	log time
7. Direct activities of the site-management team to facilitate the recovery effort	
8. Approve required recovery purchases up to defined disaster-authorization level	
9. Communicate status of the recovery on a regular basis to the command center	
10. Facilitate problem resolution/escalation	
11. Establish schedule for management coverage in the site command center throughout the recovery effort	
12. Coordinate and chair status meetings with recovery teams and the command center	
13. Provide status updates to the client-relationship management-team member	
14. Maintain timeline of recovery effort in the site command center	
15. Facilitate efforts to repair and return to primary site	

Emergency-Management Team Procedures/
Response-Team Leader

Action	Comments (log time, etc.)	Check when done
1. Receive communication on emergency situation for site		
2. BCP set up alert conference bridge using procedures in Appendix Q		

(continued on next page)

Action	Comments (log time, etc.)	Check when done
3. Contact response team as indicated on the emergency-notification list using notification procedures in Appendix C; notify BCP response-team leader of alert bridge number		
4. Communicate alert status to team members via conference bridge		
5. Prepare for declaration: • Retrieve offsite storage • Instruct team leaders to begin preparing schedules for recovery personnel and to make travel arrangements as needed		
6. If disaster is declared, communicate to response team via conference bridge and continue to step 8		
7. If disaster is not declared, communicate alert cancel to response-team members via conference bridge		
8. Management team reports to the command center; notify recovery-team leader, of your arrival and arrival of team members [insert command center location]		

Emergency-Management Team Procedures/ Human-Resources Representative

Action	Comments
Receive communication on disaster declaration at the site	log time
Contact human-resources staff using procedures in Appendix C to notify them of disaster and where to report	log time
Report to command center [insert command center location]	

Action	Comments
Establish HR representative coverage at the command center 24/7 throughout the recovery effort	
Update contingency information line using procedures in Appendix K	
If injuries or fatalities have occurred, activate HR team member who is trained to respond	
Provide resources for recovery teams by reassigning staff not involved in recovery effort or through temporary or contractor support	
Facilitate cash advances to recovery staff	
Respond to other HR needs as they arise	

Emergency-Management Team Procedures/ Finance Representative

Action	Comments
Receive communication on disaster declaration at the site	log time
Contact finance staff using procedures in Appendix C to notify them of disaster and where to report	log time
Report to command center [insert command center location]	
Establish finance-representative coverage at the site command center 24/7 throughout the recovery effort unless otherwise directed by the site-management team leader	
Activate disaster-recovery cost center	
Provide channel for authorization of expenditures by recovery team	
Record emergency extraordinary costs and expenditures	
Provide immediate cash advances to recovery staff with team approval	
Work with purchasing to facilitate the ordering of replacement supplies and equipment for immediate delivery	
Provide immediate payment for expenditures when required to facilitate recovery effort	

263

Emergency-Management Team Procedures/ Systems-Team Leader

Action	Comments
Receive communication on disaster declaration at the site	log time
Contact systems staff to notify them of disaster and to activate the technical recovery plan for the site	log time
Report to command center [insert command center location]	
Establish systems-representative coverage at the command center at the site 24/7 throughout the recovery effort	
Provide resources and support to facilitate systems-recovery efforts for site	
Provide channel for authorization for equipment expenditures by systems-recovery team	
Participate in status meetings with recovery teams and command center	
Provide leadership and direction as needed to systems team involved in the recovery effort	
Manage process required to restore systems to normal operation	

Emergency-Management Team Procedures/ Client-Relationship Representative

Action	Comments
1. Receive communication on disaster declaration	log time
2. Contact client-relationship staff using procedures in Appendix C and notify them of the disaster and where to report	log time
3. Work with public relations to develop scripts of information to be used by phone representatives and client managers in response to client concerns	
4. Contact critical customer/client companies with information regarding the disaster declaration for the site	
5. Report to command center [insert command center location]	

Action	Comments
6. Establish client-representative coverage at the command center 24/7 as needed throughout the recovery effort	
7. Obtain updated status and update the contingency information line every two hours using procedures in Appendix K	
8. Attend status meetings with client companies as requested	
9. Participate in status meetings with recovery teams and command center	
10. Bring client issues and concerns to the attention of the EMT leader	
11. Provide support and direction to the client-services team throughout the recovery effort	

Emergency-Response Team/Response-Team Leader/Site

Action	Comments (log time, etc.)	Check when done
1. Receive communication on disaster declaration for site		
2. Contact team leaders as indicated on the emergency-notification list using notification procedures in Appendix C		
3. Report to alternate site for recovery as identified in Appendix D; notify command center upon your arrival and arrival of team members		
4. Determine status of recovery		
5. Maintain recovery timeline for critical function recovery		
6. Compile list of team members from team leaders at each location and send to HR representative at command center for food, beverage, and lodging requirements during the recovery effort		
7. Provide regular status updates to the command center		

(continued on next page)

265

Action	Comments (log time, etc.)	Check when done
8. Facilitate the resolution of recovery issues as they arise		
9. Escalate issues that require management decision/approval for resolution.		
10. Identify additional resource needs (administrative and technical support) and escalate to the command center for resolution		
11. Establish schedule for recovery-team leader coverage 24/7		
12. After critical function recovery is complete, identify requirements for return to normal operations		
13. Manage team to return operations to primary site when available		

Emergency-Response Team/ Critical-Function Team Leader/ Site Recovery

Note: You want to create one of these for each critical function you will recover. Modify as needed to match your business or create a new checklist.

Action	Comments (log time, etc.)	Check when done
1. Receive communication on disaster declaration for site		
2. Contact team as indicated on the emergency-notification list using notification procedures in Appendix C; tell them to report to alternate site		

Action	Comments (log time, etc.)	Check when done
3. Report to alternate site as identified in Appendix D; notify recovery-team leader of your arrival and arrival of team members		
4. Determine status of critical-function recovery if already begun		
5. Oversee the critical-function restoration to completion		
6. Communicate recovery status to recovery-team leader to update recovery timeline for critical-function recovery		
7. Escalate issues to command center through recovery-team leader,		
8. Attend status meetings at command center		
9. Facilitate the resolution of technical-recovery issues as they arise		
10. Escalate issues that require management decision/approval to recovery-team leader for resolution.		
11. Identify additional resource needs (administrative and technical support) and escalate to the recovery-team leader for resolution		
12. Establish schedule for recovery team 24/7 including management support as needed		
13. Identify staff at each location through team leaders and give to recovery-team leader for food, travel, accommodation, and expense needs		
14. After completion of critical-function recovery, determine requirements to return to normal operations		
15. Manage team to return operations to primary site when available		

Emergency-Response Team/
LAN-Recovery-Team Leader/Site Recovery

Action	Comments (log time, etc.)	Check when done
1. Receive communication on disaster declaration for site		
2. Contact server administrators for site as indicated on the emergency-notification list using notification procedures in Appendix C		
3. Contact offsite-storage team leader to validate retrieval of server backups and delivery time to alternate site		
4. Make travel arrangements to alternate site		
5. Report to alternate site as identified in Appendix D; notify recovery-team leader of your arrival and arrival of team members		
6. Execute server-recovery plan		
7. Communicate recovery status to recovery-team leader to update recovery timeline		
8. Escalate issues to command center through recovery-team leader		
9. Attend status meetings with command center		
10. Facilitate the resolution of server-recovery issues as they arise		
11. Escalate issues that require management decision/approval to recovery-team leader for resolution		
12. Identify additional resource needs (administrative and technical support) and escalate to the recovery-team leader for resolution		
13. Establish schedule for server-support team 24/7 as needed to support the recovery efforts		
14. Identify server staff at each location through team leaders and give to recovery-team leader for food, travel, accommodation, and expense needs		

Action	Comments (log time, etc.)	Check when done
15. After completion of server recovery, return to normal operations at alternate site		
16. Manage project to restore LANs at primary site and participate in team to return operations to primary site when available		

Emergency-Response Team/Systems Team/Site

1. Receive communication on disaster declaration for site		
2. Contact systems-team members using notification procedures in Appendix C		
3. Verify that offsite-storage leader has contacted offsite vendor for retrieval of backups and delivery to alternate site		
4. Report to alternate site as identified in Appendix D; notify BCP team leader of your arrival and arrival of team members		
5. Instruct systems team to execute recovery procedures for critical systems for site; critical systems are identified in Appendix J		
6. Communicate recovery status to BCP team leader to update recovery timeline		
7. Escalate issues to BCP team leader		
8. Identify additional resource needs (administrative and technical support) and escalate to the BCP team leader for resolution		
9. Establish schedule for systems team 24/7 including management support as needed		
10. Identify systems staff at each location through team leaders and give to BCP team leader for food, travel, accommodation, and expense needs		
11. Identify replacement equipment needed to restore primary site and provide to facilities team leader		
12. Participate in team to return operations to primary site when available		

Emergency-Response Team/Offsite-Storage Leader/Site Recovery

Action	Comments (log time, etc.)	Check when done
1. Receive communication on disaster declaration for site		
2. Contact offsite vendor for delivery of offsite storage to alternate site using procedure in Appendix B		
3. Contact records team using notification procedures in Appendix C		
4. Report to alternate site as identified in Appendix D; notify BCP team leader of your arrival and arrival of team members		
5. Unpack storage boxes and recovery procedures and deliver to groups as needed		
6. Communicate recovery status to BCP team leader to update recovery timeline		
7. Escalate issues to BCP team leader		
8. Identify additional resource needs (administrative and technical support) and escalate to the BCP team leader for resolution		
9. Establish schedule for records team 24/7 as needed		
10. Identify records-team members to team leader for food, travel, accommodation, and expense needs		
11. Participate in team to return operations to primary site when available		

Emergency-Response Team/
Critical-Function-Recovery Team/Site Recovery

Action	Comments (log time, etc.)	Check when done
1. Receive communication on disaster declaration for site		
2. Contact additional recovery-team members as requested using notification procedures in Appendix C		
3. Report to alternate site as identified in Appendix D; notify critical-function team leader of your arrival and arrival of your team members		
4. Execute the recovery procedures for your critical functions in priority sequence		
5. Communicate recovery status to critical-function team leader to update recovery timeline		
6. Escalate issues through critical-function team Leader		
7. Identify additional resource needs (hardware, telephones, copy machines, office supplies, computer software, etc.) and escalate to the critical-function team leader for resolution		
8. Identify additional human-resources needs (administrative and technical support) and escalate to the critical-function team leader for resolution		
9. Establish schedule for recovery team 24/7 for duration of recovery effort as needed		
10. Identify recovery-team members to critical-function team leader for food, travel, accommodation, and expense needs		
11. After completion of critical-function recovery, identify requirements to return to normal operations		
12. Participate in team to return operations to primary site when available		

Emergency-Response Team/Facilities Team/Site Recovery

Action	Comments (log time, etc.)	Check when done
1. Receive communication on disaster declaration for site		
2. Report to site and with properties, systems, facilities, and insurance representative perform complete damage assessment		
3. Identify equipment and facility damage		
4. Communicate primary-site status to command center and estimate repair time		
5. Prepare list of equipment needs (hardware, software, office supplies etc.) to be replaced and provide to command center for approval		
6. Work with properties to contract for clean-up and repair of facility		
7. Work with finance and properties to order replacement equipment and supplies		
8. Oversee and validate facility repair to completion		
9. Validate that replacement equipment is installed and tested		
10. Participate in project to return operations to primary site and resume normal operations		

RECOVERY PLAN FOR LOSS OF BUSINESS APPLICATIONS

Note: This scenario assumes that your facility is available to you but applications upon which you are dependent are not available.

If a disaster has been declared, the following steps will be taken by the appropriate teams:

1. Business-contingency planner is notified that a disaster has occurred that will prevent all sites from connecting to business applications.
2. Business-contingency planner notifies management team of the disaster declaration.

3. Management-team members notify site response team that a disaster has been declared.
4. Management team reports to command-center locations.
5. Management team identifies impact to critical business functions.
6. Identified critical-function response teams begin manual or alternate application recovery.
7. When application is returned, recovery procedures to update application to current status are executed.
8. Client-management team leader provides statement for all employees to use when talking to customers or clients.

Command Center Locations

Management Command Center [list functions]

Primary Command Center	xxx-xxx-xxxx	Primary
Secondary Command Center	xxx-xxx-xxxx	Secondary
Tertiary Command Center	xxx-xxx-xxxx	Tertiary

Critical Function(s) Command Center [list functions]

Primary Command Center	xxx-xxx-xxxx	Primary
Secondary Command Center	xxx-xxx-xxxx	Secondary
Tertiary Command Center	xxx-xxx-xxxx	Tertiary

The command centers will become the focal point for management of the recovery process. Video-conference rooms have been specifically established as command centers to facilitate the coordination of recovery efforts and communication from multiple locations.

Loss of Data Center Plan-Activation Checklist

Action	By whom	Comments	Check when done
1. Receive communication on emergency situation	EMT leader	log time	
2. Contact management team and BCP-response team leader	EMT leader	log time	
3. Determine which functions are impacted by outage	EMT leader and management team		

(continued on next page)

Action	By whom	Comments	Check when done
4. Estimate length of outage	EMT leader and management team	Length of outage: < 1 hour > 1 hour–<2hours > 2 hours–<12 hours >12 hours–<24 hours >24 hours–<48 hours >48 hours Unknown	
5. Estimate business risk	EMT leader and management team		
6. Make decision: if no declaration, then return to normal operations and inform team alert is over; if decision is to declare, proceed to step 8	EMT leader		
7. Declare disaster, notify executive team immediately	EMT leader and management team	log time	
8. Notify emergency-response team leader identified in emergency-notification list using procedure in Appendix C	Management-team leader	log time	
9. Activate command centers	EMT leader	log time	
10. Report to management command center	EMT leader and management team	log time	

PLAN ACTIVATION
Emergency Alert

In the event that a situation or disaster occurs at the data center, the security staff would contact corporate contingency planning. Corporate contingency planning contacts the impacted business-contingency planners. Business-contingency planners are responsible for contacting the management team and assessing the emergency situation. An alert will be sent to all recovery-team members. A conference bridge may be set up by the BCP response-team leader during the damage-assessment phase for team members to contact for status of the alert.

Impact Assessment

During the impact-assessment phase, the management team will identify specifically whom and what have been affected by the disaster. The team leaders will evaluate the event that has occurred and determine which recovery teams will be required to respond to the situation. The decision to activate the disaster-recovery plan for the affected areas may be made at this point or after notification and review with the executive team.

As part of the impact-assessment process, the risk assessment to the business will be evaluated. If after assessment it is determined that activation of the recovery plan is required, notification to the executive team will be made.

Notification Procedures

Once the disaster has been declared and the decision has been made to activate the business-resumption plan, the emergency-management team will notify the BCP response-team leader. The BCP response-team leader will send another page to the response team to contact the conference bridge. Initial instructions to the response team will be sent through the conference bridge. It is the responsibility of the response-team leaders to coordinate appropriate notification procedures using the emergency-notification list. Initially, only employees who are part of the identified recovery teams will be contacted.

The notification script located in Appendix C should be used when contacting team members, particularly in the event of catastrophic circumstances. The nature and scope of the disaster may not be clearly defined at the time the decision to implement disaster recovery is made. It is important not to cause unnecessary panic among the families of team members. For this reason, as well as to prevent disclosure of the nature and scope of the problem to those outside of the company, it is imperative that information about the disaster be communicated to the team member only. If the team member is not at home, leave a message for him/her to call the phone number at the command center and do not provide any further details.

Command-Center Activation

Once a disaster has been declared, the command centers will be activated. The recovery emergency-management team leader will instruct the management teams from each location to report to the command center. The command center will be equipped with a copy of the plan document and other resources that may be needed in the event of a disaster. It is the recovery-team leader's responsibility to make certain that the command center is equipped properly and to coordinate any additional resources as needed.

Command-Center Locations

Management Command Center:

Primary Command Center	xxx-xxx-xxxx	Primary
Secondary Command Center	xxx-xxx-xxxx	Secondary
Tertiary Command Center	xxx-xxx-xxxx	Tertiary

Critical-Function Command Center:

Primary Command Center	xxx-xxx-xxxx	Primary
Secondary Command Center	xxx-xxx-xxxx	Secondary
Tertiary Command Center	xxx-xxx-xxxx	Tertiary

The command centers will become the focal point for management of the recovery process. Video-conference rooms have been specifically established as command centers to facilitate the coordination of recovery efforts and communication from multiple locations.

Note: I did not repeat the checklists for each team and team member as it would be redundant, but you want to provide the same checklist format for this type of event as well.

Note: The following pages contain common procedures or information that is referred to within the sample plan document.

Appendix A: Disaster Declaration Procedures

In the event of a declared disaster, certain individuals have the authorization to declare a disaster with the designated offsite vendor. Authorized individuals only will be allowed to make a declaration on behalf of the company. For a current list of authorized individuals, see below. The vendor will require a password for declaration. Passwords will be provided to those team members who are authorized to declare.

The following individuals, in the order shown, are authorized to declare a disaster for the company at the alternate site:

1. _____
2. _____
3. _____
4. _____
5. _____

To declare a disaster, execute the following procedures:

(Insert procedures for declaring a disaster including contacts for alternate-site declaration. Any passwords should be distributed to authorized members seperately.)

Appendix B: Offsite Procedures

Handling of Offsite Recovery Media

In the event of a declared disaster, certain individuals have the authorization to coordinate with the designated offsite vendor. Authorized individuals only will be allowed to release the data from the offsite storage location. For a current list of authorized individuals, contact the offsite-storage team leader. The offsite vendor will require a password for delivery of the offsite media. Passwords will be provided to those team members who are authorized to retrieve data.

The offsite vendor will work with one of the authorized employees to expedite the tape media to the alternate site. Management will continually be updated while shipment is in transit to the alternate site.

Contact names for offsite-storage vendors are as follows in the preferred order:

VENDOR NAME/ADDRESS/PHONE NUMBER/

Name	Phone no.	Pager no.
1. Name	XXX-XXX-XXXX	XXX-XXX-XXXX
2. Name	XXX-XXX-XXXX	XXX-XXX-XXXX

Appendix C: Call-Notification Script

This procedure is to be used by all employees when contacting other employees at home to notify them of the occurrence of a disaster. The purpose of this procedure is to standardize the information given to employees regarding a disaster and to prevent disclosure of information regarding the disaster to anyone outside of the company. Anyone making phone calls as a result of a disaster should also be cognizant of the fact that it is possible that the employee was at the site of the disaster when it occurred. Using this script will prevent unnecessary panic for the family members of the employee.

Contacting via phone:

"Hello, may I speak with _____, please?"

If employee is not home, state the following:

"When he/she returns, would you ask him/her to please contact me immediately at the following number (command center, conference bridge, or location where you will be)?"

If employee is at home, explain the following:

- Give the employee a brief description of the situation that has occurred, what it has impacted, and an estimate of the length of outage if known.
- Tell the employee where to report and when and how long he or she should expect to stay.
- Remind him or her to bring any recovery procedures along.
- If travel arrangements have been made for the employee, inform him or her of what they are.
- If travel arrangements are to be made by the employee, inform him or her of where and when he or she is expected and verify that he or she has the information to make the arrangements.
- If the employee is to remain at home, inform him or her to remain on call and prepared to report to work.
- Remind the employee that he or she is not to speak to anyone regarding the situation.

Contacting through page or text messaging to cell phone:

Alpha pagers—send text message to response team:

Alert message/disaster alert: contact xxx-xxx-xxxx, access code xxxxxx, immediately.

Declare message/disaster declared: contact xxx-xxx-xxxx, access code xxxxxx, immediately.

Numeric pagers—send bridge number and access code.

When the employee contacts the bridge, provide the same information as listed above for direct phone contact.

Appendix D: Recovery Locations and Travel Directions

Alternate Site _____

Critical function	Alternate site

Alternate Site _____

Critical function	Alternate site

Note: Provide directions to all alternate sites. Include address and phone number of site. Include maps and floor plans.

Appendix E: Hotels near the Recovery Facility

Note: If travel to the alternate site will be necessary for any team or team member, insert a list of hotels near the facility with necessary contact information so that this information does not have to be located during the event.

Appendix F: Caterers near the Recovery Facility

Note: You are most likely going to have to feed people during the early stages of recovery, so having a list on hand of caterers who will deliver to the alternate site will be very helpful. If you use the same caterers when you do an exercise, you can find out which ones are good and establish a relationship with them so at a time of disaster, they may be more willing to provide services on short notice.

Appendix G: Food Request

Recovery Location: _____

Number of individuals: _____

Meals: ____Breakfast ____Lunch ____Dinner ____Snack

Time: _____ _____ _____ _____

Number of days required _____

Any individuals with special dietary requirements? ____Yes ____No

If yes, what are they? _____

Any special requests?_____

Requested by _____

Appendix H: Travel and Accommodations Request Form

Employee name	Recovery location	Travel to/from	Date of travel	Hotel Y/N	# of nights	Company credit card Y/N	Cost center
1.							
2.							
3.							
4.							
5.							
6.							
7.							

Requested by _____ Date _____

Appendix I: Business Function Recovery Order of Priority

List functions by site in order of priority for recovery.

Site 1

Function	Priority of recovery

Site 2

Function	Priority of recovery

Appendix J: Internal Business Systems Priority

Site 1

Application	Platform (mainframe, desktop, server)	Priority of recovery

Site 2

Application	Platform (mainframe, desktop, server)	Priority of recovery

Appendix K: Updating the Corporate Contingency Information Line

To update the contingency information line, the client-relationship group will contact corporate contingency planning as listed in the emergency-notification list with the updated information as required. The corporate contingency-planning group will perform the updates. Once completed, the client-relationship group will verify the update is complete and accurate.

The information to be updated to this line is general information regarding the status of the recovery process and information for employees on when and where to report.

If employees may be at risk from the impacts of the event, the line can be converted to an "I'm ok" or "I need help" line for employees to communicate with the company about their whereabouts and whether they need any assistance from the company. This is done by notifying the corporate contingency staff and asking them to activate the process. Depending on the nature of the events, the line will then instruct employees to leave a message as to their location and contact information, or the employee can be directed to a live response.

Please note that the contingency information line is an unrestricted 1-800 number and as such could be accessed by individuals outside the company. This line is to be used for communications to employees concerning when they will be needed to report to work, not for detailed updates on the recovery effort.

Appendix L: Problem Reporting/Change-Management Procedure

Note: Document how you want to manage this process during the recovery.

Problem Ticket

Business Function or Application_____ Name_____

Problem description Include application and describe the issue/problem	Criticality Does this prevent you from performing your critical functions?	Suggested resolution If you have one	Comment

Appendix M: Purchase Requisition

Today's date / /	Disaster Recovery Purchase			Requisition Requisition Number	
Date required / /	Requisitioned name		Telephone number	Recovery location	Suggested vendor Name and address Telephone and contact
QTY	Descrip-tion	Estimated price	Actual price	Proposed delivery date	General-ledger account Company ____ Account number ___ Cost center ____

Shipping instructions	Approvals Date
_____	_____ / /
_____	_____ / /
Contact name/mail zone/phone number	

Appendix N: Cash-Advance Form

Employee name	Employee date of birth	Social Security #
Address		Corporate ID#
		Telephone #
Brief Description of circumstances under which cash advance is requested		
Signature of employee	Date	
Signature of employee manager	Date	

Appendix O: Contractor/Temporary Reassignment Staffing Form

Contractor/Temporary Reassignment Staffing Requisition

Company: _____ Division cost center _____

Phone number: _____ Mail zone: _____

Duration of REQ: _____ REQ end date: _____

Position/title: _____ Target rate: _____

What are required skills? _____

What hours will the employee work? _____

What location will the employee work at?_____

Fax to command center for approvals:

Manager_____

Division head_____

Finance _____

Senior VP, Development/operations _____

CFO_____

President _____

Appendix P: Injury Report Form

Employee name	Employee date of birth	Employee ID
Address		Company name
		Telephone #
Location at time of injury	Date of injury month/day/year __/__/__	Time of injury
Name of individual making report _____ Injured employee? Yes No Other: _____	Was employee taken to hospital? Yes No Name of hospital _____	Nature of injury
Brief description of circumstances under which injury occurred: _____ _____		
Signature of employee or individual making report		

Appendix Q: Conference Bridges

(Insert your procedures for establishing a conference bridge into this section of the plan.)

Conference bridges can be used as virtual command centers, virtual town meetings, as a vehicle for coordinating between teams recovering in different sites, and for updating the status of the recovery.

Appendix R: Inbound 800 Service

List all inbound 800 service that comes into each site and where the calls should be directed to in the event that the site is not available.

Site 1

Inbound 800 service	Redirect service to the following

SAFETY AND EMERGENCY PROCEDURES

There is a Fire

If you find it:

1. *Immediately* call 911.
2. Activate the nearest pull station located at each stairwell, exit, or lobby area.
3. Follow the evacuation procedures and instructions given by the public-address system or your fire warden.

If you hear the public-address system or fire alarm:

1. *Stay calm.* Follow the instructions broadcast over the public-address system.
2. Follow the evacuation procedures and instructions given by your manager or fire warden.
3. Do not attempt to retrieve items from your workspace.

There is Severe Weather

Follow these instructions:

1. If you are at home, call the contingency information line (800-555-5555 or 555-555-7207) for the most up-to-date information regarding a possible business interruption as well as general employee instructions or contact your manager.

2. Check your local radio and/or TV stations for broadcast announcements.
3. Remember, property damage may require that you report to work at a different location. Contact your manager for instructions.
4. If you are at work and evacuation or release is necessary, follow the instructions broadcast over the public-address system, call the contingency information line, or ask your manager.

Evacuation of Your Area is Announced

Every time you are evacuated from your site, when possible, always bring your car keys and wallets or purses with you. You may not be allowed back in the building. Follow these guidelines:

1. *Some routes may not be safe.* Follow your fire warden out of the building.
2. *Do not* use the elevators for an emergency evacuation.
3. Walk quickly when directed to do so, but do not run.
4. *Do not* go back to retrieve personal belongings or for any other reason until authorized to do so by the fire department.
5. Proceed to the predesignated evacuation site for your building.
6. Wait for further instructions from your manager, fire warden, or local emergency responders.

Medical Assistance is Needed

If someone in your area needs medical assistance, follow these instructions:

1. *Immediately* call 911.
2. Provide your name, location, phone number, and any information about the illness or injury. *Do not hang up* until the dispatcher confirms the information.
3. Don't attempt first aid if you are not qualified. It could lead to further injury.
4. Keep someone with the injured person at all times.
5. If possible, have someone stay at the call-back number.
6. If possible, have someone meet the emergency responders at the front entrance.
7. If *you* need medical assistance, *immediately* call 911 and stay at your original location until help arrives.

You Receive a Bomb Threat

Follow these instructions:

1. *Remain calm.*
2. Take notes. Note the exact time and duration of the call. Try to find out the location of the caller, the type of device, and the detonation time.
3. *Listen* for distinguishing characteristics, such as quality of voice, accent, background noise(s), age, gender, etc.—this is *very important*.
4. *Immediately* call corporate security at 555-555-2610.
5. Notify your manager and await further instructions. *Do not* discuss the call with your peers or others in the area.
6. Follow the directions of building-security officers, fire wardens, or public-address broadcasts if an evacuation is necessary.

An Unauthorized Person is in Your Workspace

If a stranger has entered your work area, follow these instructions:

1. *Immediately* report all unauthorized people to local authorities by calling 911.
2. Relate the following characteristics to the dispatcher:
   - Physical description (clothing, height, hair color, gender, age, distinguishing marks, etc.)
   - Location of sighting and possible direction the individual was heading
3. *Prevent piggybacking*—do not allow people whom you do not recognize to follow you through a door.
4. *Immediately* report any mechanical lock or card-reader problems to building security at 555-555-2610.

A Suspicious Package is in Your Workspace

Here's what to do if you spot a suspicious package or parcel:

1. *Remain calm* and *immediately* report all suspicious packages to corporate security at 555-555-2610.
2. If a biological or chemical agent is suspected, isolate employees who have come in contact with the package.
3. Remove all personnel from the area where the package is located and *do not* touch the package
4. Corporate security will ask a series of questions to help determine the appropriate response.

BUILDING AN ENTERPRISE-WIDE BUSINESS CONTINUITY PROGRAM

There is a Threat of Workplace Violence

Employees who have any concerns about the threat of workplace violence should inform their manager, human resources, or security immediately. In an emergency or a situation of immediate serious threat:

1. *Immediately* call 911.
2. Notify local building security, then call corporate security at 555-555-2111 as soon as possible.
3. *Immediately* contact your manager.

Corporate Security will take information from you and contact the threat-assessment team, which will review the situation and determine next steps.

B

Sample Initial-Response Plan for Small Sites

Business-Continuity
Initial-Response Plan

Acme Company
(Enter location)

Author:
Date:

Emergency or fire	
Security	
Medical	
Local fire/emergency services	
Corporate communications	555-555-3099
Event-management conference bridge	800-555-2113 Access code 5552779
Technology-support center	555-555-4444
Severe-weather line	800-555-7207 or 555-555-7207
Corporate travel	travel@yourcompany.com, (555) 555-2496, or (800) 555-9145
Corporate travel 24-hour emergency	1-800-555-7457, membership code _____
Local radio station	
BCP website	http://bcp.yourcompany.com

BUSINESS-CONTINUITY PLANNERS

The purpose of selecting a business-continuity planner (BCP) is to designate a single person with appropriate backup to serve in a coordination capacity for the office. Responsibilities of the BCP include liaison with the emergency-operations center, coordination of site efforts during plan development and recovery, and delegate authority to execute recovery procedures.

Name	Team role	Office phone	Cell phone or pager	Email address

ERO—EVENT-MANAGEMENT TEAM

The goal of the company emergency-response organization (ERO) is to respond to and provide management direction during significant emergency situations. For each ERO team member, please provide an alternate person who can serve as a backup if necessary.

Name	Title	Office phone	Cell phone or pager	Email address

FLOOR WARDENS

Every site must have at least two trained floor wardens, regardless of the number of employees. Larger offices should have a ratio of one floor warden to every 20 employees.

Name	Office phone	Email address

ESTABLISH CONFERENCE-BRIDGE PROCEDURES

Conference calls or conference bridges are tools designed to allow numerous parties to conduct two-way discussions on a particular topic. Usually a call-in number is established and is either published or communicated via pagers.

Action Steps for Conference Bridges

Step	Action
1	Obtain senior-management approval on strategy and cost.
2	Determine conference-bridge procedures with input from all business units.
3	Establish number with company vendor____ Conference-Bridge Services, 1-888-555-1119 or 555-555-4018.
4	Train participants on procedures and use of conference bridge.
5	Test conference bridge, capture any action items, and enhance procedures.

Conference Information	
Conference bridge #:	
Pass code:	

IDENTIFY FUNCTIONS

Identify the business functions performed at your site.

Business function	Can function be performed at home?

SEVERE WEATHER AND OTHER LIMITED SITE EVENTS

Task	Assigned to
Initial communication: 1. Report potential severe-weather situation to 1-555-555-4444 (service center) 2. Communication will be sent to appropriate ERO team to assess event with meeting instructions (time and conference-bridge number), 1-800-555-2113 Access code 5552779 or access code 5555550	Site security or site facilities Service center
Initial assessment: 1. ERO team will assess potential impact to operations and probability of impact to the site 2. ERO team will make decision or defer decision and schedule follow-up call	ERO crisis-management team ERO crisis-management team
If decision is to early release, delay start, or close site, the following steps will be taken at the direction of the site leadership: • Notify home office by contacting 555-555-4444 • Home office will update contingency information/severe-weather line • Reroute 800 numbers as needed • Update switchboard messages • Home office will prepare and send email to all other sites to inform of site impact • Home office or branch administration may at the direction of the site-management team send communication to the agency plant of the office closure • If event is expected to be long-term site outage, the site-management team will make decision to declare at alternate site using the plan-activation checklist or defer decision and schedule follow-up call	
Monitor conditions until termination of the emergency	All

WHERE TO GO IF YOU CANNOT GET BACK INTO YOUR BUILDING

Every time you are evacuated from your site, when possible always bring your car keys and wallets or purses with you. You may not be allowed back in the building.

Event impact	General employee response	BCP/recovery teams
Site unavailable	Unless otherwise instructed by your manager, when released by fire warden, go home until your manager calls you. After two hours call the contingency information line, 555-555-7207 or 800-555-7207, for further instructions	After releasing employees, gather at ___ Hotel, 100 Main Street, to discuss next steps

ALTERNATE-SITE LOCATIONS FOR OFFICE

Event	Short-term	Short-/ medium-term	Long-term
Site outage	Surviving sites, work from home	Mobile recovery unit	Mobile recovery unit and new facility

The Vendor will deliver a ready-to-use mobile recovery unit right to our location. They can get one to our site **within 48 hours of your call.** The facility will be fully operational within one hour of arrival and will then need to be prepared with our desktop images. It's a complete end-user recovery option, with almost 1,400 square feet of space that houses everything employees need to resume productivity: server and desktop environments, voice and data communications, even terminals, printers and climate support.

Seat Assignments at the Alternate Sites

Recovery facility has 50 seats preconfigured; if this is sufficient to support entire staff, no specific seat assignments are required. Otherwise, document how many seats are assigned to each business function.

Business function	# of seats

Alternate-Site Declaration—Corporate Alternate Sites

Plan-Activation Checklist

Action	By whom	Comments	Check when done
1. Contact emergency-man-agement team regarding event, which may require activation of alternate sites with instructions to call into conference bridge with time and phone number	Corporate BCP		
2. Receive communication on emergency situation from corporate BCP, which may require alternate-site activation	Site-manage-ment team	log time	
3. Contact the alternate site and alert that disaster may be declared	Corporate BCP		
4. If evacuated from the primary site and unable to reenter the facility, pro-ceed to [enter established meeting location name and address]	Site-manage-ment team and business-conti-nuity planners		
5. Assess damage	Site-manage-ment team and business-conti-nuity planners	Network equipment, building employees	
6. Estimate length of outage	Site-manage-ment team and business-conti-nuity planners	Length of outage <1 hour >1 hour–<2 hours >2 hours–<12 hours >12 hours–<24 hours >24 hours–<48 hours >48 hours Unknown	

Action	By whom	Comments	Check when done
7 Estimate business risk	Site-management team and business-continuity planners		
8. Make decision; if no declaration, then contact the alternate site and inform them alert is over; if decision is to declare, proceed to step 9	Site-management team		
9. Advise executive team immediately, confirm decision, and declare disaster at alternate site as per procedure in this document	Site-management team	log time	
10. Work with building management and real estate to select site to set up the trailer when it arrives	Site-management team, BCP, and recovery teams	log time	
11. Continue scheduled conference calls to manage event until mobile unit arrives and is configured for operations to resume	Site-management team		
12. Continue to update contingency information line to keep staff informed of progress	Site-management team		
13. Site-management team report to recovery facility to validate readiness	Site-management team		
14. Contact staff and resume operation in the recovery facility	Site-management team		

Disaster Declaration Procedures

In the event of a declared disaster, certain individuals have the authorization to declare a disaster with the designated offsite vendor. Authorized individuals only will be allowed to make a declaration on behalf of the company. For a current list of authorized individuals, see below. The vendor will require a password for declaration. Passwords will be provided to those team members who are authorized to declare.

The following individuals, in the order shown, are authorized to declare a disaster for the company at the alternate site:

1. _____
2. _____
3. _____
4. _____
5. _____

SAFETY AND EMERGENCY PROCEDURES

There is a Fire

If you find a fire:

1. *Immediately* call 911.
2. Activate the nearest pull station located at each stairwell, exit, or lobby area.
3. Follow the evacuation procedures and instructions given by the public-address system or your fire warden.

If you hear the public-address System or fire alarm:

1. *Stay calm.* Follow the instructions broadcast over the public-address system.
2. Follow the evacuation procedures and instructions given by your manager or fire warden.
3. Do not attempt to retrieve items from your workspace.

There is Severe Weather

Follow these instructions:

1. If you are at home, call the contingency information line (800-555-5555 or 555-555-7207) for the most up-to-date information regarding a possible business interruption as well as general employee

instructions or contact your manager. Remember, property damage may require you to report to work at a different location.
2. Check your local radio and/or TV stations for broadcast announcements.
3. If you are at work and evacuation or release is necessary, follow the instructions broadcast over the public-address system, call the contingency information line, or ask your manager.

Evacuation of Your Area is Announced

Every time you are evacuated from your site, when possible always bring your car keys and wallets or purses with you. You may not be allowed back in the building. Follow these instructions:

1. *Some routes may not be safe.* Follow your fire warden out of the building.
2. *Do not* use the elevators for an emergency evacuation.
3. Walk quickly when directed to do so, but do not run.
4. *Do not* go back to retrieve personal belongings or for any other reason until authorized to do so by the fire department.
5. Proceed to the predesignated evacuation site for your building.
6. Wait for further instructions from your manager, fire warden, or local emergency responders.

Medical Assistance is Needed

If someone in your area needs medical assistance:

1. *Immediately* call 911.
2. Provide your name, location, phone number, and any information about the illness or injury. *Do not hang up* until the dispatcher confirms the information.
3. Don't attempt first aid if you are not qualified. It could lead to further injury.
4. Keep someone with the injured person at all times.
5. *If possible,* have someone stay at the call-back number.
6. *If possible,* have someone meet the emergency responders at the front entrance.
7. If *you* need medical assistance, *immediately* call 911 and stay at your original location until help arrives.

You Receive a Bomb Threat

Follow these instructions:

1. *Remain calm.*
2. *Take notes.* Note the exact time and duration of the call. Try to find out the location of the caller, the type of device, and the detonation time.
3. *Listen* for distinguishing characteristics, such as quality of voice, accent, background noise(s), age, gender, etc.—this is *very important*.
4. *Immediately* call corporate security at 555-555-2610.
5. Notify your manager and await further instructions. *Do not* discuss the call with your peers or others in the area.
6. Follow the directions of building-security officers, fire wardens, or public-address broadcasts if an evacuation is necessary.

An Unauthorized Person is in Your Workspace

Follow these instructions:

1. *Immediately* report all unauthorized people to local authorities by calling 911.
2. Relate the following characteristics to the dispatcher:
   - Physical description (clothing, height, hair color, gender, age, distinguishing marks, etc.)
   - Location of sighting and possible direction the individual was heading.
3. *Prevent piggybacking*—do not allow people whom you do not recognize to follow you through a door.
4. *Immediately* report any mechanical lock or card-reader problems to building security, 555-555-2610.

A Suspicious Package is in Your Workspace

Follow these instructions:

1. *Remain calm* and *immediately* report all suspicious packages to corporate security at 555-555-2610.
2. If a biological or chemical agent is suspected, isolate employees who have come in contact with the package.
3. Remove all personnel from the area where the package is located *and do not* touch the package.
4. Corporate security will ask a series of questions to help determine the appropriate response.

There is a Threat of Workplace Violence

Employees who have any concerns about the threat of workplace violence should inform their manager, human resources, or security immediately.

In an emergency or a situation of immediate serious threat:

1. *Immediately* call 911.
2. Notify local building security, then call corporate security at 555-555-2111 as soon as possible.

In a potentially dangerous situation:

1. *Immediately* contact your manager and corporate security at 555-555-2111.

Corporate Security will take information from you and contact the threat-assessment team, which will review the situation and determine next steps.

C

Test-Planning Guide and Sample Test Plan for Business-Unit Exercises at an Alternate Site

EXERCISE CHECKLIST

The following is a list of action items to guide the BCP through planning the exercise. Some of these may not apply to your exercise. Cut/add as required.

Detail—tasks	Due date	Owner	Complete
Obtain management support			
Review business function to be tested			
Define scope of exercise			
Establish objectives for the exercise			
Identify limitations of exercise			
Build exercise plan			

Delivery—tasks	Due date	Owner	Complete
Put together scenario for exercise			
Develop the timeline of events			
Develop messages, mini-scenarios, data			
Coordinate efforts of internal and external response organizations if needed			
Secure logistics support (people, facilities, food, paperwork)			
Develop mockups, props, diagrams			
Complete exercise manual/plan			

Setup—tasks	Due date	Owner	Complete
Schedule exercise date with the appropriate alternate site			
Select the participants, controllers, and evaluators			
Distribute informational package to participants			
Conduct walkthrough of exercise if needed with the exercise team			
Brief participants on scope and limits of the exercise			
Inform all employees of the exercise if needed to dispel rumors			
Testing—tasks			
Activate recovery environment as required			
Swing production activity to recovery site as required			
Isolate users from primary site as much as technologically feasible without risking production			

Conduct the exercise			
Follow-up—tasks			
Conduct debriefing with participants			
Conduct debriefing with technical team			
Assemble exercise critiques and responder feedback			
Document and evaluate the exercise			
Generate the exercise report			
Revise the plan and training based on lessons learned			
Publish a thank-you letter to participants and attach issues list from exercise			
Review work action-issues list from exercise			
File deliverables report and issues list			

ALTERNATE-SITE TEST PLAN SAMPLE
FOR BUSINESS-UNIT TESTING

Contingency Planning
Test Plan—Alternate Site

Company/business unit:	
Test coordinator:	
Alternate-site location:	
Test date:	
Start/end time:	

(continued on next page)

303

Scope and type of test (actual, walkthrough, proof of concept, user acceptance, etc.):
  Sample text:
    • The scope of this exercise will be a full-scale exercise.
    • The scope of this exercise is limited to a technical test of the backup servers and the desktop image.
    • The exercise will be held between _____ and _____ hours.
    • The exercise will test the recoverability of the operations and client-services business functions.	

Objectives:
  Sample text:
    • Validate installation of desktop image on the desktop.
    • Move users to alternate site.
    • Isolate systems from primary site.
    • Execute transactions to production, DR, or test environment(s).	

Planned exceptions/limitations:	

Driving Directions to the Alternate Site

(Insert directions to the alternate site here—
include maps, toll information, etc.)

Timeline

Estimated start	Estimated completion	Action	Owner

Participants

Department	Seat/ phone #	Role	Contact/ participant	Phone #	Pager/ cell
Contingency planning					
Desktop support					
Desktop support					
Business-continuity team leader					
Tester					

Alternate-Site Floor Plan

(Note: Insert floor plan for the alternate site here.)

Calls to be Rerouted

Communication Conference Bridge

(Note: Insert conference-bridge number for the test here.)

Problem Reporting

Problem-reporting tickets will be located at each desk—complete the form and bring it to the box.

(Note: copy problem-reporting form from test plan and put on desktops.)

Action Items from Test

The following is a list of action items from the test:

Detail—tasks	Due date	Owner	Complete
Follow-up—tasks to be scheduled			

Problem-Reporting Tickets

Business function   **Name**_____

Problem description Include application and describe the issue/problem	Criticality Does this prevent you from performing your critical functions?	Suggested resolution If you have one	Resolved today? Y/N	Comment

Test Participant Survey

To participants: In order to help us better prepare for an emergency situation, please take a few minutes to provide feedback on the areas listed below. This will allow us to review and revise any processes that you think can be handled more effectively. Your input to this process is greatly appreciated.

Please rate the following as either satisfactory or unsatisfactory:

	Satisfactory	Unsatisfactory	Comments
Facility condition			
Hardware operation			
Staff support			
Security			
Technical instructions			

Please rate each of the following on a scale of 1 to 5, with 1 being the lowest and 5 being the highest. Please include specific comments regarding your experiences with the testing.

Test objectives were clearly stated.   1   2   3   4   5

_____

_____

Test went according to plan/schedule.   1   2   3   4   5

_____

_____

Test issues were addressed appropriately.   1   2   3   4   5

_____

_____

Overall test experience was good.   1   2   3   4   5

_____

_____

Were the directions to the alternate site accurate?   Yes   No

_____

Please list any issues that were not addressed—or that you feel need more attention.

_____

_____

Additional comments:

_____

_____

Test Evaluation

Please indicate yes or no for each item:	(Date) Y / N*	(Date) Y / N*
1. Were transportation issues (buses, parking, travel directions, flights arrangements, hotel arrangements, rental cars, etc.) addressed as part of the test?		
2. Was the alternate-site environment established independent of the primary location?		
3. Did the business unit recall and implement a sampling of stored electronic and hard-copy vital records, procedures manuals, forms, etc.?		
4. Was any technology that was restored during the test restored with backup information from offsite storage?		
5. Was the business able to connect to all required servers, directories, and applications?		
6. Did end users validate functionality?		
7. Did the business navigate all the way through each application or process?		
8. Were phone and fax numbers transferred, and did they work as planned?		
9. Does this location meet your minimum recovery capacity requirements (phones, desktops, etc.)?		
10. Have action items been addressed from the previous alternate-site test?		
11. Was your management team notified at time of test?		
12. Were critical vendors contacted at time of test?		
13. Were interdependencies contacted at time of test?		
14. Was your problem-management strategy tested during the test?		
15. Was the network available on time (for external alternate sites)?		

Please indicate yes or no for each item:	(Date) Y / N*	(Date) Y / N*
16. Was network response time acceptable?		
17. Was all information required for recovery available, and did backups have good data?		
18. Was the desktop image complete, current, and re-stored in time required?		
19. Was the business able to print?		
20. Were end-user instructions for the desktop provided?		
21. Were there sufficient number of phones and inbound and outbound trunks available and tested?		
22. Was voice recording tested (if applicable)?		
23. Were phone instructions provided to the business users?		
24. Was voicemail available at the alternate site?		
25. Were action items documented and submitted to business-unit management?		

Comments on any "no" responses:

Item #	Comment

D

Test Scenarios

External threats and hazards	Technological accidents	External threats due to location
Bomb threat	Explosion	Chemical-plant accident
Terrorist threat	Fire	Ocean storm surge
Sabotage	Computer loss/failure	Flood plain
Theft	Equipment failure	Airport disaster
Crisis at neighbor facility	Contaminated product	Major highway accident
Arson	Power failure	Major railway accident
Someone else's Crisis (on your property)	Service-provider failure (telephone, internet, water)	Military-base attack
Crisis in same industry	Hazardous byproducts	Federal-building attack
Government restriction	Chemical spill/release	Foreign-embassy attack
Supplier loss	Radiological accident	Landfill problems
No property access	EPA shutdown of facility	Hazardous neighbor
Communication failure	Gas leak	Upper-floor office evacuation issues
Transportation loss	Air-quality Problem	Cultural risk
Hostage situation	Medical problems	Unfavorable exchange rates
Political situation	Offices made unavailable	War

(continued on next page)

External threats and hazards	Technological accidents	External threats due to location
Technology failure	Process failure	Special events in area (e.g., Olympics)
Hackers	Transportation accident	Lack of skilled labor
Computer virus		High dependency on government contracts

Natural disasters	Anticipatory events	Business crisis
Hurricane	Scandal	Product problem/recall
Tornado	Poor earnings expected	Corporate takeover
Earthquake	Key customer loss	Labor strike/lockout
Flood	Key supplier loss/failure	Workplace violence
Tsunami	Hurricane forecast	Executive dismissals
Lightning	Severe-weather forecast	Sexual/racial harassment
Fire	Executive(s) departure	Whistleblowing
Drought	Executive(s) resignation	Class-action lawsuits
Heavy snowfall	Fraud	Consumer Actions
Ice/ice storms	Power shutdown	Supplier problem/disaster
Landslides/mudslides	Serious product problem	Media scare (real or not)
Dam failure	New computer virus	Shareholder suit
Infestation	Pending lawsuit	Unfavorable court ruling
Contamination	Rumors being circulated	Major promotional error
Sinkholes		
Volcanoes		
Extreme cold/heat		
Extended severe cold/heat		
Solar magnetic storms		
Epidemic/pandemic		

E

Alternate-Site Development Kit

Requirements for:

Location(s):

Completed by:

Desktop requirements:

1. How many desktops (seats) will you require in the alternate site?	#
2. What applications do you use to perform your functions? Please list all applications that you will need to access from the alternate site.	
3. List any special software that is essential to your operation. These are applications that run only on specific desktops and are specific to your operation.	Software name and vendor:
4. Do you have any modem requirements?	
5. If desktop modem is required, is outbound-only dialing sufficient?	

(continued on next page)

6. How many phones do you need?	
7. Will any of these phones require hunt or pick groups?	
8. Do you need international dialing capability?	If yes, for how many phones?
9. Do you require recorded lines?	If yes, how many?
10. Will you need to establish ACD groups?	If yes, please complete the phone information as appropriate.
11. List any inbound fax numbers that will need to be re-routed to the alternate site.	Area code+number:

Inbound numbers to be rerouted:

Phone number	Department	Target number
1.		
2.		
3.		
4.		
5.		

For each # listed above or for any ACD group that needs to be established at the alternate site, please complete the following information: *Make as many copies of this page as you need.*

Phone # _____

Number of seats assigned to this phone group_____

When phone call is answered by the alternate-site phone system, the caller hears: (for example: "Thank you for calling our company. Your call is important to us. For balances and account information, press 1; for payments press 2; to speak to a representative, press 3.")

For each path the caller can take, answer the questions below:

Name the ACD group:

If all agents are busy, the caller hears this message: _____

_____

If all agents are still busy, the caller hears this message: _____

_____

How frequently does the message repeat? _____

_____

After waiting for how long should the caller be offered the option of leaving a voicemail message? _____

_____

What are the hours of operation for the phone number? _____

_____

Is there a night-time message? If so, what is it? _____

_____

Does this group overflow to another ACD group? If so, which group?

_____

Are calls for this group recorded? _____

_____

Will your business need to receive market-data feeds at the alternate site?

If yes, please complete the information below for each feed required.

Vendor name	# of connections	Delivery

Please identify any other specific requirements you may have, including any unique requirements of your business. Consider such items as scanners, time-stamp machines, postage meters, mail carts, printing calculators, etc. Do not include items such as paper, pens, pencils, staplers, and other general office supplies.

Item	# required

Any other resources or comments?

F

Business-Continuity-Planner Job Description

Reports to: Operationally: Company President or
                                Chief Operations Officer

              Functionally: Vice President, Enterprise Risk Management

PURPOSE

The business-continuity (or -contingency) planner (BCP) directs the continuity-planning program of a Company. The BCP is responsible for ensuring that adequate contingency planning, documentation, testing, and maintenance are developed and maintained for his or her area of responsibility. The BCP acts as a focal point for all contingency-planning functions to ensure that the business continuity is supported by a current and viable plan.

GOAL

The BCP goal is to plan the integration of a series of tasks, procedures, and information that directs actions at the time of a business interruption in order to reduce confusion, improve communications, and achieve a timely continuation/resumption of business.

DUTIES AND RESPONSIBILITIES

BCP duties and responsibilities include:

1. Coordinate and support all contingency-planning efforts within the company. Coordinate all communications and follow-up with employees and management for events that may have business-interruption impact, such as power shutdowns and ongoing incidents.
2. Provide input to and act as a resource for the development, implementation, maintenance, and/or dissemination of standards, policies, procedures, guidelines, and contingency-plan documentation for the contingency-planning program in compliance with established corporate policy.
3. Coordinate, document, and maintain the identification of the business functions and the assignment of criticality and recovery time-frame requirements for his or her area of responsibility by working with business management.
4. Identify business-function resource requirements. This includes but is not limited to hardware, software, vendor information, essential personnel, and facility space.
5. Maintain currency of all contingency-planning documentation including emergency-notification lists, BCP backup names and numbers, contingency plans, test plans, schedules, and results.
6. Acquire senior management's approval of plan contents and test results annually.
7. Secure the appointment, alternate coverage, training, and viability of all contingency-planning teams. Develop, maintain, and conduct recovery-team testing/awareness/training/walkthrough of recovery plans.
8. Design and maintain the alternate sites, business components, and procedures to keep the location in a state of readiness. Coordinate the application sizing information, scheduling, and execution of tests with the recovery site. Review and direct periodic recovery-plan revisions/updates based on test results.
9. Provide primary contact for his or her assigned area to handle coordination response to emergency and/or business interruption situations. Participate in the joint decision made by all stakeholders to move to alternate sites:
   - Coordinate recovery activities in the event of disaster
   - Resolve conflicts and problems as needed
   - Maintain war-room communications

10. Coordinate companywide contingency planning, awareness, and training.
11. Provide regular status report on the progress and issues relating to exposed areas of the company/division contingency plan as well as business impact of incidents that occurred.

KNOWLEDGE AND SKILLS

Breakdown: technical: 10 percent, business 30 percent, managerial 40 percent, interpersonal 20 percent.

In-depth knowledge of how a business unit operates and understanding of its critical functions.

Coordination of resources. Direct responsibility for expenditures.

Excellent written and oral communication skills.

Excellent analytical skills, strategic outlook.

Strong understanding of business principles and practices.

Ability to handle multiple tasks simultaneously.

Willingness to manage or to personally execute necessary tasks, as limited resources require.

Executive presence.

Good motivational skills; effective at leadership through consultation and influence.

EDUCATION/EXPERIENCE

Education: Bachelors degree, advanced degree desirable
Experience: 10 or more years of management experience
Certifications: Appropriate professional certification

ACCOUNTABILITIES

Interfaces: All levels within the company, as well as clients, vendors, and regulatory and law-enforcement organizations
Decisions: Directs overall activities of assigned function; defines stated objectives and ensures compliance; delegates tasks and manages their execution

ORGANIZATIONAL RELATIONSHIPS

Immediate manager: President or V.P.
Peers: Senior functional managers; other executive management.

INDEX